# CONFOUNDING
# THE REICH

**Other books by Martin W. Bowman:**

*Fields of Little America*
*The Encylopedia of American Military Aircraft*
*The B-24 Liberator 1939–45*
*Castles in the Air*
*Home by Christmas?*
*The Bedford Triangle*
*Wellington: The Geodetic Giant*
*The World's Fastest Aircraft*
*Famous Bombers*
*Classic Fighter Aircraft*
*Modern Military Aircraft*
*Flying to Glory*
*Spirits in the Sky* (with Patrick Bunce)
*Four Miles High*
*Great American Air Battles 1942–1992*
*Eighth Air Force at War*
*Thunder in the Heavens* (with Patrick Bunce)
*The Men who Flew the Mosquito*
*The USAF at War*
*Low Level from Swanton*

As part of our ongoing market research, we are always pleased to receive comments about our books, suggestions for new titles, or requests for catalogues. Please write to: The Editorial Director, Patrick Stephens Limited, Sparkford, Near Yeovil, Somerset BA22 7JJ.

# CONFOUNDING THE REICH

## THE OPERATIONAL HISTORY OF 100 GROUP (BOMBER SUPPORT) RAF

## Martin W Bowman and Tom Cushing

PSL

Patrick Stephens Limited

First published in 1996

British Cataloguing-in-Publication Data:
A catalogue record for this book is available from the British Library

ISBN 1 85260 507 3

Library of Congress catalog card no. 95-79125

Patrick Stephens Limited is an imprint of Haynes Publishing, Sparkford,
Nr Yeovil, Somerset, BA22 7JJ

Typeset by J. H. Haynes & Co. Ltd
Printed and bound in Great Britain by Biddles Limited,
Guildford and Kings Lynn

# CONTENTS

*The time will come when thou*
*Shall lift thine eyes*
*To watch a long drawn battle*
*In the skies*
*While aged peasants, too amazed*
*For words*
*Stare at the flying fleets*
*Of wondrous birds*
*England, so long mistress of the sea*
*Where wind and waves confess*
*Her sovereignty*
*Her ancient triumphs yet on high*
*Shall bear*
*And reign, the sovereign of*
*The conquered air.*

'LUNA HABITALIS' BY THOMAS GRAY, 1737

# INTRODUCTION

On 23 November 1943, 100 Group (Special Duties) of RAF Bomber Command was formed. The object was to consolidate the various squadrons and units that had been fighting a secret war of electronics and radar countermeasures, attempting to reduce the losses of the heavy bombers – and their hard pressed crews – in Bomber Command. This secret war involved the use of air and ground radars, homing and jamming equipment, special radio and navigational aids, and intruding night-fighters to seek out and destroy their opposite numbers, the Ju 88s and Bf 110s of the Nachtjagdgeschwader now defending the vivid night skies of the Third Reich with ever increasing success.

While there were various radar counter-measures that could be activated from the ground, the airborne operations took two distinct forms. One was a force of heavy bomber aircraft flying over Germany and Occupied Europe, carrying a variety of radar and radio 'jamming' equipment, sometimes on Spoofing operations; the other was provided from the Home Defence Night-fighter Squadrons. Since June 1943, these had been carrying out high-level, freelance *Intruder* sorties specifically against the German night-fighters.

These activities conducted by specialist bomber and night-fighter crews, and the equipment they used, were cloaked under some weird and strange-sounding code-names such as *Serrate, Mandrel, Jostle, Monica* and *Airborne Cigar*. The night-fighter crews who completed a first tour on one of seven fighter squadrons in 100 Group could expect to go for their 'rest' of six months either to BSTU, the Bomber Support Training Unit, or BSDU, the Bomber Support Development Unit. In the latter, they were still expected to continue flying on operations because the new equipment could only be adequately tested on the job. In those halcyon days that meant 'over the other side'.

The losses among the Lancasters, Halifaxes, Stirlings and Wellingtons were many times greater than those of the *Serrate* Mosquitoes. The task of trying to reduce those losses was a rewarding challenge for all British night-fighter crews. It had to be pursued to the very limit and beyond. Sometimes they saw the bombers being shot down in flames around them. Sometimes they could return to base and tell their welcoming and faithful ground crews that 'they had got one' which meant that one German night-fighter would not be returning to its base that night, nor taking off the following night to hit the 'bomber boys'.

# ACKNOWLEDGEMENTS

I am enormously grateful to the following people for making it possible to include detailed information in this book. Don F. Aris very kindly allowed me to quote from his superb unpublished three-volume history of 141 Squadron which has taken him a lifetime to compile. His fellow armourer, Johnny Claxton, kindly made these available for a long period of time. Dr Theo Boiten provided enormous expertise on victories and details of German crews. As always, I am most grateful to Mike Bailey for his guidance, proofing and kind loan of much-needed books for research purposes. Bob Collis of the Norfolk & Suffolk Aviation Museum, Flixton unstintingly provided his customary expertise and furnished much valuable information on aircraft and crews, often in very detailed and painstaking correspondence. Last but not least I would like to pay tribute to Tom Cushing for his most marvellous assistance and for so very graciously giving me free rein to use his vast historical collection of memorabilia, documents and photographs at Little Snoring. Time spent at his house on Snoring airfield, served with plentiful cups of tea from his lovely wife Wendy, were some of the most enjoyable interludes during the preparation of this book.

Jerry Scutts and Philip J. Birtles, Chairman of the Mosquito Museum, provided many superb photographs. Steve Jefferson worked wonders with making prints from glass negatives. I am no less grateful to the following for their marvellous help and support throughout: Steve Adams; Michael Allen DFC; Jim Avis; Capt 'Buddy' Badley; Len Bartram; Tim Bates; Derek 'Taffy' Bellis DFC*; Frank Bocock; Eileen Boorman; Les Bostock; Bill Bridgeman; Jean Bunting; Andrew Crotch; the late S/L John Crotch DFC; S/L Joe Cooper AFC; Hans-Peter Dabrowski; S/L Mike Daniels; Ernie Frohloff; *Legion Magazine*; Richard T. Goucher; Peter B. Gunn, author of *RAF Great Massingham*; Terry Groves; Alan Hague, Curator, Norfolk & Suffolk Aviation Museum; Lewis Heath; Raymond Hicks; Leslie 'Dutch' Holland; S/L George Honeyman; Harry Jeffries; W/C H. C. Kelsey DSO, DFC; Geoff Liles; Ron Mackay; Sister Laurence May; Neville Miller; W. H. Miller DFC; Mosquito Aircrew Association; Simon Parry, Murray Peden QC; Eric Phillips; Don Prutton; Barbara and John Rayson G.Av.A; Harry Reed; S/L Derek Rothery RAF Retd; W/C Philip Russell DFC; G/C J. A. V. Short MBIM; G/C E. M. Smith DFC, DFM; Martin Staunton; Harry Welham; Graham 'Chalky' White; S/L R. G. 'Tim' Woodman DSO, DFC.

# GLOSSARY

| | |
|---|---|
| AI | Airborne Interception (radar) |
| AI Mk IV | 1.5 m fixed dipole aerials working on the 'floodlighting' principle |
| AI Mk V | as Mk IV but with pilot indication |
| AI Mk VI | as Mk V but installed in single-seat fighter |
| AI Mk VII | 10 cm radar with spirally rotating scanner; max range 5–6 miles |
| AI Mk VIII | as Mk VII but with beacon and IFF facilities; max range 7–8 miles |
| AI Mk IX | 10 cm radar having spiral scanner with facility to lock on to target; max range 10 miles |
| AI Mk X | 10 cm radar with fully rotating scanner; max range 10 miles |
| AI Mk XV | (ASH) 3 cm radar with horizontal scanner; max range 8 miles |
| ADGB | Air Defence of Great Britain |
| AM | Air Marshal |
| ASH | air-surface H (homer) |
| ASR | air-sea rescue |
| AVM | Air Vice Marshal |
| blip | radar echo or response |
| bogey | unidentified aircraft |
| Bordfunker | German wireless/radar operator |
| BSDU | Bomber Support Development Unit |
| *Bullseye* | training aircraft engaged by sector searchlights and subjected to dummy attacks by night-fighters |
| Canary | IFF used by radar sites and AA sites to identify friendly aircraft |
| CRT | cathode ray tube |
| C-scope | CRT showing front elevation of target |
| Diver | V-1 |
| *Düppel* | German code-name for *Window* after a town near the Danish border where RAF metal foil strips were first found |
| *Emil-Emil* | German code-name for *Lichtenstein* AI |
| F/L | Flight Lieutenant |
| F/O | Flying Officer |
| F/Sgt | Flight Sergeant |
| Fähnrich (Fhr) | RAF equivalent: Flight Sergeant |
| Feldwebel | RAF equivalent: Sergeant |
| *Flensburg* | German device to enable their night-fighters to home on to *Monica* |
| *Flower* | low-level night *Intruder* patrol over German airfields |
| *Freelance* | patrol with the object of picking up a chance radar contact or visual sighting of the enemy |

| | |
|---|---|
| G/C | Group Captain |
| Gee | British navigational device |
| General der Flieger | RAF equivalent: Air Marshal |
| Generalfeldmarschall | RAF equivalent: Marshal of the RAF |
| Generalleutnant | RAF equivalent: Air Vice Marshal |
| Generalmajor | RAF equivalent: Air Commodore |
| Generaloberst | RAF equivalent: Air Chief Marshal |
| *H2S* | British 10 cm radar |
| Hauptmann (Hptm) | RAF equivalent: Flight Lieutenant |
| *Helle Nachtjagd* | Light (or Bright) Night Chase; night interception in searchlight-illuminated zones |
| Horrido! | German for 'Tallyho!' |
| IAS | indicated air speed |
| IFF | identification friend or foe |
| Instep | Patrol seeking air activity in Bay of Biscay |
| Leutnant (Lt) | RAF equivalent: Pilot Officer |
| *Lichtenstein* | first form of German AI |
| *Mahmoud* | high level, bomber support sortie |
| Major | (German) RAF equivalent: Squadron Leader |
| *Mandrel* | airborne radar-jamming device |
| *Monica* | tail-mounted warning radar device |
| Nachtjagdgeschwader | (NJG) Night-fighter wing |
| NFT | night-flying training/test |
| Oberfähnrich | Warrant Officer |
| Oberfeldwebel (Ofw) | RAF equivalent: Flight Sergeant |
| Oberleutnant (Oblt) | RAF equivalent: Flying Officer |
| Oberst (Obst) | RAF equivalent: Group Captain |
| Oberstleutnant (Obstlt) | RAF equivalent: Wing Commander |
| op | operation |
| OTU | Operational Training Unit |
| *Outstep* | patrol seeking enemy air activity off Norway |
| P/O | Pilot Officer |
| Pauke! Pauke! | (German) Kettledrums! Kettledrums! (Going in to attack!) |
| PPF | Pathfinder Force |
| R/T | radio telephony |
| RCM | radio countermeasures |
| resin | aircraft identification light |
| *Rhubarb* | low-level daylight fighter sweep |
| S/L | Squadron Leader |
| *Schräge Musik* | Slanting Music; German night-fighter's guns that fire upwards at 70° |
| *Serrate* | British equipment designed to home in on *Lichtenstein* radar |
| TI | target indicator |
| Unteroffizier (Uffz) | RAF equivalent: Corporal |
| *Vapour* | airborne directing of night-fighters from a specially equipped Wellington |
| W/C | Wing Commander |
| W/O | Warrant Officer |
| WOP | wireless operator |
| WOP-AG | wireless operator/air gunner |
| *Wilde Sau* | German single-engined night-fighters operating over the RAF's target, relying on freelance interceptions from a running commentary, aided by the light from fires and searchlights |
| *Zahme Sau* | German single-engined and twin-engined fighters fed into the bomber stream on the way to the target as soon as its track was properly established |

\* indicates a bar to an existing award

# CHAPTER 1

# *SERRATE SQUADRON*

*Ist die Luftschlacht in der Steige,*
*Und die Nacht, die dröhnt und lärmt wie dumm.*
*Pauke! Pauke! Rums die Geige!*

'DAS LIED VON DER „WILDEN SAU"' BY PETER HOLM

'**M**arie-5,' sounded in the earphones of the Bordfunker crouched in the cockpit of the Bf 110G-4a night-fighter. The code-word, sent from the ground controller, indicated that the Nachtjagdgeschwader night predator was only 5 kilometres behind a British bomber. It had been picked up on German ground radar, fixed on the *Seeburg* plotting table and transmitted to the Leutnant and his Unteroffizier stalking the bomber on their *Helle Nachtjagd* (night chase). As soon as the Bordfunker picked up contact on his *Lichtenstein* C-1 *weitwinkel* (wide-angle) radar, he transmitted 'Emil-Emil' to alert his controller.

'Pauke! Pauke!' ('Kettledrums! Kettledrums!'): the Leutnant had obtained visual contact of his target. It was a Lancaster, crossing gently from port to starboard. His Bordfunker immediately transmitted 'Ich beruhe'. Then they closed in rapidly for the kill – 300, 200, 150 metres, finally opening fire from 100 metres.

Strikes peppered the fuselage and danced along the wing root. Another 2-second burst and the four-engined bomber burst into flames. Doomed, it fell away to port in a flaming death dive, impacting in a German forest. Gouts of fuel from ruptured tanks ignited and lit up the night sky with a reddish hue. The engines buried themselves deep into the earth. 'Sieg Heil!' said the pilot over R/T to ground control. The British bomber crew had unwitting been 'homed in' on: its *H2S* set had been picked up by the night-fighter's *Naxos* Z FuG 250, while its *Flensburg* FuG 227/1 homed in on the bomber's *Monica* tail-warning device.

On another night it would be the turn of the Leutnant and his Unteroffizier to be the preyed-upon. It was all part of a deadly and sophisticated electronic game in which the RAF, the Luftwaffe, aided by the scientists, pitted their wits in an ethereal, nocturnal battleground. One side gained the ascendancy until the inevitable counter-measure was found.

*On 3 December 1942, a Wellington 1C, similar to this one, of 1473 Flight, flown by P/O Edwin Paulton RCAF, went on a suicidal mission with the bomber stream to Frankfurt to pinpoint the source of German transmissions in the 490 MHz band. The Wimpy allowed itself to be attacked by a Ju 88, four of the crew were wounded and the aircraft was ditched near Deal but evidence was transmitted to England and as a result, effective countermeasures were developed by TRE. (Vickers)*

When a British listening station monitoring German R/T traffic picked up the codeword *Emil-Emil*, and special operators aboard aircraft of 1473 Flight subsequently detected transmissions on the 490 Mhz band on *Ferret* flights over occupied Europe, proof was needed that they came from enemy night-fighters. On 3 December 1942, a Wellington 1C of 1473 Flight, flown by P/O Edwin Paulton RCAF, went with the bomber stream to Frankfurt to pinpoint the source of the transmissions. If they did in fact come from German night-fighters, the crew were to allow the enemy aircraft to close in to attack and to follow his radar transmissions throughout. Pilot Officer Harold Jordan RCAF, the special wireless operator, picked up a signal which came closer until it was so loud that it nearly deafened him. It was a Ju 88.

Jordan warned the crew that an attack was imminent and F/Sgt Bill Bigoray

RCAF, the wireless operator, sent out signals to base. The 'Wimpy' took evasive action as the Ju 88 made 10–12 attacks. Four of the crew were wounded. Jordan was hit in the arm and jaw in the first two attacks but continued to work his set. In the third attack, he was wounded again, this time in the eye. Almost blind, he explained the operation of the wireless set to the navigator. Bigoray, although badly wounded in both legs, had persisted in passing on the messages from Jordan. Edwin Paulton managed to fly the badly damaged Wellington to England and ditched off Walmer Beach near Deal. Jordan was awarded an immediate DSO, Paulton and Bigoray received the DFC and DFM respectively.

The courage of the crew enabled information to be pieced together on the new radar. As a result, a new, lighter *Window* was produced. Also, the TRE

(Telecommunications Research Establishment at Malvern, Worcestershire) developed a homer using a receiver known as *Serrate*, which actually homed in on the radar impulses emitted by the *Lichtenstein* (*Emil-Emil*) interception radar. *Serrate* got its name from the picture on the CRT (cathode ray tube). When within range of a German night-fighter, the CRT displayed a herring-bone pattern either side of the time trace, which had a serrated edge. *Serrate* came to be the code-name for the high-level Bomber Support operations.

The TRE, and its airfield at Defford nearby, was the centre of all wartime RAF radar research. In 1941, it had begun work on jammers to counter the German *Freya* early warning ground radar which was first discovered at Auderville on the Cap de la Hague in February. After the famous raid on Bruneval on 27/28 February 1942 in which British paratroopers and an RAF

radar technician dismantled a complete *Würzburg* radar installation and removed it to England along with one of its operators, TRE developed jammers for the *Würzburg* also.

During 1942, some RAF night-fighter squadrons had re-equipped with the de Havilland Mosquito – 'a lethal brute with no vices' – and in October of the same year ACM Arthur 'Bomber' Harris, the AOC RAF Bomber Command, advocated that Mosquito fighters should be used in the bomber stream for raids on Germany. ACM Sir W. Sholto Douglas, AOC Fighter Command, loathe to lose his Mosquito fighters, argued that the few available Mosquitoes were needed for home defence should the Luftwaffe renew its attacks on Britain. However, on 5/6 March 1943 the Battle of the Ruhr began with an attack by 442 bombers on Essen. Between the beginning of March and the end of July, 872

*AI Mk IV radar installation in the Beaufighter Mk IF showing the nose-mounted dipole transmitter aerial and wing-mounted receiver aerials. (BAe)*

bombers were lost and 2,126 were either badly damaged or crash-landed in England. Something equally dramatic had to be done to curb the Luftwaffe night-fighter force.

Back in late 1941, a joint services committee had been established to study the future application of RCM (radio countermeasures). It had been mooted by TRE that such countermeasures could be effectively carried out in support of Main Force operations over Germany. Now, one of the first steps was to transfer a Squadron, No. 141, from Fighter Command to Bomber Support using the new *Serrate* homer. No. 141 Squadron, a long-established night-fighter home defence squadron, which had been stationed at Predannack since February, was a natural choice for the task, although it was equipped with the Beaufighter 1F which had neither the range nor the performance of the Mosquito.

On 19 June 1940, 141 Squadron had lost 10 aircrew with two injured when six Defiants were destroyed and one damaged, all by Bf 109s. The Defiants were switched to night fighting and 141 destroyed its first enemy aircraft at night on 16 September 1940. At Ayr on 26 June 1941, the first Beaufighter 1F equipped with Mk IV AI

radar was delivered to the squadron. The first operational patrol by a Beaufighter 1F of 141 Squadron took place on 25 August 1941. On 4/5 June 1942, 141 used Mk VII AI radar operationally in a Beaufighter 1F for the first time when a Dornier 217 was damaged.

In December 1942, W/C John Randall Daniel 'Bob' Braham DSO, DFC*, not yet 23, assumed command of the squadron. An outspoken individualist, unsurpassed in his sheer aggressive fighting spirit and relentless determination, Bob Braham was already a living legend, having shot down 12 enemy aircraft, 11 of them at night. The son of a WW1 RFC pilot, Braham shot down his first aircraft during the Battle of Britain and at 23 had become the youngest wing commander in the RAF. 'The Night Destroyer', as he was dubbed in the press, had an overdeveloped sense of modesty and could see no reason for the press having an interest in him. It is perhaps because he shunned publicity wherever possible, that he is not as well known as some other aces of WW2.

Posted with Braham to 141 Squadron from 29 Squadron, was F/O W. J. 'Sticks' Gregory, DFC, DFM, his navigator and radio/radar operator, who had partnered Braham in seven kills. Gregory earned his nickname as a result of having been a drummer in Debroy Somer's band. Another inspired appointment was F/L Bernard 'Dickie' Sparrowe who arrived in November 1942 as Adjutant. Flying Officer Cedric 'Buster' Reynolds, the Intelligence Officer and Flying Officer (later Flight Lieutenant) James Dougall MD, B.Ch. completed a superb team under Braham. It

*W/C John Randall Daniel 'Bob' Braham DSO, DFC*. An outspoken individualist, unsurpassed in his sheer aggressive fighting spirit and relentless determination, Braham was already a living legend, having shot down 12 enemy aircraft, 11 of them at night, with 29 Squadron (and one with 51 OTU) when, not yet 23, he took command of 141 Squadron in December 1942. (IWM)*

*On 9 May 1943, a Ju 88R-1 of IV/NJG 3 flown by Flugzeugführer Oblt Herbert Schmidt, Ofw Paul Rosenberger and Bordschütze Ofw Erich Kantvill, and fitted with Flensburg FuG 202 Lichtenstein BC AI radar, landed intact at Dyce, near Aberdeen. The aircraft is now on permanent display at the RAF Museum, Hendon. (Author)*

was not unusual for Reynolds and 'Doc' Dougall – who was known as 'The Mad Irishman' because of his wild antics – to fly on operations with their CO!

Lack of enemy air activity over England saw fighters, including Beaufighters during the moon period, employed in incursion missions in France and the Low Countries. On 13 March 1943, 141 flew the first *Ranger* patrol by night in Beaufighter 1Fs over south-west France. A *Ranger* was a deep penetration flight into enemy territory with the object of engaging any target of opportunity on the ground or in the air. (*Rangers* were normally patrols by single aircraft while *Intruders* were normally flown in pairs). Aircraft fitted with Mk VII or Mk VIII AI radar equipment were not permitted to fly over enemy territory lest their highly secret apparatus should fall into German hands. Those aircraft with Mk IV AI had to have their equipment taken out, or at least major parts of it removed. On 23 March, they flew their first *Instep* patrol, by day, over the Bay of Biscay. *Insteps* were long-range fighter protection operations to intercept attacking enemy aircraft or to report on aircraft or shipping in the Western Approaches of the Atlantic and the Bay of Biscay.

Only a few such operations had been flown, when, on 15 April, Braham and Reynolds were summoned to HQ Fighter Command at Bentley Priory near

Stanmore. The top level meeting was attended by a number of staff officers and two civilians from the TRE. AM Sir Trafford L. Leigh-Mallory, who had taken over Fighter Command in November 1942, was obviously impressed with the aggressive spirit Braham had instilled in his squadron in so short a time. He informed Braham that 141 Squadron had been selected as the first *Serrate* squadron for Bomber Support operations over enemy territory. On 30 April, 141 Squadron flew south to Wittering, their new station. *Ranger* and *Instep* operations and home defence duties continued while Beaufighter Mk VIs arrived, and *Serrate* and the *Gee* radio navigation aid equipment was installed. New crews arrived from 51 OTU at Cranfield to fly the Beaufighters. Then, on 12 May, the first six 141 Squadron crews flew to Drem in Scotland to begin *Serrate* training.

A few days before, on 9 May, a Ju 88R-1 of IV/NJG 3 was flown from Kristiansund/ Kjevik in Norway to Dyce, near Aberdeen, after its crew defected during an aborted interception of a Courier Service Mosquito off Denmark. The fiancée of the pilot, *Flugzeugführer* Oblt Herbert Schmidt, was Jewish and had been arrested and transported to a concentration camp, while his Bordfunker, Ofw Paul Rosenberger, was of Jewish descent. Bordschütze Oberfeldwebel Erich Kantvill, a Nazi, went along with the defection. This aircraft was equipped with the FuG 202 *Lichtenstein* BC AI. Examination by TRE scientists enabled them to confirm that the *Serrate* device operated on the correct frequencies to home in on the FuG 202 and FuG 212 *Lichtenstein* radars. *Serrate* could only home in on *Lichtenstein* AI radar and then only if it was turned on. The Beaufighters would also be equipped with Mk IV AI radar which would be used in the closing stages of a *Serrate* interception because *Serrate* could not positively indicate range. The Mk IV was also needed to obtain contacts on enemy night-fighters that were not using their radar.

On 14 June, 141 Squadron flew its first Bomber Support operation. Late in the afternoon, five Beaufighter FVIs equipped with *Serrate* and Mk IV AI radar flew to their forward airfield at Coltishall, Norfolk and took off again shortly before midnight for operations over Holland and Germany. Meanwhile, 197 Lancasters and six Mosquitoes of the Main Force were *en route* to Oberhausen in the Ruhr. Squadron Leader Charles V. 'Winnie' Winn DFC – an old friend of Braham in 29 Squadron – and R. A. W. Scott, and Braham and Gregory took off at 23:35 hours. Braham headed for the German night-fighter airfield at Deelen near Arnhem in Holland. The flight over the North Sea was uneventful and they patrolled Deelen in wide orbits, sometimes flying as far as Venlo – another German night-fighter airfield in Holland – and Wesel in Germany in their search for 'trade'. They found nothing and so, at 01:51 hours, Braham and Gregory set course for the coast again.

At 10,000 ft over Staveren on the north-east coast of the Zuider Zee, Gregory saw an enemy aircraft coming up behind them to attack from the port side. Braham orbited hard left to get behind him but as he did so the enemy pilot also turned to port. A dogfight ensued as each pilot tried to get the upper hand. Finally, Braham got on to

the enemy's port beam and from 400 yards opened fire with cannon and machine guns. He finished with a 5-second burst from astern at 200 yards. The enemy machine, a Bf 110, was raked along the fuselage from tail to cockpit and the port engine caught fire. Braham throttled back to attack again but it was unnecessary. The Bf 110 went into a vertical dive and crashed in flames 8 miles north of Staveren. Low on fuel, the victorious RAF crew set course for home and landed at Wittering at 03:15 hours.

Squadron Leader Winn and R. A. W. Scott had landed 35 minutes earlier having encountered no trade at Eindhoven. At 03:25 hours F/O R. C. MacAndrew and P/O L. Wilk landed at Wittering having seen no activity at Gilze Rijen in Holland. The fourth Beaufighter, crewed by F/O B. J. Brachi and his navigator/radio operator, P/O A. P. MacLeod, had returned early with technical problems. Belgian pilot, F/L Lucien J. G. LeBoutte and his navigator/radio operator, P/O H. Parrott, had an equally uneventful trip to the German airfield. The 46-year-old LeBoutte had been interned by the Germans in both world wars and was a well-known Capitaine Aviateur aerobatic pilot in the l'Aviation Militaire and a qualified fighter pilot. He was serving in the Belgian Congo in 1940 when Belgium was invaded and he returned to join the fighting but it was too late and was interned. Maj LeBoutte escaped, crossed France and went over the Pyrénées on foot into Spain. He was interned by the Spanish who finally freed him in September 1941, and the brave Belgian finally arrived in England in October. Despite his age and the fact that he wore glasses, LeBoutte was finally commissioned into the RAF as a P/O in January 1942.

Despite 141 Squadron's efforts, 17 Lancasters were lost on that night's raid. Next day, Braham was awarded a second Bar to his DFC. Bad weather that night meant no Main Force and therefore no *Serrate* operations, so 141 Squadron was stood down. On 16/17 June, Bomber Command dispatched 202 Lancasters and ten Halifaxes to Köln while six Beaufighters of 141 Squadron again attempted to draw the enemy fighter force away from the main stream with patrols over German airfields in Holland. Winnie Winn and R. A. W. Scott patrolled Gilze Rijen but were forced to return early after taking a hit by a flak burst which knocked out all their instruments. Flying Officer R. C. MacAndrew and Pilot Officer L. Wilk damaged a Bf 110 while on patrol near Eindhoven before icing caused the pilot's guns to jam. Braham and Gregory had headed for the German night-fighter airfield at Venlo where they damaged a Ju 88. Braham got in a 2-second burst from astern before his guns also jammed. LeBoutte and Parrott saw a Ju 88 west of Eindhoven but lost it in cloud. Flying Officer Leonard Florent Alexandre Louis Renson, another Belgian pilot in the Squadron, and his navigator/radio operator, P/O J. A. Pouptis, returned early before reaching the Dutch coast with a valve failure in their AI radar. (Renson was killed on 18/19 November 1943, with F/O Ken Baldwin, during an *Intruder* patrol to Hoya, Germany). A sixth Beaufighter, piloted by F/O Douglas Sawyer with his navigator/radio operator, Sgt Albert Smith, failed to return following a patrol over Gilze Rijen. Fourteen Lancasters also failed to return.

There was a two-night lull in Bomber Command operations until 19/20 June when 290 bombers raided the Schneider armaments factory and the Breuil steelworks at Le Creusot in France. Five Beaufighters of 141 Squadron flew Bomber Support operations over Holland again, this time using Ford in Hampshire as a forward base. Bob Braham and F/O Howard Kelsey's Beaufighters were fired at by flak batteries but returned safely. The Beaufighters were again called upon for Bomber Support on 21/22 June when Krefeld was attacked by just over 700 bombers. Seven Beaufighters flew to Coltishall and flew patrols over German fighter airfields in Holland but LeBoutte's and F/O Thornton's Beaufighters remained at the Norfolk base, grounded with technical troubles. Squadron Leader Charles Winn and R. A. W. Scott destroyed a Ju 88 while on patrol to Deelen but 44 bombers were shot down, most of them by German night-fighters.

On 22/23 June, 557 bombers attacked Mulheim. New tactics were employed whereby four Beaufighters were ordered to patrol 6–8 miles north of the bomber stream and the other four patrolled to the

*W/C 'Bob' Braham DSO, DFC\*, and F/O W. J. 'Sticks' Gregory DFC, DFM. Gregory partnered Braham in four of his eight victories in 141 Squadron, 14 June 1943 – 29 September 1943 (F/L Jacko Jacobs partnered him in the other four). Braham finished the war with 29 victories. (IWM)*

south. Eight Beaufighters were duly dispatched to the forward base at Coltishall from where they took off again late that night for *Intruder* operations over Holland. One Beaufighter, flown by Howard Kelsey with his navigator/radio operator, Sgt Edward M. Smith, destroyed their first enemy aircraft, a Bf 110, during a patrol to Soesterberg. Smith's *Serrate* and AI sets went unserviceable after Kelsey had fired his guns. Flight Lieutenant D. C. Maltby and Flying Officer J. E. Watts had to return early when their AI set also went unserviceable. On this and recent Bomber Support operations, Beaufighter crews reported interference from their *Grocer* equipment which made homing almost 'impossible.' Equipment problems could, in time, be corrected, but infinitely more worrying to the air force chiefs of staff was the loss of 35 bombers.

The situation was almost as bad on 24/25 June when 34 bombers were lost in a raid on Wüppertal by 630 RAF heavies. Five Beaufighters were flown to Coltishall but Winn burst a tyre and his place on the operation was quickly taken by the ever eager Bob Braham who flew to Coltishall with Sticks Gregory in the navigator's seat. They took off from Coltishall at 23:45 hours and headed for Gilze Rijen. At Antwerp, a cone of about 30 searchlights pierced the sky, accompanied by a heavy flak barrage. At Gilze, Braham and Gregory found to their satisfaction that the flarepath and visual *Lorenz* south-east/north-west runways were lit up like beacons. After a few minutes, the lights were doused, to be replaced with a decoy set of lights to the south-west. Braham and Gregory were not diverted from their task. They could see the exhausts of twin-engined German night-fighters orbiting the area and Gregory spotted a Bf 110 chasing a Beaufighter. Braham allowed the pursuer to almost get within firing range before coming up 1,000 ft behind it. At 600 ft dead ahead, he pumped a 3-second burst of cannon and machine-gun fire into the Bf 110. There was a white glow and it burst into flames. Braham followed it down and pumped another 2-second burst into the

*The enemy. Messerschmitt Bf 110G-4/R1 night-fighter of NJG 3 equipped with early type FuG 202 Lichtenstein BC radar. The equipment worked on 490 MHz and could operate as far as 2½ miles.*

doomed Bf 110 before it hit the ground and exploded.

On 25/26 June, six Beaufighters were employed on Bomber Support operations as 473 bombers bombed Gelsenkirchen. Winnie Winn and R. A. W. Scott, and Kelsey and Smith set out from Coltishall to patrol the German night-fighter airfield at Rheine in Germany while the other four Beaufighters were to head for the airfields at Deelen, Twenthe and Venlo in Holland. Ninety miles out to sea, Winn suffered an engine failure and was forced to return to Coltishall on one engine. LeBoutte and Parrott, and F/O R. J. Dix and Sgt A. J. Salmon aborted with radio malfunctions soon after leaving the English coast and returned to Wittering. Kelsey and Edward Smith caught a Bf 110 flying east in a gentle curve to the south and gave chase before the enemy crew could creep up on them. For ten minutes both aircraft tried to out manoeuvre each other. Finally, Kelsey got behind his adversary and from 900 ft gave him a 3-second burst of cannon and machine-gun fire. First, the enemy's port engine caught fire and there were strikes on his fuselage and starboard engine. Then as Kelsey overshot him, he lifted his right wing to avoid collision and a shower of large burning pieces flew off the enemy aircraft and struck the Beaufighter, fortunately doing no more damage than making some dents and scratches under the wings and fuselage. The enemy machine went down over Hardenburgh in a ball of flame. On the debit side, Bomber Command lost 30 aircraft this night.

In an attempt to rack up more losses in the bomber streams, Oblt Hans-Joachim 'Hajo' Herrmann, a bomber pilot, began forming a Kommando on 27 June using Fw 190A fighters fitted with 300-litre (66-gallon) drop tanks for Wilde Sau attacks on heavy bombers over the Reich. Hermann had reasoned that enemy bombers could be easily identified over a German city by the light of the massed searchlights, Pathfinder flares and the flames of the burning target below. By putting a mass concentration of mainly single-seat night-fighters over the target, his pilots could, without need of ground control, visually identify the bombers and shoot them down. Three Geschwader, JG 300, JG 301 and JG 302, which formed 30 Jagddivision, were raised to carry out Wilde Sau tactics. These units were equipped with the Focke Wulf 190F-5/U2 and the Bf 109G-6/U4N. Additional FuG 25a and FuG 16zy radio equipment and the GuG 350 Naxos Z radar-receiving set were installed. The 30 Jagddivision operated until March 1944, picking up H2S radar emissions from up to 30 miles away.

Meanwhile, on 28/29 June, when Harris sent 608 bombers to Köln, 25 failed to return. Six Beaufighters of 141 Squadron operated but without success. Bob Braham and Sticks Gregory had a close encounter with two Ju 88s at 18,000 ft near Beverloo during their Intruder patrol near Venlo. One of the Junkers attacked from behind while the other approached the Beaufighter from straight ahead. At a range of 1,000 ft, the under gun opened up, firing three quick bursts of red tracer and continuing until the Beaufighter passed underneath. Braham's left engine burst into flames and continued burning for some minutes until he switched off the engine. He managed to elude his adversaries by diving and weaving hard to starboard into cloud.

In all, 141 Squadron flew 46 Serrate sorties during June, destroying five enemy aircraft for the loss of one Beaufighter. On 10 occasions, aircraft had been forced to return with failures of radar equipment, instruments or an engine. It was obvious that despite its impressive firepower and rugged airframe which could absorb great punishment, the Beaufighter was not going to be the answer to successful Serrate operations. Enemy aircraft picked up more than 4 to 5 miles away on Serrate were out of range for the Beaufighter VIF which did not have sufficient speed to chase and close from this distance. Its lack of manoeuvrability in combat was a worrying factor and the aircraft's reduced time on patrol cut down the opportunities for interception. The much vaunted Mosquito was not available for *Serrate* operations and 141 Squadron was forced to continue using the Beaufighter, at least for a few more months.

In July, 141 Squadron flew 66 *Serrate* Bomber Support operations on 10 nights. Flying Officer H. E. 'Harry' White and his navigator/radio operator Flying Officer Mike Seamer Allen damaged a Bf 110 near Aachen while on patrol to the German airfield at Eindhoven on 3/4 July when 653 bombers went to Köln. White blasted the night-fighter at 200 yards dead astern in a 2-second burst and then gave the enemy a second burst of cannon and machine-gun fire before diving violently away to port to avoid collision. The enemy aircraft was not seen again and they could only claim a 'damaged'. Thirty RAF bombers failed to return, 12 of them shot down by Hajo Herrmann's Fw 190A-4s employing *Wilde Sau* tactics.

As a 17-year-old, Harry White had enlisted in the RAF in 1940 having lied about his age. On 4 August 1940, Sgt White, as he then was, crewed up with 18-year-old AC2 Allen at 54 OTU Church Fenton. In September 1941, they were posted from the OTU to 29 Squadron at West Malling where they started defensive night patrols in Beaufighters. Harry White was then only 18¼. After only six weeks, they were posted to 1455 Flight (later renumbered 534 Squadron) at Tangmere, a Havoc and Boston *Turbinlite* squadron. Young Harry was commissioned as a Pilot Officer on 26 March 1942. They operated on *Turbinlites* on home defence until 19 January 1943 with no success at all, but before he was 21 Harry White's bravery had earned him a DFC*. When the *Turbinlite* units were disbanded, Harry and his Navigator were posted back to a Beaufighter squadron, 141 at Ford. Much

to their disappointment, they were attached to a Ferry Unit at Lyneham and spent four frustrating months ferrying new Beaufighters from Britain to Egypt, eventually rejoining 141 at Wittering on 15 June 1943.

The only enemy aircraft destroyed in July – 15/16 July– fell to White and Allen, their first victory. The two men took off from the forward base at West Malling on an *Intruder* patrol to Juvincourt, one of six Beaufighters providing Bomber Support for the Main Force of 165 Halifaxes whose target was the Peugeot Motor Works at Montbeliard, a suburb of Sochaux. Eight miles south-east of Rheims, Harry White and Mike Allen saw a Bf 110 flying straight and level at 10,000 ft. The Beaufighter, which was 2,000 ft above the enemy machine, flown by Major Herbert Rauh of II./NJG4, dived and got dead astern and slightly below before White opened fire from 750 ft, closing to 600 ft. The 2-second burst of cannon and machine-gun fire hit both engines and the fuselage. A moment later, the aircraft exploded in flames, broke in two and struck the ground. Michael Allen recalls:

As it went down in flames we started to congratulate ourselves and for the next ten minutes the Beau flew itself, whilst we continued to tell each other what clever chaps we were and how easy it was to shoot down enemy aircraft . . . and how many more we were going to get! [White and Allen would become the most successful fighter team 141 Squadron ever had]. After all, we had been flying together for two years with 'NO JOY' at all, so a little celebration was justified! But as usual, we overdid it and nearly got ourselves shot down in the process!

In our exuberance (shooting down an enemy aircraft was just like scoring a try in Rugby . . . the feeling was just the same!) we flew over Dreux. 'A searchlight came on and tried unsuccessfully to pick us up and there was a good deal of heavy flak, far too accurate for comfort. . .'(so reads our combat report). We managed to extricate ourselves from the mess into which our carelessness had led us and 're-crossed the coast at Ouistreham at 02:45 hrs . . .' On landing back at Wittering, the excitement of our ground-crew matched our's [sic] of earlier in the night which had nearly cost us so dear! As the immortal Group Captain Cheshire said '. . . the moment you think everything is all right and I'm clear . . . that is the time to watch out for trouble . . .'

Losses to the main force had reached such proportions (275 were shot down in June) that Bomber Command was at last given permission to use *Window*. This was the code-name for strips of black paper with aluminium foil stuck to one side, cut to a length equivalent to half the wavelength of the *Würzburg* ground, and *Lichtenstein* airborne radars, and dropped by aircraft one bundle a minute to 'snow' the tubes. Although *Window* had been devised in 1942, its use by Bomber Command had been forbidden until now for fear that the Luftwaffe would use it in a new Blitz on Great Britain. When 'Bomber' Harris launched the first of four raids, code-named *Gomorrah*, on the port of Hamburg on 24/25 July, *Window* was carried in the 791 bombers for the first time. Led by H2S PFF aircraft, the bombing force reigned down 2,284 tons of HE and incendiaries on the dockyards and city districts of Hamburg, creating a fire-storm which rose to a height of 2½ miles. The *Himmelbett* (literally translated, 'bed of heavenly bliss', or 'four-poster bed' because of the four night-fighter control zones) GCI control system and the German night-fighters had no answer to the British countermeasures. Only 12 bombers, just 1.5 per cent of the force, were lost. Hamburg had been destroyed once before by fire, in 1842. Over four nights in July–August 1943, 3,000 bombers dropped 10,000 tons of HE and incendiary bombs to totally devastate the city and kill 50,000 of its inhabitants.

No. 141 Squadron's Beaufighters did not participate in the Hamburg operation on 24/25 July but five were used on the night of the second raid on 27/28 July when only 17 aircraft from the force of 787 aircraft were lost, and eight took part on 29/30 July, when 28 out of 777 bombers were shot down. Seven Beaufighters flew *Intruder* patrols on the fourth and final night of the raids on Hamburg on 2/3 August when 30 out of 740 bombers were lost.

By the late summer of 1943, the majority of the German night-fighter force was in complete disarray. *Window* rendered useless the *Würzburg* ground radar, the *Lichtenstein* AI airborne radar in the night-fighters, and the radar-predicted AA guns and searchlights. Crews took advantage of this ascendancy. On 9/10 August, Bob Braham notched his fourth victory since joining 141 Squadron, and his sixteenth overall, when he destroyed a Bf 110 on a patrol to the German fighter airfield at St Trond in Belgium. Sticks Gregory, who as usual flew as his navigator and operated the radar, was then rested and replaced by F/Lt H. 'Jacko' Jacobs DFC, who had been instructing at 51 OTU, Cranfield. On 12/13 August, when Bomber Command attacked Turin with 656 aircraft, 141 Squadron flew *Serrate* sorties over France. Squadron Leader F. P. Davis and Flying Officer J. R. Wheldon destroyed a Ju 88 about 30 miles south-west of Paris. Three nights later, Winnie Winn and F/O R. A. W. Scott's Beaufighter was hit by machine-gun fire from a Wellington over France but Winn was able to belly-land at Ford, without flaps or undercarriage. One other crew was intercepted by a Mosquito and fired on by AA gunners near Chichester. Flight Sergeant M. M. 'Robbie' Robertson and Flight Sergeant Douglas J. Gillam were shot down by return fire from a He 177 over France and were taken prisoner.

On 16 August, 141 Squadron began receiving the first of a few, albeit war-weary, Mosquito Mk II aircraft fitted with Mk IV AI radar. The first *Serrate*-equipped Mosquitoes would not arrive until 16 October and even these were of the 'clapped out' variety. Also on 16 August, Howard Kelsey and Edward Smith, notched their third victory when they destroyed a Ju 88 and claimed a Bf 110 as a 'probable' when they jumped a formation of two Ju 88s and a Bf 110 near Etampes flying at 17,000 ft during an *Intruder* patrol to Châteaudun. The second Ju 88 was damaged in the encounter.

No. 141 Squadron's greatest operation so far, however, came on 17/18 August when Bomber Command attacked the secret experimental research establishment at Peenemünde on the Baltic which was developing the V-1 pilotless flying bomb and the V-2 rocket. Some 597 bombers were dispatched and the bombing, carried out in moonlight to aid accuracy, was orchestrated for the first time by a Master Bomber, G/C J. H. Searby. The German night-fighter force operated in large numbers employing large-scale *Zahme Sau* (Tame Boar) tactics for the first time. *Zahme Sau* had been developed by Oberst Victor von Lossberg of the Luftwaffe's Staff College in Berlin. The *Himmelbett* ground network provided a running commentary for its night-fighters, directing them to where the *Window* concentration was at its most dense. Although the ground controllers were fooled into thinking the bombers were headed for Stettin and a further Spoof by Mosquitoes aiming for Berlin drew more fighters away from the Peenemünde force, some 40 Lancasters, Halifaxes and Stirlings, or 6.7 per cent of the force, were shot down.

Ten of 141 Squadron's Beaufighters patrolled German night-fighter bases in Germany and Holland this night. Bob Braham and Jacko Jacobs destroyed two Bf 110s of IV./NJG1 from Leeuwarden. Four

Bf 110s of this unit under Lt Heinz-Wolfgang Schnaufer had taken off to intercept what they thought were heavy bombers. (Schnaufer and Ofw Scherfling aborted after engine failure.) Braham's first victim was Fw George Kraft, a night-fighter ace with 14 victories. He and his radar operator, Uffz Rudolf Dunger bailed out into the sea. Dunger was rescued two hours later but Kraft's body was washed ashore in Denmark four weeks later. Braham's second victim was the Bf 110 flown by Fw Heinz Vinke, a night-fighter ace with over 20 victories. The radar operator, Fw Karl Schödl and the gunner, Uffz Johann Gaa – both of whom were wounded – and Vinke bailed out into the sea. Only Vinke, who was picked up after 18 hours in the water, survived. He and Dunger later formed a crew with Uffz Vinke and had scored 54 victories when they were shot down on 26 February 1944 and he, Dunger and Walter were killed.

Harry White and Mike Allen had a close shave when, during their first contact, the enemy aircraft, a Bf 110, got on their tail and gave them a short burst of tracer which fortunately passed just over the top of them. Twenty minutes later, the Mosquito crew got on the tail of a Bf 110 and Allen gave it brief burst. Strikes were recorded before it dived away but they could only claim a 'damaged'. (Their total number of victories was increased by one in the postwar years when Martin Middlebrook's research for his book *The Peenemünde Raid* revealed that the Bf 110, from 111/NJGI, flown by Hauptmann Wilhelm Dormann, a pre-war Lufthansa pilot, with radar operator Obfw Friedrich Schmalscheidt, had in fact been destroyed. Schmalscheidt was killed when his parachute did not fully open. Dormann also bailed out and suffered severe head injuries and burns. He never flew operationally again.) There was no mistake with the third contact, which was exploded by Harry White's raking fire, but the two men identified it as a 'Ju 88'. It was actually a Bf 110 of 12./NJG1 flown by Lt Gerhard Dittmann and Uffz Theophil Bundschun, who were both killed.

Signs were that the German night-fighter force was beginning to overcome the RAF radar countermeasures, for on 23/24 August, when 719 bombers attacked Berlin, 62 aircraft were shot down, 56 of them by German night-fighters of JG 300 employing *Wilde Sau* tactics. This represented a loss rate of 8.6 per cent, the heaviest loss suffered by Bomber Command thus far. No. 141 Squadron put up 10 Beaufighters which patrolled bases in Holland and Germany but to no avail.

At the end of August, Wittering became a little crowded with the influx of American personnel of the 20th Fighter Group, whose 77th and 79th Squadrons moved into the satellite airfield at King's Cliffe. The 55th Fighter Squadron was to be based at Wittering. The 20th was equipped with the P-38 Lightning. The CO, Maj D. R. McGovern from Providence, Rhode Island, had served in the Pacific flying P-39 Airacobras and had destroyed five Japanese aircraft. He and Bob Braham became friends. On 20 September, Braham and Jacko Jacobs in a Mosquito engaged in a local friendly dogfight with a P-38. Braham found that even though the Mosquito was worn out and meant for training and with his inexperience of the aircraft, it was, in his opinion, superior to the Lightning.

During September, 141 Squadron flew 56 *Serrate* sorties on 11 nights. Flying Officer Harry White and Flying Officer Mike Allen scored their fourth kill when they destroyed a Ju 88 on 6/7 September. On 15/16 September, 141 Squadron dispatched seven Beaufighters to Ford to provide support for the raid by 369 aircraft on the Dunlop rubber factory at Montluçon. A Beaufighter crewed by F/Lt Robert W. Ferguson and F/O R. W. Osborn developed engine trouble on an *Intruder* patrol to the airfield at Chartres and had to ditch in the sea. Ferguson's body was never found.

Osborn was found after 36 hours in a dinghy by a Walrus and returned to Wittering.

The month closed with two more memorable sorties by Bob Braham. On 27/28 September, during an *Intruder* patrol to the Bremen area, he and Jacko Jacobs chased a Do 217 10 miles west of Hannover. The Dornier stood no chance and was quickly dispatched in flames. Braham recorded in his logbook that this operation was 'bags of fun'. He also stated that they received a hit on their aircraft by flak as they crossed from Holland over the island of Texel. Braham's twentieth victory, and the eighth while with 141 Squadron, occurred on 29/30 September when Maj McGovern flew as a passenger with Braham and Jacobs on what was Braham's last operation with 141 Squadron. They set off from Coltishall at 19:20 hours and carried out an *Intruder* patrol to Twenthe in Holland. Over the Zuider Zee they saw an enemy aircraft and shortly thereafter recognized it as a Bf 110. It took Braham 10 minutes of fierce manoeuvring before he could finally out-turn the enemy aircraft and 5 miles west of Elburg give him a 3-second burst from astern. Although he did not know it, his adversary was Hptm August Geiger of 7./NJG1 who had 53 victories. Geiger received hits all over his aircraft before it exploded into a mass of flames and dived straight into the Zuider Zee.

After a few minutes, Braham and Jacobs got a visual on a Ju 88 about 3 miles south of Zwolle, which was also turning and climbing for a position to attack, just as Geiger had tried to do. He was no more successful than Geiger had been. Braham gave the Junkers a 2-second burst of cannon and machine-gun fire from 150 yards astern before his cannons infuriatingly jammed. Strikes were observed on both wing roots and there was an explosion in the fuselage which burnt for 1 or 2 seconds before the Ju 88 dived away sharply to the right and disappeared from sight. Braham could only claim a 'damaged'. Much to his chagrin, after this operation Braham had to take a rest at the insistence of AOC 12 Group, AVM Roderick Hill. Wing Commander K. C. Roberts, late of 151 Squadron, arrived at Wittering to take command. Braham left the squadron as the top ace night-fighter pilot. That 141 Squadron had been selected as the first *Serrate* squadron was down to this exceptional pilot who was a magnificent example to his men.

A convivial evening was held at the George Hotel, Stamford to celebrate the Squadron's victories. By the end of the evening, everyone except Doc Dougall, who was left behind, drove back to Wittering. The Mad Irishman did not fancy a long walk back to the airfield and so looked around for alternative transport. At the back of the hotel, he saw three bicycles, one a man's, one a woman's and one meant for a very small child, all belonging to the landlord. For a wheeze Dougall rode, with great difficulty, the child's cycle all the way back to the station, and during the next few days proceeded to cycle around the camp on it. Unfortunately, the landlord did not see the funny side of what was just a high-spirited prank, and made an official complaint. At his subsequent court martial Dougall was accused of actually stealing the cycle! He was acquitted but posted to Balloon Command within days. He had the whole Squadron's respect for his medical expertise and also for his courage in flying on some operations with Braham.

During October, 141 Squadron flew 49 *Serrate* Bomber Support operations on nine nights. It was a very disappointing month for the squadron with a large number (15) of early returns caused by problems with radar, engines and the weather. One Beaufighter was lost. Operationally, November proved equally disappointing. Bad weather prevented Bomber Command flying any operations from 12–17

November. On 18 November, it was announced that with effect from 15 November, Wittering came under the Command of the Air Defence of Great Britain on the reorganization of Fighter Command into ADGB and the Tactical Air Force. Night *Intruder* operations using Mosquitoes had begun in April–May 1943 when five squadrons had begun operations, and three more had begun day *Rangers* (daylight cloud-cover patrols). In May, 60 OTU at High Ercall had been expanded and made responsible for all *Intruder* training. Beginning in June, Mosquitoes of 605 Squadron began successful, albeit small-scale, Bomber Support *Flower* attacks on German night-fighter airfields during raids by Main Force bombers. *Flowers* supported bombers by disrupting the *Himmelbett* chain. Long-range *Intruder* aircraft fitted with limited radar equipment were used, and these proceeded to the target at high altitude, diving down whenever they saw airfields illuminated. This type of operation if correctly timed, prevented the enemy night-fighters, already short of petrol, from landing at their bases.

In August, Mosquitoes of 25 and 410 Squadrons began *Mahmoud* sorties (single Mosquitoes employed as bait for enemy night-fighters in their known assembly areas) over enemy territory. The enemy fighter would be allowed to stalk its prey, picked up by *Monica* radar built into the tail of the Mosquito, then its crew would circle and shoot down the unsuspecting German crew using AI Mk IV for direction. Mosquito operations were extended to include loose escort duties for the Main Force. On 18/19 November, Bomber Command began the main phase of The Battle of Berlin and for the next four and a half months, ACM Sir Arthur Harris attempted to destroy the German capital. A new RAF Group would figure largely in the bombing campaign and the role of 141 Squadron was expanded.

# CHAPTER 2

# *THE BATTLE OF BERLIN*

*Mitten in dem stärksten Feuer,*
*Swischen Fliegern, Flak und Mordsradau,*
*Ja, das wird dem Tommy teuer:*
*Die Horridos der „Wilden Sau"!*

'DAS LIED VON DER „WILDEN SAU"' BY PETER HOLM

Over the Reich the German battle-cries, 'Pauke! Pauke!' and 'Horrido!' ('Tallyho!' – St Horridus was the patron saint of German fighter pilots), were still being heard all too often as the Nachtjagdgruppen infiltrated the bomber streams and wreaked havoc among the heavy bombers. This was despite extensive countermeasures and day and night *Ranger* and *Intruder* patrols. The introduction of *Window* had changed the whole method of German night defence and the manner in which their night-fighters operated. *Zahme Sau* tactics in particular had reduced the chances of successful interceptions by the *Serrate* equipped Beaufighters of 141

*Focke Wulf 190 fighters similar to this one were employed in* Zahme Sau *and* Wilde Sau *night-fighter tactics against RAF bombers*

25

Squadron, especially when the target was as far away as Berlin where the Beaufighter's short range proved a severe handicap. The Mosquito could reach Berlin but re-equipment for the Wittering-based squadron was slow.

In October 1943, 141 Squadron had only received three elderly Mk IIs each of which had seen extended operational service with other squadrons before being issued to 141 Squadron. One had been badly damaged on operations and one other had twice been involved in flying accidents. The Merlin 21s were also well used and over the next few weeks maintenance problems were the bane of the fitters' lives as they struggled to keep airworthy the few Mosquitoes in their charge. Finally, in February 1944, all reconditioned engines were called in and while stocks lasted, only Merlin 22s were installed. There were also troubles with the Mk IV AI radar and *Serrate* installed in the Mosquitoes. Flying Officer MacKenzie of the TRE at Malvern was attached to 141 Squadron on 13 November to assist in locating the trouble with the radar equipment in the Mosquitoes.

One of the first Mosquitoes and crew were written off on 13 November during a practice flight and camera-gun exercise with a Stirling. Flying Officer J. D. Bridge and Flight Sergeant L. J. W. Cullen had just made a camera-gun attack on the bomber and had broken away when the Mosquito appeared to go into a vertical dive. Pieces of the aircraft were seen to break away and it finally hit the ground near Polebrook and exploded. Two days later, a second Mosquito was lost during a test flight. Engine failure was blamed as the cause of the crash which killed F/O D. F. A. Welsh and his navigator, F/O W. C. Ripley. No. 141 Squadron dispatched its first Mosquito on 18/19 November when Bomber Command attacked Berlin with 440 aircraft and Mannheim/Ludwigshaven with 395 aircraft. Thirty-two bombers failed to return. Next night, 141 dispatched two Beaufighters and a single Mosquito flown by S/L Winn DFC and F/L R. A. W. Scott.

*Mosquito NF II DD737, the type which began to equip 141 Squadron in October 1943. The first three received were elderly machines which had seen extensive operational service with other squadrons and the Merlin 21s were well used. There were also troubles with the Mk IV AI radar and* Serrate *installed in the Mosquitoes.*

*100 Group was formed on 23 November 1943. Its badge has the head of one of the Gorgons, three-winged monstrous sisters of Greek mythology who had live snakes for hair, huge teeth and brazen claws. The motto* Sarang Tebuan Jangan Dijolok *is Malay for* Confound and Destroy. *(G/C Jack Short)*

fighter force. The primary duty of 100 Group was to reduce the escalating losses being suffered by the heavy bomber force over Germany. Addison had previously commanded 80 Wing RAF, which as a wing commander, he had established at Garston in June 1940. At that time, the Air Ministry had a complete picture of the main blind-bombing and navigation aids used by the Luftwaffe. Between June 1940 and the winter of 1941 *X-Gerät* (X-equipment) blind-bombing aid (of which it had first been aware in 1939) and *Knickebein* (Bent Leg), which could be used by bombers equipped with the *Lorenz* blind-approach aid, were successfully jammed and rendered useless. The *Y-Gerät*, used only in the He 111H-4s of III/KG 26, was also jammed effectively before this unit took part in Barbarossa, the invasion of Russia.

All returned safely. On 22/23 November, 764 bombers attacked Berlin again and 141 Squadron dispatched three Mosquitoes and two Beaufighters. Two of the Mosquitoes and the two Beaufighters returned early with various equipment failures and only one Mosquito reached its patrol area at Salzwedel.

The first unit to move to 100 Group, from 3 Group at Gransden Lodge, was 192

Despite the early problems, the Mosquito would become the main offensive weapon in 100 Group (Bomber Support), which was created on 23 November under the command of Air Commodore (later AVM) E. B. Addison, at Radlett, Herts. It had become obvious that the RAF needed a specialized bomber support force to integrate radio countermeasures (RCM) and ELINT (electronic intelligence), and a long-range

*On 23 November, Air Commodore (later AVM) E. B. Addison established 100 Group HQ at Radlett, Herts. Its primary duty was to reduce the escalating losses being suffered by the heavy bomber force over Germany. Addison had previously commanded 80 Wing RAF which, as a wing commander, he had established at Garston in June 1940.*

*Derelict Bylaugh Hall near Swanton Morley, Norfolk pictured in 1994. In its former glory, it served as the headquarters of 100 Group throughout the war from 18 January 1944 onwards. (Author)*

Squadron. Its Blind Approach Training Development Unit had started to fly on the German *Ruffian* and *Knickebein* beams. No. 192 had been formed at Gransden Lodge on 4 January 1943 from 1474 Flight for the ELINT role with three Mosquito Mk IVs, two Halifax Mk IIs and 11 Wellington Mk Xs to monitor German radio and radar. The squadron had always been part of the Y-Service and, as such, its primary object had been a complete and detailed analysis from the air of the enemy signals organization. It arrived at Foulsham in Norfolk on 7 December.

Addison's HQ would not move to the county until 3 December when it was established at RAF West Raynham, 8 miles from Fakenham. A permanent HQ, at Bylaugh Hall near Swanton Morley, would not be ready for occupation on 18 January 1944, when 2 Group HQ moved to Mongewell Park near Wallingford in Berkshire, becoming part of 2nd Tactical Air Force. Late in November, W/C Roberts was informed that West Raynham would also be the new home for 141 Squadron, which would become the first operational

squadron in 100 Group, and that the squadron would be moving to Raynham on 3 December. There, 141 Squadron really got down to conversion from Beaufighter VIs to Mosquito IIs. The Squadron diarist reported:

TRE were sublimely happy with their *Serrate* aerial design for the Mosquitoes. Everybody knew the design was perfect – except the aircrew who were troublesome enough to find it almost impossible to direction find in a turn. This resulted in the Squadron having to operate, half Beaus and half inadequate Mosquitoes, and consequently many opportunities were lost. Spirits flagged. Despondency set in among the overworked Radar mechanics. Perhaps the one thing which served to restore confidence more than anything else was that an informal chat in the Mess between F/O Pollard (Squadron Radar Officer) and the AOC, which resulted in a Mosquito being placed exclusively at Pollard's disposal for experimental purposes. Within a fortnight this cutting of red tape bore fruit and a new and satisfactory aerial system was designed.

*Mosquito NF II DD750 of 239 Squadron showing* Serrate *wing-mounted receiver aerials. No. 239 began receiving Mosquito night-fighters on 11 December 1943. Mk IIs given to 100 Group had usually seen long service and this aircraft was no exception, serving with 157, 25 and 264 Squadrons. Mechanical troubles plagued the* Serrate *squadrons until finally, in February 1944, all reconditioned engines were called in and, while stocks lasted, only Merlin 22s were installed. (Philip Birtles)*

The fitting of these new aerials was a difficult and tedious operation. TRE were worried. de Havilland's representative was worried. In fact everyone was worried except Pollard, who proceeded to get on with the job slowly but surely with many a strip of tinfoil over the leading edges and vast quantities of Bostik (who in the Squadron will ever forget Bostik night in the Mess? One W/Cdr at Group still wears his neatly parted hair as if it were rubberized). Eventually, the job was done – and well done – and the squadron were completely converted to Mosquito II.

In the meantime, on 6 December, 141 Squadron was joined by the advance party of 239 Squadron which had been training at Ayr and Drem for *Serrate* Bomber Support operations. No. 239 had been reformed at Ayr in September 1943. Its previous function had been Army Co-operation, so that all aircrew for its new role of the offensive night-fighting had to be posted in. With W/C P. M. J. Evans DFC as

Squadron Commander, S/L Black and S/L Kinchin as flight commanders, and F/L Carpenter and F/L 'Jacko' Jacobs DFC* as N/R Leader and navigation officer respectively, the 18 crews began their training. The squadron diarist recorded:

They were all anxious to press on but a deplorable absence of aircraft made practice flying a very great rarity. It was not until well into October that a dual-controlled Mosquito became available, and as late as the last week in November Form 540 contained the pathetic entry: 'Training was carried out in the Mosquito.' Most of the flying personnel were experienced AI crews from Fighter Command, and their enthusiasm on being posted to a Squadron destined for offensive work was somewhat lessened as week after week dragged by with the operational goal seemingly as far away as ever.

On 9 December, 239 Squadron moved to West Raynham and on 11 December two operational Mosquito IIs equipped with Mk IV AI forward-looking and backward-looking *Serrate* equipment and the Gee navigational aid, arrived. The squadron trained at every available opportunity when the weather allowed. Meanwhile, 169 Squadron, the third equipped with *Serrate*, moved from Ayr to Little Snoring on 7 and 8 December. The squadron had been reformed at Ayr on 15 September under the command of W/C E. J. 'Jumbo' Gracie DFC, 'a little fire-eater' who, as a F/L flying Hurricanes in 56 Squadron in the Battle of Britain, had shared in the destruction of a Bf 110 on 19 July 1940. Later, in the Mediterranean, he flew Spitfires from the carriers *Eagle* and *Wasp* to reinforce units on Malta. He finally commanded a Wing at Takali before returning to England to command 169 Squadron. The groundcrew were all retained from the old Mustang squadron and aircrew were posted in, mostly made up of volunteers from night-fighter squadrons. A Mosquito II and a Beaufighter were delivered towards the end of October, followed by further Beaufighters. All aircrew underwent a course with 1692 Flight at Drem and all

pilots went on to the Rolls Royce Engine Handling Course.

For 12 nights from 4 December, not one heavy bomber had operated because of a full moon and bad weather. When Bomber Command resumed operations on 16/17 December with an attack on Berlin by 483 Lancasters and 15 Mosquitoes, two Beaufighters and two Mosquitoes of 141 Squadron took off from West Raynham on 100 Group's first offensive night-fighter patrols in support of the heavies. It was hardly an auspicious occasion and became known as 'Black Thursday'. Bomber Command lost 25 Lancasters and a further 34 Lancs were lost on their return to England due to very bad weather causing collisions, crashes and some bale-outs after aircraft ran out of fuel. One of the Mosquitoes was flown by S/L (later W/C) Freddie 'Cordite' Lambert with his navigator/radio operator, F/O Ken Dear. Lambert had picked up the nickname Cordite while flying Westland Wapitis policing the North West Frontier. Later, he had commanded 110 Squadron in India, flying Vultee Vengeances against the Japanese. The two Beaufighters and Lambert and Dear patrolled the airfield at

*100 Group airfields in Norfolk November 1943 – May 1945. 100 Group was disbanded in December 1945.*

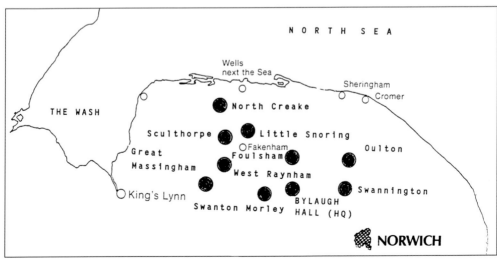

Hoya. One of the Beaufighters was forced to return to base early after *Serrate* and AI both failed near the German border, while the second Mosquito aborted with engine trouble on the way over the Dutch coast. Flight Sergeant Coles and Flight Sergeant J. A. Carter reached Hoya but had to abort the operation when their back hatch blew open during a hard turn to port. They turned for home and were chased for about 20 minutes by what was presumed to be an enemy night-fighter.

Lambert and Dear pressed on in their Mosquito II. From 30 miles within the Dutch coast and all along the route they received indications of some 18–20 aircraft, all about 10 miles distant. Nevertheless, they proceeded as ordered to Hoya where, at 19:20 hours Dear picked up a *Serrate* contact 10 miles ahead and 25° to port. The enemy aircraft was flying at about their height of 21,000 ft. It had clearly picked up the Mosquito because the next indication they had was when the bogey closed, and some 5 minutes later an AI back blip at a range of 2,000 ft was picked up slightly to port. Lambert peeled off to port and lost height. He levelled off at 10,000 ft hoping that the enemy would reappear in front or allow him to turn and get behind it. The blip split into two and Dear suspected that there were two enemy night-fighters tailing them. A violent dogfight ensued and the enemy aircraft fired a long burst from close range and two more bursts from within 2,000 ft but without doing any damage. Throughout the fight the enemy aircraft clung on like a leech. Finally, the enemy machine overshot beneath the Mosquito as both turned hard to starboard. The enemy aircraft was close enough to be identified as a Bf 110. Lambert immediately gave the Bf 110 a burst of 40 rounds from his cannons lasting about 2 seconds, opening at 900 ft and ceasing fire at 1,200 ft from slightly above and with 1½ rings of deflection. Several strikes were observed on the enemy machine and Lambert claimed a

*Sitting duck for a* Zahme Sau *night-fighter. A Lancaster is silhouetted against the night sky over Berlin on 13 December 1943.*

'damaged'. He tried to follow up the attack but the Bf 110 was now lost to view and the AI set had packed up. Lambert and Dear returned to Norfolk and put down at Downham Market before returning to West Raynham.

The next heavy raid by the Main Force took place on 20/21 December when 650 bombers attacked Frankfurt. Again, losses were high. Some 41 bombers were lost, despite a diversionary raid on Mannheim by 54 aircraft. No. 141 dispatched two Beaufighters, one of which returned almost immediately because of intercom trouble. On 23/24 December 390 bombers returned to Berlin. No. 141 Squadron was still going it alone on the *Serrate* beat and managed only three Beaufighters for the night's operation. One Beaufighter was forced to abort on reaching their patrol area at Hassalt when the *Serrate* equipment became inoperative. The 21-year-old pilot,

F/O Bernard Gunnill, and 22-year-old F/Sgt Harry Hanson, his navigator/radar operator, took off from West Raynham at 00:35 hours on Christmas Eve and were never seen again. Both these young men are buried in the Schoonselhof Cemetery at Antwerp in Belgium.

The third Beaufighter, flown by Howard Kelsey with Edward Smith, had also taken off at the same time as Gunnill and Hanson. They stooged around for some time on their patrol track at Uckerath, Germany, picking up numerous weak *Serrate* contacts. At 01:55 hours at 20,000 ft, two *Serrate* contacts were made hard to starboard at 10 miles range but they were above them and as the Beaufighter was already at 20,000 ft, Kelsey declined the chase. He patrolled Uckerath to no avail and then turned towards Düren. At 02:15 hours at 23,000 ft Smitty picked up a *Serrate* contact slightly below them and 10 miles to the north. Kelsey turned the Beaufighter and chased the contact at 300 mph IAS, which was flying south very fast. At 5 miles range the enemy turned east. Smitty obtained contact on the AI at a range of 14,000 ft. Visual contact was obtained some minutes later. It was a Ju 88 burning green and white resins. Kelsey had the impression the Junkers was drawing away so he let fly with a burst of cannon and machine-gun fire from 1,000 ft. The Ju 88 slowed and

Kelsey pumped another 7-second burst into it, closing to 300 ft. Strikes were seen all over the aircraft, which turned steeply to port and dived straight down with flames streaming from both engines and the fuselage. It exploded on the ground where the glow of the burning pyre could be seen through the 10/10ths cloud.

Immediately afterwards, Kelsey and Smith's Beaufighter was hit by flak at 19,000 ft. The port engine began to run very roughly and various parts of the leading edges and wings were damaged. Smith picked up more *Serrate* contacts but Kelsey was unable to give chase because of the damage to the aircraft. However, when a contact was picked up just 5° below and 5° to starboard, Kelsey turned head on into the enemy's path. It passed 300 ft to starboard and the RAF crew set off in pursuit. Disappointingly, the enemy aircraft managed to lose them by its sheer speed and disappeared in the Moll area. Kelsey got back on course for home and recrossed Schouwen at 03:10 hours at 15,000 ft in a dive. He gave out a Mayday signal but he managed to land back at West Raynham at 04:00 hours without further mishap. Their victory was the fourth they had chalked up since joining the squadron.

On Christmas Day 1943, there were no operations flown and RAF personnel

*F/L Howard Kelsey and P/O E. M. Smith pictured in front of their Beaufighter VIF V8744 of 141 Squadron at RAF Wittering. On 23/24 December 1943, they scored the first 100 Group victory when they shot down a Ju 88 of 4./NJG1 based at St Trond. It crashed near Bergisch-Gladbach, near Cologne. Oblt Finster, pilot, and Staffel Kapitän, was KIA. Fw S. E. Beugel, WIA, bailed out. (Tom Cushing Collection)*

*Mosquito Mk VI HJ716 in flight with a stopped port engine. Much to the chagrin of 141 Squadron, which put up with the troubles associated with the Mosquito II, its Merlin engines and its fickle radar equipment longer than anyone else, 239 Squadron was the first* Serrate *Squadron to receive brand new Mk VI Mosquitoes, in December 1943. No. 169 Squadron began equipping in June 1944 and it was not until August that 141 finally received some Mk VIs.*

enjoyed themselves with football matches between teams of officers and NCOs and an excellent Christmas lunch served to the men by the officers in the Airmen's Mess. In spite of the festivities, 141 Squadron was suffering its most dispirited period since it had suffered such tragic losses to its Defiants during the Battle of Britain. The main reason was the failure of its Mosquito aircraft. The squadron had continued to receive old models. Engines and radar were in such poor condition that on Boxing Day all Mosquitoes were temporarily grounded until modifications were completed by de Havilland engineers. The squadron diarist noted that: 'Experimental work is still proceeding with the Mosquito aircraft and most difficulties have or are being solved.'

Despite this optimism, engine and radar problems still grounded the Mosquitoes when on 29/30 December Bomber Command went to the 'Big City' again with a force of 712 bombers. Most of the Beaufighters had been transferred to other units in anticipation of converting completely to the Mosquito, so 141 Squadron could only operate two Beaufighters this night. Diversionary *Spoof* raids on Düsseldorf, Leipzig and Magdeburg by Mosquitoes succeeded in drawing away a large percentage of the German nightfighters and helped keep losses down to 20 heavy bombers. In the hands of the long range fighter squadrons in 100 Group and cured of all its operating problems, the Mosquito would ultimately provide much of the support Bomber Command needed.

# CHAPTER 3

# *THEY SLAY BY NIGHT*[1]

*Denn – munter ist die „Wilde Sau"!*
*Und wenn es runst und kracht, dann weiß er es genau:*
*Das war ein Flugzeugführer von der „Wilden Sau"!*

'DAS LIED VON DER „WILDE SAU"' BY PETER HOLM

On 1/2 January 1944, Bomber Command returned to the Big City with a force of 421 Lancasters. Twenty-eight Lancasters failed to return. The following night, 383 Lancasters returned to Berlin and 27 bombers were shot down. Throughout the two nights of sustained operations, 141 Squadron was only able to put up two Beaufighters and none at all on the first night of the new year. On 5/6 January, meanwhile, when 358 bombers raided Stettin, with the loss of 16 heavies, 141 Squadron mounted its last Beaufighter *Serrate* sortie of the war when F/L D. V. Anderson and P/O Johnson took off in a Beaufighter VIF for a bomber support patrol to the Frisian Islands. They landed back at West Raynham without incident.

On 7 January the first Mosquito fitted with new modifications was flown to Hatfield from West Raynham for final approval by de Havilland, while W/C Roberts drove to Radlett to expedite the delivery of new equipment. Three days later, a completed Mosquito went to each of the three *Serrate* squadrons. Nos 239 and 169 Squadrons were still under training but two Mosquitoes in 141 Squadron were aloft on *Serrate* duty on 14/15 January when 498 bombers hit Brunswick. A staggering total of 38 bombers failed to return. Almost predictably, there were problems with the *Serrate* Mosquitoes. The Mk II crewed by S/L Freddie Lambert and F/O Ken Dear suffered a port engine failure 20 miles inland of the Dutch coast and was forced to land on one engine at Coltishall. Squadron Leader F. P. Davis and Flying Officer J. R. Wheldon developed faulty inter-communications which forced them to abandon a AI contact chase in the Hoya area. They also had to contend with ominous orange coloured flashes along the length of the cockpit for 15 minutes on the return flight before they landed at 21:50 hours without further mishap.

[1] We Slay By Night is the motto of 141 Squadron.

All three *Serrate* squadrons operated for the first time on 20/21 January. Once again, the war-weary Mosquitoes posed problems for overworked ground staff. At West Raynham six Mosquito IIs were prepared for operation but heavy mist and fog delayed night flying tests until 16:00 hours. These revealed that four were unserviceable, mostly with AI radar and *Serrate* problems. By this late stage, only two Mosquitoes, crewed by S/L J. W. Murray DFC DFM and F/L G. S. Bliss, on their 'freshman' trip, and F/Sgt Ivan D. 'Doug' Gregory and F/Sgt Derek H. 'Steve' Stephens, were cleared for flying. At Little Snoring, W/C Jumbo Gracie, CO of 169 Squadron, and his navigator, F/L Wilton W. Todd, climbed aboard the only squadron Mosquito Mk II fit for duty. No. 239 Squadron also could only muster one Mosquito; F/L Jackson S. Booth DFC and F/L Tommy Carpenter flew the sortie. 'What did you get?' they were asked on their return to West Raynham. 'Back!' they said.

A number of contacts with bogeys were made but no enemy aircraft fell to the guns of the Mosquitoes. Some 35 bombers, however, were shot down by the German defences, which operated the *Zahme Sau* tactics to excellent effect.

*Window* seemed to have been rendered counter-productive by the German night-fighter force. The following night, 21/22 January, when 648 bombers attacked Magdeburg, 20-year-old F/Sgt Desmond Byrne Snape RAAF and F/O I. H. Fowler RCAF of 141 Squadron, one of five Mosquito II crews airborne this night (the fifth was from 239 Squadron), tussled with a Ju 88 during their patrol in the Brandenburg area. German night-fighters shot down 57 bombers. Maj Prince zu Sayn Wittgenstein, Kommodore of NJG4 and a night-fighter ace with 83 or 84 victories,

shot down four or five of the bombers flying a Ju 88G this night and was then shot down and killed by the rear gunner of a Lancaster. Hptm Meurer, CO of 1/NJG1, was also killed when his He 219 Uhu (Owl) was accidentally rammed by a Bf 110.

The 169 Squadron B Flight Commander, S/L Joseph Aloysius Hayes 'Joe' Cooper, and his navigator were flying their freshman *Serrate* op after having been posted from 141 Squadron. Cooper had been one of Bob Braham's flight commanders at West Raynham where he had crewed up with F/L Ralph D. Connolly, an Income Tax Inspector from Dulwich, London. They went to the Dutch Islands; 'to get flak up their arse' on the 21st. Joe Cooper's favourite mount was HJ711 'VI-P', as it significantly was coded. 'Mount' is the operative word. In the early 1930s, Lance Corporal Joe Cooper, or 'Trooper Cooper,' had been a cavalryman in the 4th Hussars. When it mechanized in

*169 Squadron crest designed by S/L Joe Cooper, B Flight Commander. (Author)*

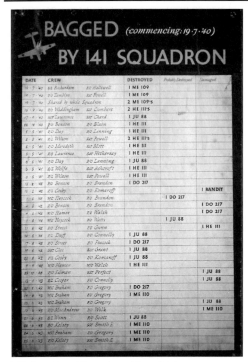

*141 Squadron Victories tables which were once on display at West Raynham (Author)*

1936, Cooper decided he did not wish to drive tanks – he wanted to fly aeroplanes – so he borrowed £25 from a friend and bought his discharge from the Army. He applied for, and surprisingly got, a short service commission in the RAF. 'I'd left school at 14 without the School Certificate but to their credit, the RAF took me in', he recalls. Apart from being a keen horseman, Cooper was an accomplished boxer and he became Lightweight Boxing Champion of the RAF in 1938/39.

Cooper soloed on the Tiger Moth and went on to fly Audaxes and Harts, Blenheim night-fighters and then Beaufighters in 141 Squadron where he was B Flight Commander. 'The Beaufighter was for men not boys,' he fondly recalls. 'I could out-turn the Mosquito in a Beau.' Flying a Beaufighter he and Connolly damaged a Ju 88 on the night of 18 January 1943. In 169 Squadron, Cooper had no problems converting to the new steed, which he christened, *P-Pluto*.

Cooper recorded in his log book: '2 *Serrate* contacts. Chased one. No luck. One AI contact. Behind. Turned on it. Everything blew up. Jinked my way home very startled.'

The next major raid by RAF Bomber Command took place on 27/28 January when a force of 515 bombers attacked Berlin. Again, losses were high. Thirty-three Lancasters were shot down. No. 141 Squadron dispatched seven *Serrate* Mosquitoes and 239 and 169 Squadrons sent off three and two Mosquitoes respectively. However, none of the Mosquitoes recorded any successes, mainly because five crews experienced engine failures and had to abort, while two other aircraft suffered AI failures. On 28/29 January seven Mosquitoes were dispatched from West Raynham. One returned early with equipment failures and 22-year-old F/L Basil 'Johnny' Brachi and his navigator, 37-year-old F/O Angus P. MacLeod of 239 Squadron, failed to return.

During a patrol to Berlin their Mosquito lost its starboard engine over enemy territory and then the port engine started cutting out and finally quit over the North Sea. Crews from 239 and 141 Squadrons conducted an extensive sea search but the two crewmen were never found. (MacLeod's body was later washed ashore in Holland where he is buried.)

Joining the search between 17:10 and 21:20 hours were Harry White and Mike Allen, who had only just returned from their successful sortie at 06:00 hours. Both men had joined 141 Squadron at the same time as Brachi and MacLeod. White and Allen had picked up AI contacts on an enemy aircraft which turned out to be a single-engined machine, probably a Bf 109. White had dispatched it with a 5-second burst of 20 mm cannon fire from astern and below. The enemy aircraft burst into flames and exploded, diving through haze. The other success of the night went to F/O Munro and F/O Hurley of 239 Squadron, the first Squadron victory using *Serrate*.

On 30/31 January, Berlin was attacked again, this time by a force of 534 aircraft. Thirty-three bombers were shot down. Two Mosquitoes were put up by 169 Squadron, including *P-Pluto*. Joe Cooper and Ralph Connolly went all the way to Berlin in VI-P. Joe Cooper recalls:

I had to orbit 50 miles from Berlin on one of the German beacons. We tootled along and just got into position when I picked up a blip in front of me. He was orbiting slowly. Turning down the gunsight I could see the shape. There was no moon and it was very, very dark. I got into position, slightly below, and astern, went up to him and gave him the treatment; cannon – a lot of cannon. We were at about 25,000 ft. He was a complete flamer. Actually, I gave him a bit more. 'That's for Coventry,' I said. But I got in too close. I was mesmerized by it all. Rafe said, 'Look out Joe, you're going to hit the bastard.' I pulled the 'pole' back hard and the result was I stalled and went into a spin. We were not allowed to spin or aerobat the Mosquito because of our long-range belly tanks which moved the centre of gravity of the aircraft. I put on the usual drill; full opposite rudder, stick forward. I'd done this before but never in a Mossie. Went straight into a spin the other way! I went into the spin about five times, heading for the ground all the while. During the spins I could see this 110 out of the corner of my eye; most extraordinary!

One's thoughts were, what a bloody shame. This is going to be the first Hun the Squadron's got and I won't be there to tell the boys. I wonder who's going to hit the ground first, me or him? What a bloody

*FuG 212* Lichtenstein *C-1* Weitwinkel *radar-equipped Bf 110G-4a night-fighter. On the night of 30/31 January S/L Joe Cooper and F/L Ralph Connolly scored the first 169 Squadron victory when they shot down Bf 110G-4 Wrk Nr 740081 D5+LB of Stab III/NJG3, which crashed at Werneuchen, 20 kms east of Berlin. Oblt Karl Loeffelmaan, pilot, KIA. Fw Karl Bareiss, radar operator, and Ofw Oscar Bickert, both WIA, bailed out.*

shame the boys aren't going to know. I told Rafe, 'Bail out. We've had it!' He had an observer-type parachute under his seat. In the spin he couldn't bend down to pick it up! He took his helmet off and put it on again. I said, 'Get out!' Rafe replied, 'If you can get us out of this spin, I could!' I thought, 'I'll try something else.' I centralized the pole and the rudder and eased it out of the dive. At 7,000 ft I straightened up. I had not been frightened but boy was I frightened now. Our radar blew up in the spin. I said to Ralph 'You can kneel and look backwards and keep an eye out for the Huns!' We had light flak all the way back to the coast. Approaching Snoring I called up the tower. 'Is S/L Ted Thorne in the tower?' I asked. 'Yes,' they said. I said, 'Tell him he owes me ten bob.' (I had bet Ted 10 shillings I would get a Hun before him!) Ted took the camp

Tannoy – it was one in the morning – and announced, 'For your information everybody, S/L Cooper is coming into land and he's got the first Hun!' When I landed there were 300 airmen and WAAFs around *P-Pluto*! Most extraordinary! I gave them a little talk and off we went.

On 30/31 January five Mosquitoes from 141 Squadron were also on patrol and one of the crews, F/Lt Graham J. Rice and F/O J. G. Rogerson, destroyed a Bf 110. Two aircraft returned early with engine trouble while F/L John C. N. Forshaw and P/O Frank Folley discovered to their dismay that the cannons would not fire when Forshaw had a Bf 110 in his sights at a range of 900 ft. Howard Kelsey and Smitty Smith chased six or seven *Serrate* contacts at heights varying from 22,000 ft to 6,000 ft

*Fw 190 pilots stand by one of their aircraft. These single-engined fighters were employed in* Wilde Sau *and* Zahme Sau *tactics and were responsible for the loss of 78 bombers on 19/20 February on the operation to Leipzig. F/O Harry White and F/O Mike Allen destroyed a He 177 Beleuchter (Illuminator) which was being used in conjunction with these tactics, on 15/16 February and F/L H. C. Kelsey DFC\* and F/O E. M. Smith DFC, DFM destroyed a Fw 190 over Berlin on 24/25 March (via Hans-Peter Dabrowski)*

but failed to get close to their prey to open fire. After 30 minutes over the target their AI began to develop a 'squint' so they turned for home.

There were no major raids undertaken by Bomber Command during the first two weeks of February 1944 but the *Serrate* squadrons were tasked to support a raid by small forces of Mosquitoes on Berlin, Aachen and Krefeld on 1/2 February. Flight Sergeant Snape and Flying Officer I. H. Fowler returned early after the oxygen supply failed. Just after taking off from West Raynham for practice night flying, a Mosquito flown by S/L A. Black of 239 Squadron crashed at Hill Farm, Great Dunham. Black and his navigator, W/O J. K. Houston, were both killed. Four enemy aircraft were shot down in February. Three of them were accredited to crews in 169 and 239 Squadrons but the first kill that month came on 15/16 February when 891 bombers resumed the attack on Berlin in the biggest raid on the capital so far.

Harry White DFC and Mike Allen DFC took off from West Raynham at 19:20 hours and flew to Berlin. Although the city was covered by 10/10ths cloud they could see the city from 70–80 miles away, illuminated by a concentration of red and green skymarkers dropped by the Pathfinders. As the Mosquito approached, the attack began in earnest. Clouds of *Window* cascaded down like sleet, searchlights illuminated the cloud-top and fighter flares could be seen. There were a few enemy *Serrate* fighters abroad too as the bombers approached from the North from over Denmark. After bombing they turned on to a westerly heading. *Window* added to the general confusion on the AI tubes and several chases that were initiated, were soon broken off again because of *Window* identification or contacts turning into friendly aircraft.

After patrolling the target area for seven minutes a white light was observed ahead, crossing on the same level and moving gently to starboard. White and Allen followed the light through a gentle turn and closed the range using full throttle because the enemy aircraft seemed to be drawing away from them. Mike Allen, meanwhile, had obtained contact on an aircraft closing from 7,000 ft distance. The Mosquito was closing much too fast to open fire, so White throttled back, turned hard starboard 45° and hard port until contact was regained at a range of 3,000 ft. White gently closed the range to 800 ft and opened fire from dead astern with a 3-second burst, placing in the centre of his sight the only part of the enemy aircraft that was visible, the tail light. Mike Allen read out the range. Strikes were observed on the fuselage and starboard engine, and the enemy aircraft caught fire. Harry White fired a second burst as the enemy aircraft turned gently to starboard. More flames appeared and in the illuminated sky they could quite easily make out the doomed machine to be a He 177. This special *Beleuchter* (illuminator) was dropping flares in an attempt to reveal targets to the *Wilde Sau* night-fighters. The He 177 spiralled down on fire, followed to 12,000 ft by the Mosquito before the Heinkel disappeared in cloud. Harry White had fired 306 rounds of 20 mm cannon shells, 92 from each of three guns, and 30 from the fourth cannon (which then jammed). It was the sixth enemy aircraft destroyed by the White–Allen partnership.

Some 43 bombers were lost on 15/16 February and on 19/20 February, *Zahme Sau* tactics were the cause of the very heavy loss of 78 bombers on the operation to Leipzig. The German night-fighters attacked the Main Force stream all the way into and out of the target area and the *Serrate* Mosquitoes were hard pressed to ward off the attacks. It was clear to Harris that Berlin was becoming too costly a prize and he abandoned operations to the Big City.

*Navigator/radio operator F/O Mike Seamer Allen of 141 Squadron. On 4 August 1940, 18-year-old AC2 Allen, as he then was, crewed up with Sgt Harry White at 54 OTU Church Fenton. In September 1941, they were posted to 29 Squadron at West Malling where they started defensive night patrols in Beaufighters. They became the most successful crew 141 Squadron ever had. (Michael Allen)*

*H. E. 'Harry' White DFC\*, pilot in 141 Squadron. At 17 years old, Harry White enlisted in the RAF in 1940 having lied about his age. He was commissioned as a Pilot Officer on 26 March 1942. Before he was 21, his bravery had earned him a DFC and Bar. (via Michael Allen)*

On 21 February, W/C K. C. Roberts was replaced as CO of 141 Squadron by W/C F. P. Davis, promoted from S/L, the B Flight Commander. That night, the bomber force went to Stuttgart. Only four of the 598 bombers were lost. Flying Officer E. A. 'Tex' Knight and Flying Officer D. P. 'Paddy' Doyle of 239 Squadron shot down a Bf 110 but Munro and Hurley, who had scored the Squadron's first victory less than a month earlier, were lost in a fatal crash on their return from operations. (On 25/26 February, Knight and Doyle were posted missing.) On 23/24 February, a 141 Squadron crew was shot down while supporting the Bomber Command raid on Schweinfurt. Pilot Officer Desmond Snape

was killed and his navigator Flying Officer I. H. Fowler was made a PoW. Fowler was sent to Stalag Luft III at Sagan. Snape is buried at Loppersum General Cemetery in Holland.

On 24/25 February, Harry White and Mike Allen had a lucky escape during their patrol in the Heligoland–Freyburg area. Mike Allen recalls:

We were chasing something which we presumed was a hostile aircraft when the port engine failed (141 had been re-equipped with old Mosquitoes and had been experiencing a number of engine failures and several crews had gone 'missing' without any trace, we suspected with engine

*141 Squadron at West Raynham.* Back row, left to right: *1–8 unknown; F/L J. A. H. Edwards; u/k; P/O D. J. Calder; P/O E. A. Lampkin; u/k; F/Sgt R. J. Pearson (?).* Middle row, left to right: *F/Sgt G. W. L. Stanley, I/C B Flt groundcrews; P/O I. D. Gregory DFC; F/O A. C. Newton; u/k; F/O J. G. Rogerson; 6–8 u/k; F/O R. W. Osborn; P/O D. H. Stephens DFC; F/O R. E. Smith (?); F/O J. E. Harper (?); F/O R. W. A. Marriott; F/O N. Barber; u/k; F/O C. E. Booth; F/O R. D. S. Gregor USAAF; F/O M. R. Colhoun (?); F/Sgt Rand, I/C A Flt groundcrews.* Front row, left to right: *u/k; F/L G. D. Bates; F/L J. V. Thatcher; u/k; S/L D. V. Anderson, B Flt Commander; G/C G. F. W. Heycock DFC, Station Commander; W/C C. V. Winn DFC, squadron CO; S/L J. G. Rice DFC, A Flt Commander; F/L R. A. W. Scott DFC; F/L P. A. Bates (?); F/L J. K. Havilland; F/L J. D. Peterkin (?); u/k.* (Harry Welham)

failure). This meant we had lost the chance of making an attack on a German night-fighter and that we were faced with a long journey home on one engine (about 350 miles) during which we would be unable to maintain our height. (We were between 20,000–23,000 ft when the engine failed.) We turned round onto 270 (we had been heading east when chasing our target) and set course for home, steadily losing height down to 12,000 ft as we flew over the Danish Peninsular, skirted the island of Sylt, on across the North Sea, and leaving the Dutch islands well away on our port side.

We were about level with the Islands of Ameland and Terschelling and I had already picked up the Radar Beacon (known as 'Mother') at West Raynham when Harry managed to pick up R/T contact with Sector Control. We were still cross at having to abandon our chase so when Harry got hold of the Ground Controller he showed the poor little WAAF on the other end no mercy and let fly (he never had much patience with the Controllers anyway). The girl answered our 'Mayday' call and asked if we needed any help. Harry called back and without any preamble, said, 'Creeper 24 here. Returning on one . . . and tell the boys it wasn't any f***g flak or bastard fighters that got us . . . Listening out!'

They still had about 150 miles to go. Harry White made a single-engined landing at night without incident.

It was a night of mixed fortunes for the

*On 18/19 March 1944 two Junkers Ju 88s were shot down by 141 Squadron crews, F/O Harry White DFC and F/O Michael Allen DFC, and F/O J. C. N. Forshaw and P/O F. S. Folley. One was Ju 88C-6 Wrk Nr 750014 R4+CS of 8./NJG2, which crashed at Arheilgen near Darmstadt, 25 kms south of Frankfurt. Ofw Otto Mueller, pilot, Ogefr Erhard Schimsal, radar operator, Gefr Günter Hanke, air gunner, were all KIA.*

*Serrate* Squadrons. A Ju 88 was claimed damaged by F/L John Forshaw and P/O Frank Folley. Jumbo Gracie and Wilton Todd were shot down in the Hannover area. Six weeks later, news was received that Gracie had been killed. Todd was a PoW in Stalag Luft III. (He later designed the memorial to the 50 airmen murdered by the Gestapo.) On 28 February, night-fighter ace and A&AEE test pilot W/C R. Gordon Slade arrived to take command of 169 Squadron. With him came his navigator, Philip Truscott. Truscott, who hailed from Canterbury, had been Slade's observer on 22/23 August 1942 when they notched the first blood to 157 Squadron by shooting down a Do 217 of KG2 over Suffolk. London-born Slade had joined the RAF in 1933 and had learned the deadly art of night fighting in 604 Squadron at West Malling under W/C John Cunningham. Slade's tenure of 169 would be short – just under three months – but Truscott remained with the squadron, until he was killed flying with W/C Neil Bromley, Slade's

successor. (G/C Slade OBE, FRAS, left the RAF in July 1946 and took the post of Chief Test Pilot for Fairey Aviation, retiring as Chairman of Fairey Hydraulics in 1977.)

On 25/26 February, F/O N. Munro and F/O A. R. Hurley, who had scored the first *Serrate* 239 Squadron victory on 28/29 January, crashed at Manor House Tittleshall, Norfolk on returning from operations. Munro was killed in the crash and Hurley died in No. 53 Mobile Field Hospital at Weasenham a few hours later. February had proved a bad month for the three *Serrate* squadrons and to compound it, 17 Mosquitoes had returned early with engine failures. On 27 February, W/C F. P. Davis, CO of 141 Squadron, went to 100 Group HQ at Bylaugh Hall and returned with the very good news that all reconditioned Merlin 22 engines in the Mosquitoes were to be returned and, in future and while stocks lasted, only new engines were to be fitted when replacements were required. Ground staff worked from 8 a.m. until 10 p.m. for days on end in order to give the squadrons a fresh lease of life.

In March 1944, the *Serrate* Mosquito squadrons destroyed six aircraft, while a seventh, He 177A-3 of 3./KG100, was destroyed by W/C Freddie Lambert and F/L Morgan of 515 Squadron, on 5 March. It crashed near Chateaudun, France killing Lt Wilhelm Werner and crew. Four of the victories went to 141 Squadron crews. On 18/19 March Harry White and Mike Allen destroyed two Ju 88s during a patrol in the Frankfurt area which was the target for 846 bombers. F/O John Forshaw and P/O Frank Folley also bagged a Ju 88. On 19 March, Harry White and Mike Allen went to 100 Group HQ at Bylaugh Hall to receive congratulations for their double victory from G/C Roderick Chisholm, the Senior Air Staff Officer. Chisholm said that they would be sent to 51 OTU at Cranfield on 23 March to give a talk on the Squadron's operations in a mission to try and garner volunteers for new *Serrate* crews, particularly from among the flying instructors on the completion of their rests. On 22/23 March, when Bomber Command again dispatched 816 aircraft to Frankfurt, S/L E. W. Kinchin and F/L D. Sellars of 239 Squadron destroyed a Bf 110. (Both failed to return from operations on 20 March.) The following night, F/L Butler and F/Sgt Robertson of 239 Squadron were added to the grim reaper's total following a support operation for Mosquitoes bombing Dortmund. The night of 24/25 March was one of mixed fortunes. Bomber Command dispatched 811 bombers to the Big City in a finale to the Battle of Berlin; 72 bombers failed to

return. (The Berlin offensive cost 625 bombers shot down and 2,690 crews killed and 987 crews made prisoners of war.) To these cold, harsh statistics can be added the loss of the *Serrate* crews who supported them. Flight Lieutenant Armstrong and Flying Officer Mold of 239 Squadron were posted missing, later to be declared PoWs.

On 25/26 March, the marshalling yards at Aulnoye in Northern France were the target for 192 bombers. A 141 Squadron crew, F/O Francois Emile D. Vandenplassche, a Belgian, and his navigator, 20-year-old F/O George Mamoutoff, the son of Russians living in London, lost their port engine when it caught fire during a patrol to Aulnoye. Mamoutoff bailed out at 1,400 ft and the Belgian followed. Vandenplassche evaded capture and made a remarkable home run via the Pyrénées, Spain and Gibraltar. He arrived back in Britain on 2 May. Mamoutoff is

*F/L R. G. 'Tim' Woodman. On 30 March 1944, he and his observer, Pat Kemmis DFC, had a very eventful night in their Mosquito while the fatal raid on Nürnberg by Bomber Command was in progress. A devastating loss of 95 bombers was recorded; Woodman saw 44 of them go down. (Tim Woodman)*

buried at Choloy War Cemetery.[2]

On the afternoon of 30 March, Mosquito crews in 100 Group were briefed for the part they would play in the raid that night on Nürnberg. Flight Lieutenant R. G. 'Tim' Woodman, who had previously flown Beaufighters in 96 Squadron at Honiley before joining 169 Squadron, recalls:

Briefing showed the bombers' track going south across France, then turning east to a point north of Nürnburg where the bombers turned again on to their target. They were to leave the target in a south-westerly direction, then out west and north and back to England. We immediately protested that as the bombers entered Germany between Mannheim and Frankfurt they would be passing between two German marker

beacons which would be heavily stacked by German night-fighters waiting to pounce. And having established the track of the bombers other night-fighters would be vectored in from the north and up from the Munich area. Only a month earlier I had shot down a 110 which was orbiting, along with other night-fighters, the south one of these two beacons. We knew from a captured map sent to us by the Resistance the positions of 22 of these German night-fighter marker beacons. Our request that the track of the bombers be changed was passed to the SASO, Air Commodore Rory Chisholm DSO, DFC at 100 Group, who passed it on to Bomber Command. But they refused to change.

At the next briefing our escort counter-measures patrol lines were on the map, planned by Group. I saw that my route and patrol was at 20,000 ft, from the North

*B Flight, 169 Squadron at Little Snoring sit for the camera in front of a 515 Squadron Mosquito.* Back row, left to right: *Harry Reed; Logan; D. C. Dunne; Bob Tidy RCAF; Dickie Drew.* Middle row, left to right: *P. A. J. 'Pete' Dils; W/O Hays; F/O Pat Kemmis; Len 'Tiny' Giles; F/O Stuart Watts; Robinson; F/L R. W. 'Dick' O'Farrell.* Front row, left to right: *F/L Ralph Connolly; F/L R. G. 'Tim' Woodman; S/L Joe Cooper, B Flt Commander; F/O Gordon E Cremer; F/L A. Paul Mellows. (Joe Cooper)*

Sea down over the Netherlands, then west of the Ruhr and to cross ahead of the bomber stream as it entered Germany, to take up a patrol on its south side at 10 miles range. I was to engage any German night-fighters approaching from that direction. We were informed that the main bomber formation would have climbed to 15,000–20,000 ft and that it would be some 5 miles wide. To me it was utterly incomprehensible: I was being treated like a destroyer escorting a convoy. At 10 miles range I would only have some 2 minutes to try and intercept on a dark night before a German night-fighter entered the bomber stream where contact would be lost. I begged Group to let me get ahead of the bombers (fly in low down undetected) and go straight to one of those marker beacons, with another crew flying to the other one, and shoot at least one down and scare off the rest. Again the Group SASO tried with Bomber Command and again our request was turned down. We foresaw a night of heavy casualties, possibly as great as some recent ones which had reached 70+ bombers shot down. The Station Commander, G/C Rupert Leigh (he had done a couple of *Serrate* operations himself), enjoined us all to press on even if we had radar failure which in the past had been an acceptable excuse for abandoning an operation and returning to base. Even one Mosquito's presence might save a bomber or two.

I took off and climbed out over the North Sea. It was a dark night; the moon would rise after the raid was over. At 18,000 ft flames and sparks burst out from the inner side of the starboard engine and back across the wing. This was a disaster. I throttled back the engine, cut my speed almost to stalling, but did not stop the engine. The fire died down and I now had to make a possible fatal decision. The engine instruments were OK. Go on or go back? The golden rule was: never open again an engine which has been on fire. But I did. I had lost height to 13,000 ft, carefully opened up the throttle and the engine roared away smoothly. No sign of fire

so I decided to press on. Over the Netherlands my observer, Pat Kemmis DFC, spotted on radar another aircraft coming up behind me. I guessed, rightly, that it was F/O Harry Reed from my squadron who had caught up with me. He was indeed trying to intercept me thinking I was much further ahead. I put the nose down and at full throttle lost him but ran into flak over Aachen, which I had to avoid. Back at 20,000 ft again and expecting shortly to cross ahead of the bomber stream Pat started picking up radar contacts coming from the right. It was the bombers. We had lost time getting there and they were being carried along on a wind which was much stronger than forecast. There was nothing for it but to cross through the stream. This required skilful monitoring of the CR screens by Pat as he could see a dozen or more blips at the same time, whilst I saw the dark shapes of the Lancs and Halifaxes crossing below, ahead and above me. And instead of the bomber stream being 5 miles wide it was more like 50. Some had already been shot down and before I reached the far side of the stream they were being shot down on my left.

On the south side of the stream Pat immediately picked up *Serrate* contacts but before I could intercept these Hun night-fighters they had entered the bomber stream. I went back in among the bombers and told Pat to get me a *Serrate* contact dead ahead. But for the final interception it was necessary to switch over to Mk IV AI radar and each time Pat did so he had a dozen or more blips on his screens – bombers plus among them the German night-fighter. Masses of *Window* were also being tossed out of the bombers which also jammed our radar. We tried three times but each time came up below a bomber, the rear gunner spotting us the third time, his tracer coming uncomfortably close whilst his pilot did a corkscrew. It was hopeless, we were doing more harm than good. Ahead bombers were being shot down one after another, some going all the way down in flames, some blowing up in the air, the rest blowing up as they hit the ground. I counted 44 shot down on this leg to Nuremburg. What was happening behind I could only guess.

I flew on to Nuremburg and saw that the bombing had been widespread, a number of fires in the city, with a separate area where bombs and incendiaries had obviously landed in the countryside. I prowled around until the last of the bombers had gone but got no more *Serrate* contacts. Then I saw the odd bomber still being shot down to the south-west as they were making their way home. I flew down that way towards Stuttgart, then ahead and low down I saw a bomber on fire. I went down to his height, 8,000 ft, and it was a Halifax with its rear turret on fire. I kept formation with him but far enough away for the crew not to see me until the fire died down and went out. Silently wishing the crew the best of luck (they did in fact make it back) I turned and went back to Nuremburg. I was inwardly raging at the incompetence of the top brass at Bomber Command.

Back at 20,000 ft again I prowled over the city again hoping the odd German might still be around. Pat picked up a contact on radar. I intercepted it but it was another Mosquito. I called them up and told them I was on their tail but got no reply. Later I discovered there were two other Mosquitoes over Nuremburg at that time: F/O Mellows from my own Squadron and a Mosquito from 192 Squadron, also from 100 Group. [F/Sgt J. Campbell and F/Sgt R. Phillips of 239 Squadron shot down Ju 88C-6 Wrk Nr 360272 D5+? of 4./NJG3, which crashed 10 kms SW of Bayreuth. Oblt Ruprecht Panzer, pilot, WIA, radar operator and air gunner, all baled out safely.

It was time to start the long haul back with the moon already up and the clouds closing in. Near Frankfurt my starboard engine caught fire again and this time I had to shut it down and feather the prop. We could maintain a height of 7,500 ft, just above the clouds, with Pat keeping a lookout to the rear for anyone on our tail. But all the Huns had landed, sated with kills. Back at base they discovered that the engine exhaust gasket had been blown doing a lot of damage from the intense heat inside the cowling. But for the delay of the earlier fire I am sure I would have ignored orders, got ahead of the bombers and tackled those German night-fighters on one of those beacons. For the next couple of raids on Germany I was invited to Group by Air Cdre Rory Chisholm DSO, DFC to help plan *Serrate* operations, and on my future operations I was permitted to freelance. [A staggering total of 95 bombers (11.9 per cent) were lost from a force of 795 dispatched to Nuremberg, Bomber Command's worst night of the war.]

# CHAPTER 4

# *THE OFFENSIVE SPIRIT*

*Mossies they don't worry me,*
*Mossies they don't worry me,*
*If you get jumped by a One-nine-O,*
*I'll show you how to get free.*
*Keep calm and sedate,*
*Don't let your British blood boil.*
*Don't hesitate,*
*Just go right through the gate,*
*And drown the poor bastard in oil!*

As we have seen, there were a few men with offensive spirit in 100 Group, including those at West Raynham. On 11/12 April, F/L N. E. Reeves and W/O A. A. O'Leary of 239 Squadron destroyed a Do 217. On 18/19 April, Harry White (promoted Flight Lieutenant on 14 April) and Mike Allen of 141 Squadron gave chase during a *Serrate* patrol to Swinemünde and the western Baltic but their intended victim escaped. Their ninth kill would have to wait just a little longer. Altogether, 18 Mosquitoes operated from West Raynham this night, including 10 from 141 Squadron, its best effort so far.

On 20/21 April, Harry White and Mike Allen were one of eight 141 Squadron Mosquitoes dispatched to patrol over France. (Five B-17s of 214 Squadron, including one captained by the CO, W/C

McGlinn, flew their first jamming operation this night. No. 214 Squadron's role was to jam enemy R/T communication between the *Freya* radar and the German night-fighters. Among other counter measures, they also jammed the FuG 216 tail warning system.) Harry White wrote:

We took off and set course over base at 6,000 ft at 22:52 hours and continued unevent-fully on course until 23:50 hours when our first *Serrate* contact was obtained to starboard and below, crossing starboard to port. We gave chase going down hill and obtained an AI contact at 12,000 ft range which was found to be jinking considerably. Height was decreased to 12,000 ft and range closed to 1,500 ft when *Serrate* and AI contacts faded. We turned starboard and back to port hoping to regain contact – no joy. Enemy aircraft switched off *Serrate* as we broke away. Throughout this attempted interception our elevation was behaving most erratically and it is believed that the enemy aircraft was directly below us at 1,500 ft when contact faded, the usual reason for fading blips.

The gyro having spun during the interception, I had little idea of where this interception had taken me, so set course towards the estimated position of Paris which I hoped shortly to see illuminated and fix my position. At 00:20 hours various contacts were obtained on the bomber stream leaving the Paris area. Window was much in evidence. At 00:25 hours an AI contact at 15,000 ft to port and below was obtained a few miles west of stream and chased. We decreased height and followed contact through gentle port and starboard orbits reducing height to 12,000 ft and eventually closing range to 600 ft where I obtained a visual on four blue-white exhausts, later positively identified at 300 ft as a Ju 88. For five minutes I followed enemy aircraft patiently through gentle port and starboard orbits at 200 indicated air speed, eventually opening fire, still turning, at 500 ft with a 1-second burst allowing 5° deflection; no results. Enemy aircraft, completely clueless, continued to orbit. Apparently clueless also, I tried again with a 1-second burst, again no results. A third burst was fired as enemy aircraft peeled off to starboard and disappeared from view. I have no idea why I continually missed enemy aircraft and can only attribute it to the dot dimmed out from the gunsight and gremlin interference.

At 01:00 hours, being in the proximity of the bomber stream, second attack on Paris, we obtained another *Serrate* contact starboard and below which we followed for 3 minutes. This *Serrate* momentarily faded and enemy aircraft was presumed to be orbiting, at least turning. This was confirmed within a few seconds by a head-on AI contact at 15,000 ft range well below.

We turned behind and closed rapidly to 600 ft, and there obtained a visual on four quite bright blue exhausts, identified from 300 ft as a Do 217 now flying at 10,000 ft. Enemy aircraft was now turning very gently port and was followed for 5 minutes not wishing to repeat above. At 450 ft only exhausts could be seen, though these, unlike the Ju 88, quite clearly. Not wishing to approach closer I opened fire at this range with a 2-second burst and was gratified to see enemy aircraft exploded with a blinding flash and disintegrate. Several pieces were flung back at us and I instinctively ducked as they splattered over the windscreen and fuselage. Apart from two broken Perspex panels, which were causing more noise than worry, we appeared to be OK, but visions of damaged radiators caused some concern for the first minutes. We had no trouble in that respect and returned uneventfully to base.

It is almost certain that White and Allen's victim was Do 217N-1 Wrk Nr 51517 of 5./NJG4, which crashed near Meulan, north of Paris. Ofw Karl Kaiser, pilot, and Uffz Johannes Nagel, radar operator, both WIA, bailed out. Gefr Sigmund Zinser, air gunner, KIA. The Mosquitoes had done their work well. Only eight bombers were lost on the attacks on the French railway yards.

On 22/23 April, F/Lt Tim Woodman and F/O Patrick Kemmis of 169 Squadron were aloft again as the bombers went to Düsseldorf. Tim Woodman recalls:

The Y-Service had informed us that when the bombers were approaching targets in northern Germany and the Ruhr, night-fighter squadrons in the Munich area were being directed to the suspected target area. On this night, therefore, I flew from the Ruhr towards Munich as the bombers approached the Ruhr. We picked up a *Serrate* contact coming towards us and when it was within AI range turned port and came up underneath him. He had not spotted us on

P/O Tim Woodman, who with F/O Pat Kemmis, accounted for a Bf 110 at Compiègne on 18/19 April 1944, and another at Köln on 22/23 April. (Tim Woodman)

gunsight but it did not light up. I changed the bulb and it still did not work, so I banged the sight with my gloved fist and the socket and bulb fell out on its lead, blinding me with its brilliant white light as it lit up. I switched off and fired a short burst at the 110 tail light but with no strikes.

We were fast approaching the Ruhr searchlight zone so I fired a longer burst, stirring the stick as I did so to spread the shells. There were a number of strikes and the 110 seemed to have blown up. Black sooty oil covered my windscreen and when his radar. It was a 110 with a small white we got back we found the nose and starboard light on his tail. And there were four other wing damaged. Pat, on radar, said he could aircraft flying in formation with him, two to see large pieces going down to the ground. port and two to starboard. I switched on the But the Ruhr searchlights were after me and

*169 Squadron at Little Snoring in front of a 515 Squadron Mosquito VI. Front row, left to right: F/L A. Paul Mellows; R. Dunn; F/L Ralph Connolly; Hodgson; F/L R. G. Tim Woodman; S/L Joe Cooper; W/C N. B. R. Bromley OBE, squadron CO (destroyed a Bf 110 on 22/23 May 1944 and a Do 217 on 8/9 June; MIA 6/9/44); S/L Ted Thorne; F/L Philip Truscott (MIA 6/9/44); F/O E. Cremer; Salmon; Reg Dix. Centre row, left to right: W. H. 'Andy' Miller; G. Shipley; Bob Tidy; W. S. Logan; Len 'Tiny' Giles; P/O Freddie C. Bone; Pat Kemmis; Stuart Watts; F/O P. G. 'Bill' Bailey; P/O Pete Johnson; Southcott USAAF; Robinson; Murphy; F. Staziker; W/O Hays. Back row, left to right: Bonnett; Harry Reed; Pamment; u/k; R. W. 'Dick' O'Farrell; P. A. J. 'Pete' Dils; F/L S. L. 'Dickie' Drew; 'Hoppy' Hopkins. (Tom Cushing Collection)*

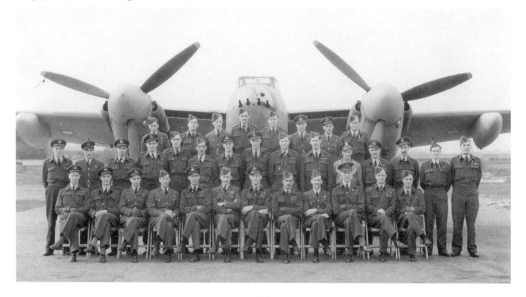

I did not want them to recognize me as a Mosquito. The Y-Service came to my aid. I reached back and pressed the trigger of a fixed Very pistol. Red and green Very lights spread across the night sky. The searchlight crews counted them and doused their searchlights. I had fired off the German 'colours of the day', the Y-Service supplying us with this information. It was the only time I did so. Immediately after the war I was sent to Germany and Denmark to test fly their aircraft and to check up on their radar and other electronic devices. This particular Me 110 I was told was probably a Luftwaffe night-fighter escorting Me 109 *Wilde Sau* fighters to the bombers' target area. Seeing their escort aircraft shot down they would all have dived down to ground level, not knowing what was behind them. Maybe this is what my observer saw on radar.

Thirty-seven bombers were lost this night.

On 23/24 April during a *Serrate* patrol to the Baltic, F/L Graham Rice and P/O Ron Mallett of 141 Squadron shot down a Fw 190 employing *Zahme Sau* tactics against RAF bombers carrying out mine laying in the Baltic. It was Rice's second victory on the Squadron. A few nights later, on 26/27 April, when Bomber Command attacked Essen, a 239 Squadron crew shot down a Bf 110. However, one of 141 Squadron's ace night fighting crews was lost when S/L John Forshaw, A Flight CO, and his navigator, P/O Frank Folley, failed to return. Both men are buried in Rheinberg War Cemetery, only about 45 kilometres from Essen. The following night, 27/28 April, 239 Squadron Mosquitoes landed back at West Raynham and submitted claims for three enemy aircraft destroyed. John Forshaw's chosen replacement, S/L Victor Lovell DFC, and his navigator, W/O Robert Lilley DFC, failed to return from a patrol to Stuttgart/Friedrichshafen.

In May, steps could be taken to increase the strength of the ECM and Mosquito

Special Duties Squadrons in 100 Group, which now became known as Bomber Support. A lack of enemy air activity in the Western Approaches had permitted the transfer of Mosquito XIIs and XVIIs of 85 Squadron and Mosquito XIXs of 157 Squadron to Addison's command. These flew in to the recently completed base at Swannington (and in June, 23 Squadron would arrive from the Mediterranean to operate from Little Snoring, 169 Squadron and 1692 Flight moving to Great Massingham). No. 85 Squadron had been commanded by W/C John Cunningham and 157 had been the first unit to be equipped with the Mosquito. All three squadrons were expert in the *Intruder* role. Corporal B. W. Salmon was a radar mechanic in 157 Squadron, one of many whose work kept the aircraft flying and capable of efficient and effective operations. He recalls:

At the time, the aircraft were fitted with radio altimeters; either LORAN or *Gee* position-fixing radar; and, most important for the night-fighters, AI, which enabled the crew to find and attack enemy aircraft in the dark, or cloud conditions. Few members of the public were aware of the advanced nature of this equipment, and its contribution to the success of the campaign. The other important item was IFF, Indicate Friend or Foe, which enabled ground defences such as the anti-aircraft radars to identify our own aircraft. Unfortunately, when this was damaged in action, as it sometimes was, the result could be disastrous. We did discover that the radar equipment was an effective tool for spotting rain clouds and thunderstorms and we also used the wave guides when testing the AI equipment to 'cook' sausages which we placed on the end of sticks and held in front of the transmitter. This must have been the first microwave cooker!

While the 'new' Mosquito squadrons

wrestled with the growing pains of joining a new Group, and adapting to their new roles, there was no lack of trade for the existing Mosquito squadrons. On 8/9 May, Tim Woodman and Pat Kemmis of 169 Squadron were aloft as the bombers hit targets in northern France and Belgium. Tim Woodman recalls:

We could clearly see the bombers, as many as ten at a time, but no sign of German night fighters. We sniffed around for 109s and 190s over the target area but saw none. I saw three Halifaxes weaving like dingbats, up at 6,000ft. Below the leading bomber was a twin-engined aircraft climbing up to it.

The Bf 110, flown by Lt. Wolfgang Martstaller, and his radar-operator/air gunner, of I./NJG4, had taken off from Florennes at 0300 hours. In a letter to his parents on 12 May, Martstaller wrote:

The sky was fully lit, so we could easily see the Tommy. Our crew saw at least ten bombers. However, we could only concentrate on one aircraft. When I was near him and fired (and my burst of fire bloody well blinded me!) the Schwinehund fired off a flare with a signal pistol, so than an enemy night fighter could post us).

Woodman fired a 2-second burst and Martstaller dived into the darkness, Kemmis following him on *Serrate*. Marstaller soared up in a steep climb and Woodman fired from 800 yards Woodman continues:

This time he opted out and took us on a chase across the French countryside at treetop height, not seeing him as he flew away from the moon but following him on *Serrate*.

Martstaller wrote:

I went into a steep dive to almost zero feet (at night!), but still we could not escape from the Mosquito's attention.

Woodman continues:

He made the mistake of flying towards the moon and I saw the moonlight glint off his wings. I fired and got some strikes on his fuselage and wings as he flew across a wide open space which looked like an aerodrome. He went into a steep turn and firing 50 yards ahead of him to allow for deflection I hit him again. White smoke poured from his port engine and closing to 150 yards I gave him another 2 seconds burst and hit him again.

Marstaller concludes:

I was fortunate to spot a field in which to belly-land. We were slightly injured from shrapnel. When we found that we were OK, we then saw a large explosion two miles away from us. Next day this turned out to be my Viermont [four motor bomber], with seven crew members (F/Lt Chase and crew of Lancaster ND587 of 405 Squadron burned to death. We were so happy!

(Marstaller was killed in a crash on St Trond aerodrome in August 1944).

At 00:10 on 10/11 May F/O Vivian Bridges and F/Sgt Donald Webb of 239 Squadron attacked Bf 110 3C+F1 Wrk Nr. 740179 of 1./NJG4 near Courtrai, setting one engine on fire. It crashed at Ellezelles, Belgium. Oblt Heinrich Schulenberg, pilot, and Ofw. Hermann Meyer, radar operator, bailed out near Flobeq. Meyer was wounded and badly concussed and spent three weeks in hospital and four weeks more at home.

On 11/12 May, 429 bombers of the Main Force made attacks on Bourg-Leopold, Hasselt and Louvain in Belgium. Harry White and Mike Allen reached double figures by bringing down a Ju 88 a few miles north of Amiens, while Lucien LeBoutte, and F/O Ron Mallett destroyed a Ju 88 30 miles south-west of Brussels. This was LeBoutte's first and only kill during his time on 141 Squadron. 'The Major', as he was called, flew over 50 *Instep*, *Ranger*, night-fighter and *Serrate* patrols and damaged three trains in strafing attacks. Officially, he was 'tour expired' and Mallet himself was on his third tour. On 24 May, LeBoutte and Mallett were both awarded the DFC.

Bridges and Webb added another victory on 12/13 May when 239 Squadron dispatched *Serrate* patrols to Belgium in support of the bombers raiding Hasselt and Louvain again. They destroyed Ju 88 C6 Wrk Nr 750922 of 5./NJG3, which crashed at Hoogcruts near Maastricht. Uffz Josef Polzer and crew were killed. Also, F/O W. R. Breithaupt and F/O J. A. Kennedy downed a Bf 110.

On 15/16 May P/O Wilfred Handel 'Andy' Miller and P/O F. C. 'Freddie' Bone of 169 Squadron destroyed two Ju 88s and a Bf 110 near Kiel when Mosquitoes of 8 Group mined the Canal. This brought the Welsh pilot and the 38-year-old Birkenhead policeman's score to five enemy aircraft destroyed while in 100 Group (they had got a Bf 110 on 5/6 February and another on 22/23 April) and eight all told.

On 22/23 May, F/L D. L. Hughes and F/O R. H. 'Dickie' Perks of 239 Squadron destroyed a Bf 110. Two nights later, Breithaupt and Kennedy added a Ju 88 to their score and damaged a Bf 109, while in the Aachen area, the Hughes and Perks, and F/L Denis J. Raby DFC and F/Sgt S. J. 'Jimmy' Flint DFM pairs each destroyed a Bf 110. On 27/28 May, 239 Squadron sent up eight Mosquitoes on Bomber Support. The A Flight Commander, S/L Neil Reeves DFC*, and P/O A. A. O'Leary destroyed Bf 110 Wrk Nr 140032 G9+CR of 7./NJG1. It crashed at Spannum in Holland at 01:15 hours. Uffz Joachim Tank (26, pilot) was slightly wounded. Uffz Ludwig Serwein (21, radar operator) and Gefr. Otto Morath (23, air gunner), were killed.

Meanwhile, F/L Harry White, now OC Station Flight, and F/L Mike Allen were one of seven Mosquito crews in 141 Squadron which supported the Main Force raids on Aachen and Bourg-Leopold. At 02:35 hours a little to the west of Aachen, two AI contacts were obtained by Allen at 14,000 ft and 12,000 ft, crossing right to left. At a range of 8,000 ft the two blips merged into one and Allen remarked to White: 'A bomber's about to be shot down in front of us at any minute.'

'Still crossing,' White wrote, 'we turned to port in behind this contact and at 1,200 ft, obtained a visual on two white exhausts.

We had not increased speed as range was closing quite rapidly but as we assumed the

*F/L David 'Taffy' Bellis DFC* and F/L Denis Welfare DFC* in front of Mosquito DZ256 at West Raynham on 12 June 1944 showing the damaged tail which was caused by burning petrol from a Bf 110 they shot down north of Paris. (Taffy Bellis)*

line astern position, the exhausts faded from sight and range was increased to 8,000 ft before, at full throttle, we were once more able to decrease the range slowly to 1,200 ft again, obtaining a visual on two white exhausts. We closed to 600 ft where I was able to identify this target as a Me 109. I closed further to 300 ft and opened fire with a 2-second burst from 15° below. It exploded with a colossal flash which completely blinded me for about a minute and a half. I asked Mike to read my instruments for me but his attention was at that moment elsewhere. The flash had attracted his attention from his box and he looked out in time to see a second Me 109 slip slowly by under the starboard wing. With his head now well in the box, Mike commenced reading off the range as this 109 emerged from minimum range behind. But even the best navigator cannot carry out an interception with the help of a blind pilot and the range had increased to 6,000 ft astern before I could even see my instruments. We turned hard port but contact went out of range at 14,000 ft.

Although the second Messerschmitt Bf 109 had escaped, the eleventh victory of Harry White and Mike Allen was duly recorded in 141 Squadron's record book.

On 14 June, Harry White with Mike Allen, and Howard Kelsey with Smitty Smith, were posted to the Bomber Support Development Unit (BSDU) at Foulsham. (On 28/29 July 1944, Harry White and Mike Allen returned briefly to West Raynham to fly *Serrate* patrols with nine other Mosquitoes of 141 Squadron. During the sortie they shot down two Ju 88s to bring their tally to 13, the highest score in the Squadron's history.) Lucien LeBoutte DFC, the very popular Belgian member of the Squadron, was also posted. He joined the Staff of the Belgian Inspector General

with promotion to wing commander. Replacements arrived at West Raynham during May–June. Two of them, W/O A. L. Potter and his navigator, F/Sgt R. E. Gray, had only just joined 141 Squadron when they were killed on a training flight on 29 May, over North Farm, Clenchwarton near King's Lynn when their Mosquito exploded in mid-air.

*Serrate* Mosquito victories were still coming thick and fast in May 1944. On 30/31 May, 239 Squadron at West Raynham dispatched 10 Mosquitoes on *Serrate* sorties. Bridges and Webb, and F/L Denis Welfare and F/L David B. 'Taffy' Bellis, shot down a Bf 110 apiece. The latter crew had become operational by the middle of March. Their previous experience of night fighting was on defensive operations with 141 Squadron at Tangmere and Acklington in 1942. Taffy Bellis recalls:

On the night of 31 May we picked up a *Serrate* transmission north of Paris. Our first priority was to make certain that the

*One of 239 Squadron's Record of Victories, which hangs in the RAF Museum at Hendon. (Author)*

transmission did not come from a fighter homing on us from behind! We then manoeuvred our Mossie to get behind the transmitting aircraft. To our dismay, it switched off its radar before we were in AI range. However, we kept on the same course and picked up an AI contact a minute or so later and converted this to a visual and the shooting down of an Me 110.

In all, 239 Squadron destroyed 10 aircraft during May and now led the three *Serrate* Mosquito squadrons with 19 victories; 141 Squadron had 13 and 169 Squadron at Little Snoring had 12.

On 4/5 June, the eve of D-Day, 239 Squadron sent out six Mosquitoes (with one early abort). W. R. Breithaupt and J. A. Kennedy returned to West Raynham having destroyed a Ju 88. Ten 515 Squadron Mosquitoes were over Occupied Europe on Ranger patrols, patrolling and bombing enemy airfields in France and strafing road, rail and canal traffic. Two Mosquitoes were shot down, including one flown by the A Flight Commander. In return, a Ju 88 and a Bf 110 were claimed destroyed. Despite this success, radar failure was occurring regularly on operations. In Tim Woodman's opinion it was due to a number of causes chief of which were inexperienced ground servicing technicians, old equipment, lack of new parts for replacing those which became unserviceable, and radar valves which were not designed for operating at the high altitudes which we reached. Newly installed aerial systems continually gave wrong altitude readings so that one did not know whether the target was up or down. And, of course, they would not release centimetre AI for our use, and when they did it was to bring in two night-fighter squadrons from Fighter Command, most of the crews having little experience of operating over enemy territory.

The campaign to acquire the British designed, American made, AI Mk X culminated in the arrival in 100 Group of 85 and 157 Squadrons at Swannington. At the beginning of May, 85 Squadron equipped with AI Mk X and already well trained in its use had been engaged in defensive night fighting, while 157 equipped with AI Mk XV had supported Coastal Command's daylight anti-U-boat patrols in the Bay of Biscay. AI Mk X, unlike Mk IV, had no backward coverage at all. From the point of view of the Mosquito's own safety, some kind of backward warning equipment had to be fitted before it could be used on high-level operations. To provide a quick interim answer BSDU began a modification of *Monica 1*. Until the tail warner was fitted, 85 and 157 Squadrons would be trained for low-level airfield intrusions. This would mean that the AI Mk X squadrons would eventually be in a position to play a dual role – either high-level or low-level work, which would help considerably in the planning of bomber operations.

The Mosquito Mk XVIIs of 85 Squadron and 157 Squadron's Mk XIXs officially began operations on D-Day, 5/6 June, when 16 sorties were flown. Twelve Mosquitoes in 85 Squadron operated over the Normandy beachhead, while four in 157 Squadron patrolled night-fighter airfields at Deelen, Soesterberg, Eindhoven and Gilze Rijen in Holland. No. 515 Squadron also operated over the Normandy invasion beaches and patrolled over German airfields in Holland. One of the dozen Mosquitoes dispatched by 141 Squadron (two returning early) was one crewed by W/C Winnie Winn, the new CO, and R. A. W. Scott. Five Mosquitoes were dispatched by 239 Squadron (two returning with problems). Denis Welfare and Taffy Bellis patrolled a known beacon near Aachen and destroyed a Bf 110. Mosquitoes of 100 Group continued their support of the invasion forces on 6/7 June. On 8/9 June, West Raynham was the scene of mixed emotions. Flying Officer A. C. Gallacher and Warrant Officer G. McLean in 141 Squadron told of the destruction of an unidentified enemy aircraft over northern France after they had chased it into a flak barrage at Rennes where it was brought down by a single burst. A popular Free French crew, F/L D'Hautecourt and his navigator P/O C. E. Kocher, returned from their seventh operation, patrolling over their homeland, on one engine and died shortly after swinging off the runway and crashing into two fighter aircraft. Both Frenchmen had only been with the Squadron since February.

Also on 8/9 June W/C Neil Bromley and F/L Truscott of 169 Squadron, which had just recently moved from Little Snoring to Gt Massingham, shot down Do 217 K-3 Wrk Nr 4742 6N+OR of Stab III./KG100. Oblt Oskar Schmidtke (pilot) and his crew were killed. Flight Lieutenant Clements and Pilot Officer Pierce of 141 Squadron safely abandoned their Mosquito in the Wisbech area after losing their port engine over Reading while returning from a sortie to northern France. A 239 Squadron crew overshot the West Raynham runway with the starboard throttle jammed and crashed in a field but both crew scrambled out

unhurt. Next day, F/Sgt Humpreys and his navigator set off from Massingham on a cross-country flight. Near Gayton Mill, Humpreys lost control and the 169 Squadron Mosquito crashed. Humpreys was killed but his navigator managed to bail out successfully.

On the afternoon of 11 June, during another training flight, a Mosquito crewed by F/L P. A. Riddoch and his navigator, 33-year-old F/O C. S. Ronayne, a new crew who had just joined 141 Squadron, disintegrated in mid-air 2 miles south of Chippenham village between Mildenhall and Newmarket. Riddoch was blown out of the aircraft and his parachute opened in the action. He suffered a dislocated right shoulder, fractured jaw and lacerations to his face and eyelids but recovered in the White Lodge EMS Hospital at Newmarket. Ronayne was found dead from multiple injuries. (A subsequent enquiry found that the cause of the accident was structural failure.) That night, Irishman W/C Charles M. Miller DFC and two Bars, CO of 85 Squadron, with F/O Robert Symon, shot down a Bf 110 over Melun airfield. Denis Welfare and Taffy Bellis of 239 Squadron

*Mosquito XIX MM652 of 157 Squadron which, with 85 Squadron, moved to Swannington and 100 Group in May 1944 equipped with AI Mk X radar. Until* Monica 1 *tail warning radar was fitted, 85 and 157 Squadrons were trained as low-level airfield intruders*

were also on patrol, between Paris and Luxembourg, on radar watch for night-fighters. Taffy Bellis recalls:

We picked up a German airborne radar transmission about 10 miles away on our *Serrate* apparatus and homed on to it. We made a contact 10,000 ft away with our own AI and in a few minutes converted it to a visual, showing clearly the twin fins and faint exhausts of a Me 110. We attacked from about 50 yards and the Me immediately blew up. Our Mossie flew into debris and was enveloped in burning petrol. Fortunately, the fire did not get hold, but our Mossie was clearly damaged. We jettisoned the escape hatch ready to bale out quickly and called UK on the Mayday channel. The emergency control at Coltishall were most helpful with radio bearings, etc. However, Denis was able to control the aircraft and our *Gee* navigation equipment seemed to be work-ing OK. Thus we decided to dispense with Coltishall's help and return to base, where eggs and bacon never tasted so good! I shall never forget Denis' skill, the ability of the Mossie to take punishment, the spectacular film from the camera gun of the engagement, and last but not least, the discomfort of flying some 300 miles home in a plane without an escape hatch.

Meanwhile, the first airfield intrusion results with AI Mk X were very promising and it was found that at a height of 1,500–2,000 ft AI contacts at ranges of 3 miles or so could be obtained and held. During June, from 176 sorties dispatched, of which 131 were completed, 38 AI contacts were reported leading to the destruction of 10 enemy aircraft and the damaging of three others. All these combats, save one of those leading to damage claims, resulted from 62 sorties flown between the nights of 11/12 June and 16/17 June.

On 12/13 June, F/L James Gilles 'Ben' Benson DFC and F/L Lewis 'Brandy' Brandon DSO, DFC opened the scoring for 85 Squadron with a Ju 188 near Compiègne, while F/L Micky Phillips and F/L Derek Smith contributed with a Bf 110. Benson had been one of the replacements posted to 141 Squadron in July 1940 after the debacle of 19 June when six Defiants were destroyed and one damaged by Bf 109s. He suffered a suspected fractured skull following a crash in his Defiant during a night landing in January 1941, but fully recovered and had crewed up with Brandy Brandon to form another highly successful Mosquito night-fighter team. Benson and Brandon destroyed two enemy aircraft and damaged two more before being posted as instructors.

The next victories of 157 and 85 Squadrons occurred on 14/15 June. A Ju 88 trying to land at Juvincourt was shot down by F/L J. Tweedale and F/O L. I. Cunningham of 157 Squadron, and F/L H. B. Thomas and P/O C. B. Hamilton of 85 Squadron also brought down another Ju 88 near Juvincourt. Third victory of the night went to F/L Branse Burbridge and F/L F. S. Skelton, who destroyed a Ju 188 flown by Major Wilhelm Herget south-west of Nivelles. Another inspired 85 Squadron pairing, S/L F. S. 'Gon' Gonsalves and F/L Basil Duckett, shot down a Bf 110 on 15/16 June. Not to be outdone, F/L Jimmy Mathews and W/O Penrose of 157 destroyed a Ju 188 the same night. On 17/18 June, at 02.30 hours F/O R. C. Kendall DFC* and F/L C. R. Hill of 85 Squadron destroyed a Bf 110 of NJG1 at Soesterberg. All three crew were killed.

Burbridge and Skelton bagged another Ju 88 on 23/24 June. The 23-year-old Bransome Arthur Burbridge and Frank Seymour 'Bill' Skelton were deeply religious men. Burbridge had been a conscientious objector on religious grounds for the first six months of the war before joining up. Both were commissioned from the ranks and served individually on

Havocs in 85 Squadron in October 1941 and January 1942 respectively. They only crewed up on their second tour on the Squadron in July 1943. Their first victory was a Me 410 Hornisse on 22/23 February 1944. A first-class team in every sense of the word, the two men were totally dedicated to their task. Many more victories were to follow but these were put in abeyance when both Mk X Squadrons packed their bags on 25–27 June, and left Swannington to return to West Malling for anti-*Diver* patrols since the V-1 offensive was now threatening London and southern Britain. Mk X radar was accurate enough to track flying bombs but the Mosquitoes had to be modified to cope with the rigours of anti-*Diver* patrols. They received strengthened noses to match the Doodlebugs' extra turn of speed and stub exhausts were fitted in place of the exhaust shrouds. Engine boost pressure was adjusted to plus 24 lb and the Merlin 25s were also modified to permit the use of 150-octane petrol so that the aircraft could reach around 360 mph at sea level. Just over 130 successful *Intruder* patrols, out of 176

dispatched, had been carried out by the two squadrons before they were transferred (they would not return to Swannington until 29 August).

Meanwhile, 141 Squadron dispatched seven Mosquitoes to France on 14/15 June. Pilot W/O Harry 'Butch' Welham with his navigator/radio operator, W/O E. J. 'Gus' Hollis, scored their first victory since joining 141 from 29 Squadron when a Me 410 fell to Welham's guns north of Lille. Although he had volunteered in 1939, the 28-year-old pilot had been classed 'reserved occupation' because of working on camouflage paints at ICI at Stowmarket, and had not joined the RAF until 1940. Further success for the Suffolk-born pilot and his Welsh navigator would follow two weeks later. However, the *Serrate* squadrons did not always have it all their own way. On 16/17 June, the night Bomber Command began its campaign against the V-1 sites in the Pas de Calais, F/O M. J. G. LaGouge and F/O L. A. Vandenberghe of 141 Squadron lost an engine to enemy fighter action over Belgium and flew home

*W/O Harry 'Butch' Welham* (left) *and W/O E. J. 'Gus' Hollis* (right) *of 141 Squadron, who destroyed a Me 410 on 14/15 June 1944 and a Ju 88 on 27/28 June (Harry Welham)*

on the other one. Approaching West Malling, they were mistaken for an enemy intruder and the runway lights were extinguished. LaGouge retracted his undercarriage and opened up his one remaining Merlin in an attempt to go round again but he crashed and the aircraft soon burned out. Miraculously, both men survived and were detained in hospital for only one night.

The next night, 17/18 June, more attacks were made on V-1 sites in northern France. The twenty-third kill of 239 Squadron was chalked up by F/L G. E. Poulton and F/O A. J. Neville when they destroyed a Ju 88 near Eindhoven and damaged another. Much to the chagrin of 141 Squadron, which had put up with the troubles associated with the Mosquito II, its Merlin engines and its fickle radar equipment longer than anyone else, 169 Squadron had begun receiving brand new Mk VI Mosquitoes for some weeks now. Even so, two or three NFTs were often needed

before an aircraft was fit for operations. Considerable trouble was experienced with the Mk IV aerial system fitted to the Mosquitoes and was only solved with the fitting of Beaufighter aerials. No. 169 had still managed to destroy 10 enemy aircraft in April–May and in June it shot down four more aircraft.

On 21/22 June, Bomber Command attacked synthetic oil plants in Germany. Losses were high with 44 out of 139 aircraft dispatched to Wesseling near Köln being lost. Another eight were lost on the strike on Scholven/Buer by 132 bombers. Four Mosquitoes of 141 Squadron and seven of 239 Squadron took off from West Raynham and F/O R. Depper with F/O R. G. C. Follis from the latter, destroyed a He 177. The 141 Squadron Mosquito flown by P/O Peter Coles and P/O Jim Carter was hit by flak after veering into the Düsseldorf area and they limped home with a broken petrol feed. Approaching West Raynham their undercarriage failed. In the Control Tower,

*'Butch' Welham and 'Gus' Hollis of 141 Squadron in Mosquito NF Mk II DZ240 shooting down a Me 410 on 14/15 June. They also bagged a Ju 88 south of Tilberg in the same aircraft on 27/28 June, possibly Ju 88G-1 Wrk Nr 710455 of 4./NJG3, which crashed at Arendonk, Belgium. Uffz Eugen Wilfert and crew were KIA. (painting by Harry Peters)*

W/C Winn was in radio contact with the crew for 45 minutes but his instructions failed to do the trick. Finally, when one wheel was locked in the down position, and the other swinging in the wind, Winn ordered them to bail out. They landed 10 miles south-west of the station and were returned in an Army car. Their Mosquito crashed at Hill House Farm near Swaffham.

On 24 June, Bob Braham with his navigator, F/L Walsh DFC, flew in to West Raynham for a day *Ranger* from the station on 25 June to Denmark (one of several such 'arrangements' Braham had made since leaving the squadron). Braham scored his twenty-ninth victory. He would get no more. Braham had just completed an attack on a German Staff car on a road on Fyn Island, when he was attacked by two Fw 190s. In one of them was Lt Robert Spreckels. The Mosquito's port wing and engine were set on fire. Braham tried to crash land on the shore of a fiord when he was attacked again but he managed to set it down and fortunately the aircraft did not explode. Walsh and Braham made a run for it and got behind sand-dunes. Troops from a nearby radar station advanced towards them and opened fire with automatic weapons. Unhurt, Braham and Walsh were marched away into captivity. At 10:00 hours next day an ASR search was initiated, and 141 Squadron crews took part, including Paddy Engelbach and Ron Mallett, but their search was in vain. That night, Dennis Welfare and Taffy Bellis of 239 Squadron destroyed a Ju 88 near Paris.

On 27/28 June, the Mosquito *Serrate* squadrons helped support 1,049 bombers making attacks on V-1 sites and other targets in northern France. At West Raynham, 11 Mosquitoes of 141 Squadron and eight Mosquitoes of 239 Squadron took off between 22:00 and 23:05 hours and set out across the sea towards France to provide bomber support. At 22:35 hours, W/C Charles V. Winn and his navigator/radio operator, F/L R. A. W. Scott, led 141 Squadron off, followed at 10 and 5 minute intervals by the remaining 10 Mosquitoes.

Flying Officer W. P. Rimer with Warrant Officer H. J. Alexander had to return soon after take off when their AI set failed. Pilot Officer Coles with Pilot Officer J. A. Carter patrolled Beacon Mücke hoping to pick up signals from German night-fighters (otherwise known as 'bashing the beacons'), but also had to abort after both *Serrate* and AI went unserviceable. Problems with engine vibration and instruments and R/T failure made a return to base equally expedient. Francois Vandenplassche with P/O M. K. Webster, were one crew who patrolled and chased but returned empty-handed. It was Vandenplassche's first operation since his return to the squadron after his evasion from occupied France when he bailed out on 25/26 March 1943.

Meanwhile, S/L Graham Rice with F/O J. G. Rogerson had had better luck. They crossed the coast of France at 23:50 hours and flew on at 14,000 ft amid 8/10–9/10 broken cloud. Above them the sky was clear. They patrolled the Florennes area, picking up several AI contacts well below which appeared to be orbiting. They flew on to Beacon Emil and orbited but failed to pick up any contacts so they carried on to Beacon Goldhammer which was flashing. They orbited but drew a blank and returned to Emil. On patrol north of the beacon in the Cambrai area, Rice and Rogerson spotted red Very flares and decided to investigate. Then they spotted another four. Half a minute later, Rogerson picked up a target on AI contact at maximum range, slightly below them. Rice closed to 4,000 ft and wheeled hard to starboard to close in from behind. At 1,500 ft dead ahead and slightly above they saw the silhouette of a Ju 88. The moon came out from behind the clouds and temporarily blinded them so that they lost

*Leavesden-built Mosquito II HJ911 in which S/L G. J. Rice and F/O J. G. Rogerson of 141 Squadron destroyed a Ju 88 at Cambrai on the night of 27/28 June 1944 and a Bf 110 NW of Amiens on 7/8 July. (BAe)*

visual contact for a few moments. Rice followed on AI for 15 minutes as the enemy aircraft weaved into the moonlight. Rice and Rogerson closed to 400 ft to confirm the identity of the German aircraft before dropping back to 600 ft and opening fire from dead astern. Both the Junkers' engines burst into flame which died out. Rice pumped another salvo into the doomed aircraft and it went down in a steep dive to port, blazing furiously. It was their third victory.

'Butch' Welham and 'Gus' Hollis used their well-established rapport to track and hunt an AI contact 5 miles north of Eindhoven. Their Mosquito, DZ240, was the same aircraft they had used to shoot down their first enemy aircraft on 14/15 June when a Me 410 had fallen to the Mk II's guns. Clearly painted in large white letters on the pilot's side of the Mosquito's nose was the double entendre 'SHYTOT'. Welham reduced height to 14,000 ft and closed in on the contact. He recalls:

The target, a Ju 88, appeared dead ahead, slightly above but we looked as if we were going to overshoot. Gus came on the intercom and in his lilting Welsh accent said, 'Throttle back, pull the nose up, Butch.' His nose was in his set, keeping track of the fir-tree-shaped blip on the *Serrate* scope. 'Left, left, right, right,' he ordered. 'Thirty degrees above. Dead ahead, 2,000 ft.' I steered to the ideal spot, 400 yards behind (the four 20 mm Hispanos were synchronized for 400 yards). I lined him up through the circular gunsight, my right thumb ready to press the firing button on top of the stick and aimed between the cockpit and engine. Gus said clearly, 'Go on, shoot!' I said, 'OK,' and let fly a 2-second burst. As the cannons fired beneath our feet the seats vibrated and dust flew up from the floor all around the cockpit. A fire started in the engine and the wing and the kite went down in a spiral burning all the while, exploding on the ground about 6 miles south of Tilburg.

We continued to patrol and at about 01:43 hours about 10 miles west of Gent, we chased another AI contact at maximum range. It developed into a series of tight orbits and contact turned out to be 2,000 ft behind. We did an exceedingly tight turn and found we now had two contacts ahead, one 1,500 ft behind the other. A bandit was being chased by a Mossie. I closed in to about 4,000 ft when the nearest one started flashing IFF. We abandoned the chase as we did not want to put a friendly fighter off. On the way home we picked up the beacon at West Raynham and Gus, as usual, after picking it up on the *Serrate* set, said, 'There it is Butch,' and went off to sleep.

It brought 141 Squadron's total victories to 17. Three aircraft were destroyed by 239 Squadron without loss or early return to bring its total to 29. Denis Welfare and Taffy Bellis got a Me 410 near Paris, W/C R. M. J. Evans and F/O R. H. 'Dickie' Perks, and F/L D. R. 'Podge' Howard and F/O Frank 'Sticky' Clay all destroyed a Ju 88 apiece. Two crews failed to return to West Raynham: F/L Herbert R. Hampshire with W/O Alan W. Melrose, who were on their first operation, and Paddy Engelbach with Ronald Mallett DFC, all of 141 Squadron. Engelbach and Mallett patrolled north Holland for an hour and the navigator could tell they were being picked up by a German night-fighter. The pilot turned south then Mallett suddenly ordered, 'Hard on to the reciprocal.' Engelbach wrote:

As I threw the aircraft over I asked if there was anything behind. The answer was a series of judders as my tail was shot off and I went into a spin. I pulled the aircraft out but was immediately hit again. At about 2,500 ft the aircraft disintegrated and I was thrown out through the canopy. I opened my

parachute after a long search for it, and my fall was broken at about 20 ft and I landed unhurt. Mallett was killed. The Germans said that the aircraft that shot me down was a Heinkel 219.

Paddy Engelbach ended up a prisoner of war and came upon old acquaintances from 141 Squadron behind the wire. One of them was W/C Bob Braham for whom he had searched on 26 June after Braham had been shot down during a day *Ranger* to Denmark. Engelbach[3] returned to 141 Squadron at the end of the war and in his flying logbook when recording his search for Braham, he inserted, 'Found him in Dulag Luft!'

[3] Paddy Engelbach was killed taking off in a Venom from West Raynham in February 1955. At that time he was CO of 23 Squadron.

On 17/18 June 1944 F/L Geoffrey E. Poulton and F/O Arthur John Neville of 239 Squadron destroyed Ju 88 G-1 Wrk Nr 710866 R4+NS of 8./NJG2 which crashed at Volkel airfield. Lt. Harald Machleidt (pilot) was killed, Uffz Kurt Marth (radar op) WIA and Gefr Max Rinnerthaler (air gunner) KIA. (Tom Cushing Collection)

# CHAPTER 5

# 'MOSKITOPANIC'

*We were hungry tired and dirty,*
*From our shoulders rifles hung,*
*Our clothes were torn, our faces bronzed*
*By long hours in the sun.*
*Here was to be our station,*
*For the war was not yet won,*
*When we came to Little Snoring*
*That fateful June had just begun.*

S. F. RUFFLE

The mere presence in the circuits of 'Mr Micawber-like' Mosquitoes 'waiting for something to turn up', as they lurked one by one to cover the whole night period, was enough to cause morale-sapping 'Moskitopanik' throughout Germany in the summer of 1944. On 5/6 July 1944, Mosquito Mk VIs of 23 Squadron flew their first *Intruder* operation from Little Snoring since returning from the Mediterranean, with sorties against enemy airfields. No. 23 Squadron had joined 515 Squadron at the secluded Norfolk base in June after flying *Intruder* operations from Sicily and Sardinia. The main role of 515 and 23 Squadrons was flying low-level day and night *Intruders*, mostly concentrating on active German night-fighter bases. Although 515 Squadron had been based at the remote Norfolk outpost since 15 December 1943, it had only been introduced to this role early in March 1944.

Before then, 515 had operated from Northolt, Heston and then Hunsdon, during which time it had conducted *Moonshine* operations using Defiant aircraft. *Moonshine* was the code-name given to an operation which was calculated to alert the enemy defences by causing the approach of a large force of aircraft to be registered on their early warning radar equipment. The large force was, in fact, one Defiant carrying special radar devices. These tests were highly successful and a Flight called The Defiant Flight was formed in June 1942 attached to RAF Northolt, under the direction of 11 Group, Fighter Command. From September–

*From September–December 1942, 515 Squadron, equipped with Defiant Mk IIs, mounted operations with* Moonshine *equipment to confuse the enemy. Flying the aircraft are F/Sgt Louden (C); F/Sgt T. S. Ecclestone (M); W/O Preston (K) and S/L J. L. 'Artie' Shaw (B), all of whom flew 515 Squadron Mosquitoes at Little Snoring. Shaw (and F/Sgt Stanley-Smith) were killed on D-Day, and P/O Louden was shot down and made PoW on 4 September 1944. (Tom Cushing Collection)*

December 1942, as 515 Squadron, and equipped with Defiant Mk IIs, operations with *Moonshine* equipment were conducted which succeeded in confusing the enemy. On occasions, 300 plus enemy fighters were drawn up by the *Spoof*, entirely in the wrong position to ward off bombing attacks by other British aircraft. In December 1942, the role of the Squadron was changed to manipulating a *Mandrel* screen by night, in support of the bomber offensive. *Mandrel* was an American jamming device and was used ahead of RAF night raids and US 8th Air Force daylight raids. Eight pre-determined positions were 515 patrolled nightly by Squadron which operated from forward bases at West Malling, Tangmere

and Coltishall. This work continued until July 1943 when it was decided to re-equip the Squadron with Beaufighters.

On 27 January 1944, S/L Freddie 'Cordite' Lambert was promoted wing commander and posted to take command of 515 Squadron. A few days later, information was received from 100 Group HQ that the squadron's work on *Mandrel* was finished and that it would be re-equipped with Mosquito Mk VI aircraft for low-level *Intruder* sorties over enemy airfields. The air gunners were posted away and new crews were brought in to train for *Intruder* work. Beginning on 29 February 1944, 515 Squadron's Beaufighters and Blenheims were replaced by Mosquito IIs for training. Some of 605 Squadron's Mk VI Mosquitoes were operated by 515 on detachment at Bradwell Bay and it was in one of these aircraft that W/C Lambert with F/L E. W. Morgan, shot down an He 177 in the first squadron sortie on 5 March.

In April, W/C B. R. 'Sammy' O'Brien Hoare DSO DFC*, CO of 605 Squadron, assumed the post of Station Commander at Snoring. Despite losing an eye before the war when a duck shattered the windscreen of his aircraft, Sammy Hoare became one of the foremost *Intruder* pilots in the RAF. He had commanded 23 Squadron during March–September 1942 and on 6 July had flown the Squadron's first Mosquito *Intruder* sortie. In September 1943, he had assumed command of 605 Squadron, destroying a Do 217 on his first operation, and in January 1944 had notched the Squadron's 100th victory when he downed

a Ju 188. At Snoring, 23 and 515 Squadron crews took bets on which one of Sammy's eyes, one blue, one brown, was real. No. 23 Squadron was commanded by the audacious and admired W/C A. M. Murphy DSO*, DFC, Croix de Guerre with Palm. In the Mediterranean, 'Murphy's Marauders' had been more akin to his private Air Force. Alan Michael Murphy, affectionately known as 'Sticky', had taken over 23 Squadron in December 1943.

Sticky was born on 26 September 1917 at Cockermouth in Cumberland. After spending his early life in South Africa, his father's health forced the Murphys to return to England where Alan went to Seafield Preparatory School at Lytham on the north-west coast until about 1931. Whilst there he played cricket and soccer. Murphy was an outstanding athlete. He

*W/C Sticky Murphy DSO, DFC (left centre) and G/C Sammy Hoare DSO, DFC (right centre) two of the RAF's top* Intruder *pilots of the entire war, pictured during a function at Little Snoring with local farmer, Mr Whitehead (right), where Murphy commanded 23 Squadron and Hoare was Station Commander. (Tom Cushing Collection)*

*Sticky Murphy pulls down the dice in the bar at Little Snoring. The bar was designed by Wilton Todd who also designed the memorial to the 50 at Sagan. The large dice was counterbalanced by a scrubbing brush. When the 23 or 515 Squadrons were on ops the dice was lowered. 'Dicing with death'. A lowered scrubbing brush* (bottom) *meant that all ops were cancelled – scrubbed. This was usually the sign of a good booze-up. (Jean Bunting/Tom Cushing Collections)*

jumped high and long, as well as being a top hurdler and 440-yard man. He represented the RAF at athletics, and in a triangular match between Cranwell, Woolwich and Sandhurst, he created a long-standing record for the long jump of 23 feet 1¼ inches in 1938. Commissioned as a pilot Officer in July 1938, Sticky continued his training on 185 Squadron with the Fairey Battle, then trained others in the north of Scotland at an OTU as Station Navigation Officer. In March 1941, Sticky joined 1419 Special Duty Flight at Stradishall, with the primary duty then of dropping secret agents throughout Occupied Europe for intelligence and Resistance activities. Sticky Murphy became one of the pioneer pilots in 138 Squadron, one of the 'Moon Squadrons' which flew the short take-off and landing Lysander to infiltrate and exfiltrate 'Joes' in Europe.

On 1 June 1942, he was rested and attached to the Air Ministry but flew various types of aircraft, and enjoyed his married life in the London area. On 20 June 1943 after almost a year, he arrived at High Ercall for conversion to Mosquitoes, and for a rapid course on intruding. Passing this course, he was given an 'Exceptional' grading by W/C 'Mouse' Fielden, who had been Sticky's CO on 161 Squadron. In late

September 1943, Sticky landed in Malta to join the veteran 23 Squadron which had been the scourge of the Axis Powers in the area throughout that year, harassing the retreating enemy armies and air forces in North Africa, and in Sicily and Italy throughout 1943. Sticky Murphy quickly became the commander of B Flight. He followed the squadron motto *Semper Aggressus* (Always have a Go) which he was more inclined to translate in terms of the ANZACs at Gallipoli, with their war-cry 'Right lads. After the bastards!'

Soon, he became CO of 23 Squadron, which quickly loved him for his humanity, his daring leadership and natural charm, bombing, strafing and intruding from Bordeaux on the Atlantic coast to Udine on the borders of Austria and Yugoslavia. At Little Snoring, the ebullient coryphaeus and his daring crews took the friendly Norfolk hamlet by storm and the locals to their hearts. Always one for a drink and a party, Sticky's discordant rendering of 'Rip My knickers Away' heralded the real singing sessions. What he lacked in melody, which was to the tune of 'Yip Aye Addy Aye Ay . . .', he made up for with his usual attack. 'We're a Shower of Bastards', the traditional squadron song, usually followed. One of the navigators, Bucky Cunningham, was a professional cabaret

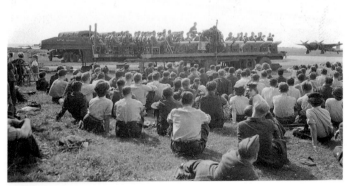

*The Glenn Miller AAF band prepare to play at RAF Twinwoods, where a Mosquito can be seen to the right of the improvized bandstand. Twinwoods was a satellite of 51 OTU Cranfield and many aircrew, including Tommy Smith, who were posted to 100 Group passed through here. (via Connie Richards)*

musician and songwriter, and he added original material to the repertoire, such as 'My Gal Sal is the Queen of the Acrobats' and 'She's got two of everything'. No. 23 Squadron left its mark in social as well as operational circles, and Sticky's exploits remain legendary in the memories of the local people of that time.

'The atmosphere that came over,' recalls F/L Tommy Smith, one of the new pilots at this time, 'was one of lots of fun and games; booze and bawdy songs, prangs and shows and strafing, and not much care for others or the agonies of war.'

This was all far from the truth. The average aircrews were dedicated, hardworking players in a dangerous game, fully aware of the risks, conscious of the death and destruction they handed out, apprehensive of the agonies of grief and despair their own families would feel on learning they were missing or dead; and also dreading the possible manner of their own death, torn to shreds by bullets or shrapnel, or roasted alive in a flamer.

Tommy, formerly a Glaswegian accountant, had earlier completed a tour of ops with 96 Squadron on Defiants and Merlin-engined Beaufighters, which ended with a trip to the RAF Head Injuries Hospital in Oxford and a non-operational medical categorization. He spent his 'rest' as a PPCI (Permanent President of Courts of Inquiry), or 'Prang Basher', in No. 81 and No. 9 Groups which administered the OTUs of Fighter Command. This was a congenial if grisly occupation; congenial because the instructors in OTUs were all operational pilots 'on rest' who were always ready for a party or a session, and included an ever-changing rota of old friends or people who knew old friends; grisly because only fatal accidents required a PPCI, and detailed investigation of prang after prang gave a jaundiced view of flying operational aircraft.

Everyone had the same burning ambition to get back on ops and Tommy was no different. 'I drank my way up the medical profession until I got to an AVM neurologist, who signed me A1 again on the grounds that I was much more likely to be written off by the Hun than by any neurological shortcomings!' From the vantage point of Group HQ, he had decided that the best business to be in was Mosquito *Intruders*, so after a brush-up at Cranfield OTU, he got a posting to the Bomber Support Training Unit at Great Massingham, then on to 23 Squadron at Little Snoring.

Compared to the Merlin Beaufighter, the Mosquito fighter-bomber was a dream. Although very functional, with a cockpit ranged around you like the console of the 'Mighty Wurlitzer', the Beaufighter felt like a flying dump-truck. By comparison, the Mosquito with its compact, well-appointed accommodation, felt like a luxurious two-seater sports car, and although I felt it was underpowered, it had so clean lines that once it got up speed it went like a bomb and really felt like a fighter. Like all high-efficiency twins, it had a few bad points. It didn't swing on take off like the Beau, but could drop a wing when near the stall, and I had investigated more than one Mossie prang where this had occurred, spreading a trail of firewood for half a mile. When a Mosquito crashed, it really crashed.

Tommy Smith had crewed up with Arthur Cockayne, a schoolmaster from Walsall, whose wife was a schoolmistress. 'Cocky', who was in his mid-thirties, pretty old for aircrew, had been called up late in the war and had trained on Catalinas at Pensacola in Florida before becoming a 'radar detective' on bombers in 100 Squadron in a lively way. On their freshman sortie, to Höörne on the Zuider Zee, they were caught in searchlights which were not supposed to be there, and the following night went on one of the Squadron's

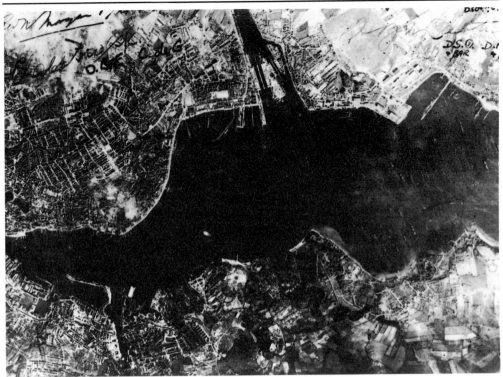

On 12 May, three Mosquito crews in 515 Squadron carried out anti-flak patrols on the Kiel Canal in support of mine-laying aircraft by drawing fire from the gun emplacements. Here, the Mosquitoes are drawing fire at 1,500 ft while Mosquitoes of 692 Squadron release mines just above the canal. Signatures include Dambuster Micky Martin (top right). (Tom Cushing Collection)

'transport bashing' operations. Tommy Smith recalls:

Each crew was allocated bits of railways and canals. I got a stretch of the Weser–Elbe Canal from Hannover to Magdeburg and a railway line from Shoningen to Hildesheim, and it proved to be a hectic bloody caper for me! We set off doing all the things the 'Old Hands' had briefed us to do. Across the sea high enough for comfort, pull up to dive flat-out over the enemy coast, then weave across the map at 1,000 ft above the scenery. Of course, since the scenery could undulate more than 1,000 ft it was all very dicey!

There was a pearl grey sky with the moon thankfully behind cloud. (Bright moonlight was no good for low level map reading.) The canal showed up as a pallid streak. In moonlight it would have been black. The

Hun blackout was very good; there were no lights anywhere but people soon woke up. Mosquitoes are the noisiest of aeroplanes, and every boy scout along the canal began firing tracer. They seemed to be hose-piping us from all sides, but they did not put on enough deflection and they missed us. I must have shot at a dozen barges but they were all either carrying scrap iron or cement. All of a sudden there was a colossal 'crump'. I said, 'What the hell's going on Cocky?'

Laconically, he replied in his old man's voice, 'There's a balloon on our tail and its firing at us!'

I honked the Mosquito around in a split-arse turn and looked up. On our tail there appeared to be a great big black balloon, with two lines of tracer coming out of it! The enemy gunners had depressed their 88 mm flak guns to rooftop level, and the 'balloon'

*W/O T. S. Ecclestone and his navigator F/Sgt J. H. Shimmon of 515 Squadron who destroyed two unidentified enemy aircraft during a day Ranger to Belgium on 26 April 1944. (Tom Cushing Collection)*

was actually a flak-burst cloud, and the two lines of tracer fire were coming from the ground below. I learned to fly a little higher after this.

Although they carried out all the normal tasks of *Intruders*, 23 and 515 Squadrons also performed any odd task dreamed up by 100 Group HQ, the Station Commander, Squadron Commanders, or even, on occasion, the crews themselves. All were likely to form a part of the curriculum. The *Intruder* crews of 23 and 515 Squadrons were excellent pupils. On 12 May, 515 Squadron carried out anti-flak patrols on the Kiel Canal in support of mine-laying aircraft by drawing fire from the gun emplacements to themselves and away from the mine-layers. The support given by the squadron to the mining of the Dortmund–Ems canal by No. 8 Group has been classified as one of the most important mine-laying operations of the war. Ten Mosquito crews in 515 patrolled the heavily defended canal area, and by drawing the fire away from the mine-layers or strafing the gun positions from very close range,

silenced the opposition and enabled the mining of one of Germany's most important waterways to be achieved without the loss of any Mosquitoes.

Several enemy aircraft were claimed destroyed by 515 Squadron during June, including two He 111s, a Ju 34, a Bf 110G and a Ju 88. The Bf 110, Wrk Nr 440076 G9+NS of 8./NJG1, was destroyed on 21 June by S/L Paul Rabone DFC and F/O F. C. H. Johns during a *Day Ranger* to northern Holland and the Frisians. The Bf 110, flown by 21-year-old Uffz Herbert Beyer, had just taken off from Eelde airfield. Rabone and Johns came in from astern and promptly attacked with a 3½-second burst of cannon. No strikes were observed, so Rabone fired again. This time the 2-second burst hit the starboard engine and pieces flew off. Later, Rabone wrote graphically:

Before the Hun got his breath back a delightful third burst of cannon was presented at 50 yards range at a height of about 100 ft. This created havoc – the Me 110's starboard wing and starboard engine

*P/O C. W. Chown RCAF and his navigator F/Sgt D. G. N. Veitch of 515 Squadron, who, on 27/28 June 1944, destroyed Ju 88 Wrk Nr 300651 B3+LT of 9./KG54 during landing approach at Welschap (after a mine laying opreation in the invasion area). The Ju 88 crashed into a house, killing three children, and Uffz Gotthard Seehaber, pilot, Gefr Kurt Voelker, Ogefr Walter Oldenbruch and Ogefr Hermann Patzel. (Tom Cushing Collection).*

burst into flames, the port engine belched forth black smoke, and the enemy aircraft dived into the ground enveloped in a mass of flames, smoke and destruction . . . Mosquito landed at Little Snoring at 16:30 hours after a most enjoyable afternoon's sport.

Beyer, Uffz Hans Petersmann (21, Radar Op.) and Ogfr Franz Riedel (20, Air Gunner) were all killed.

Paul Rabone bailed out six times in his RAF career, but his luck and Johns's finally ran out when they failed to return from a day Ranger on 24 July, their first, and last, since transferring to 23 Squadron.

On 27/28 June, P/O C. W. Chown and Sgt D. G. N. Veitch of 515 Squadron set off from Little Snoring to patrol Gilze–Volkel–Venlo–Eindhoven. After three quarters of an hour, during which they bombed Venlo airfield and created a 'substantial fire emitting flashes for the odd 15 minutes' they returned to Eindhoven for a second look. There was no cloud and visibility was 'good'. At 02:13 hours they were over the airfield which had its north-south flarepath well lit. On their approach, four red cartridges were fired from the air and the runway lights changed pattern. Four airfield identification bars were lit at

*W/O R. E. 'Bob' Preston and his navigator, F/Sgt Fred Verity of 515 Squadron, who destroyed a Ju 88 near Coulommiers on 4/5 July 1944. (Tom Cushing Collection)*

*W/O Bob Preston's Mosquito FB Mk VI PZ163 of 515 Squadron at Little Snoring. (Tom Cushing Collection)*

the southern end and then almost immediately three of the bars were switched off and a single red cartridge was fired from the ground followed by a white light flashing. Just then, a green light flashing dashes appeared in the air to the west of the airfield.

Chown and Veitch, their Mosquito at 1,500 ft, gave chase and spotted the outline of an aircraft with a green bow light and red downward identification light under the tail. They closed to 200 yards and recognized it as a Ju 88. Chown delivered a stern attack with a 2-second burst of cannon fire which recorded one strike on the Junker's fuselage. Chown closed to 150 yards and delivered a second stern attack with burst of about 3 seconds. The Ju 88 immediately exploded and scattered debris through the sky as it disintegrated. Chown and Veitch orbited the scene and took photos of the burning enemy night-fighter before breaking away and returning home. The pilot had destroyed the Ju 88 with 200 rounds of 20 mm cannon.

On 4/5 July, W/O R. E. Preston and Sgt F. Verity of 515 Squadron took off on a night *Ranger* to Coulommiers airfield via Southwold and North Beveland. They reached the enemy night-fighter base at 02:05 hours but the base was inactive so they stooged around for three quarters of an hour before returning. This time their approach signalled the double flarepath to be lit. Obviously, the base anticipated that one of its fighters was returning. Preston reduced height to 1,000 ft. Verity obtained a visual sighting of the enemy aircraft at 300–400 yards range. It was a Ju 88, and it was on a southerly course at about their height. Preston gave chase but the Junkers

started weaving before turning starboard and diving. Undeterred, Preston followed. As the Ju 88 pulled out of its dive at treetop height, it appeared right in his sights and Preston gave it a 3-second burst of cannon at 200 yards. It set the Ju 88's starboard engine on fire and the aircraft instantly disintegrated, scattering burning debris into the air like an exploding firework. Preston circled the scene before bombing the airfield with two 500 lb GP bombs which exploded in the south side of the airfield. There was no opposition and only four inefficient searchlights vainly probed the cloudy sky. Not satisfied with their night's work, Preston and Verity attacked two small freighters moored side by side in the Zuid Beveland Canal at the Westerschelde lock gates with a 3-second burst of cannon fire. Strikes were seen on the bow of one of the ships.

On 5/6 July, Sticky Murphy and three other Mosquito Mk VIs of 23 Squadron flew the first Squadron *Intruder* operation from Little Snoring since embarkation leave, with sorties against enemy airfields. Five other crews took part in an uneventful night *Ranger* on 6/7 July. On 7 July, Sticky Murphy and Jock Reid flew a day *Ranger* to France and attacked a convoy of nine vehicles, claiming one destroyed and a damaged railway engine near Ath. Eight

*F/O Bruton, F/O D. W. O. Wood's navigator on the successful day* Ranger *on 10 July 1944 when they shared a destroyed Ju 88 victory with Adams and Ruffle. Wood was killed and Bruton made a PoW when their Mosquito was shot down on 1 September. (Tom Cushing Collection)*

*Pictured at Little Snoring are, from left to right: W/C Freddie Lambert RCAF, 515 Squadron CO; S/L Paul Rabone; F/O F. C. H. Johns, S/L Price, Intelligence officer; P/O Chown RCAF. Lambert with F/L E. W. M. Morgan destroyed an He 177 on 5 March 1944 and a Bf 109 with F/O 'Whiskers' Lake AFC on 6/7 September 1944. Rabone and Johns destroyed a Bf 110 on 21 June and a Heinkel 111 nine days later (both were killed on 24 July 1944). (Tom Cushing Collection)*

other crews flew patrols that night over France, Holland and Belgium and carried bombs for the first time. An enemy train was destroyed by F/L D. J. Griffiths. Eindhoven was bombed by P/O K. M. Cotter RNZAF but no results were observed due to flak from the airfield. Le Culot was bombed by W/O T. Griffiths, and a large red glow was seen. A railway junction near Barnefeld was bombed by F/O D. Buddy Badley RNZAF. No flashes were reported but great volumes of smoke appeared. Only the weather stopped 23 Squadron flying on 9–11 July and adding to the impressive score of enemy vehicles it had run up in the Mediterranean.

During a day *Ranger* on 10 July, 515 had more success. At 15:03 hours, F/L R. A. Adams and P/O F. H. Ruffle, and F/O D. W. O. Wood and F/O Bruton, took off and crossed Happisburgh before heading across the North Sea at zero feet for their patrol area in northern Holland and north-west Germany. Both Mosquitoes roared in over the Dutch coast and 'beat up' a German Army encampment at Herslake, 15 miles west of Quakenbrück soon after crossing into Germany. Strikes were recorded on huts and the Mosquito crews reported 'general confusion among the Bosche privates'. After this exhilarating interlude both crews flew in the direction of Schwishenahner airfield. At 16:37 hours and at zero feet, a Ju 88 night-fighter, clearly on a NFT, was spotted 3 miles in the distance at 800 ft altitude making its approach to land. The Junkers, quite unconcerned, turned left and lowered its undercarriage. Wood and Bruton approached to within about 250 yards, and from below and astern, pumped a 2-second burst of cannon into the enemy machine. Its starboard engine immediately burst into flames and started down. The airfield defences opened up on the Mosquitoes with some light flak. Adams and Ruffle went in and finished it off with a further burst of 2–3 seconds of cannon fire. The Junkers hit a tree near the airfield and exploded. Both crews landed safely back at Snoring at 18:14 hours.

In July, 515 flew over 40 day and night *Rangers*. The third victory that month occurred on a day *Ranger* on 14 July when Wood and Bruton again figured in a shared kill, this time with F/L A. E. Callard and Sgt Townsley. Their victim was a Ju-W 34 single-engined four-passenger transport which was unfortunate enough to be in the wrong place at the wrong time as the pair of Mosquitoes approached, 12 miles east of Stralsund. Callard and Townsley went in first and gave it a 1-second burst from about 150 yards. At this range the Mosquito was hit by flying pieces of debris but no lasting damage to the British machine was done. The Ju 34 ,on the other hand, never stood a chance. It went into an almost vertical climb and stall-turned before 'fluttering' to the ground. There was no telling what high ranking officers were on board, if any, but just in case, Wood and Bruton made absolutely certain by giving the smouldering embers a 1-second burst until it exploded. None of the occupants would be keeping their appointment at a top-level meeting, or climbing into their night-fighters later that evening, that was for sure.

No. 23 Squadron was getting its eye in

too. On the morning of 14 July, Sticky Murphy with S/L H. F. Smith carried out a *Ranger* patrol and took the opportunity to shoot up some German troops on the beach at Stadil. Another famous pilot at Little Snoring at this time was S/L Harold B. M. 'Mickey' Martin DSO, DFC, who had joined 515 Squadron in April and was supposed to be 'resting' after flying Hampdens and Lancasters (including *P-Popsie* on the famous dams raid of 18 May 1943). Group Captain Leonard Cheshire has written: 'I learned everything I knew of the low flying game from Mick. He was the ideal wartime operational pilot. He had superb temperament, was quite fearless and innovative in his thinking. He was meticulous in his flying discipline and never did make a mistake.' On an operation over the Ruhr, Cheshire broke silence to enquire about the weather. From a Mosquito came Martin's voice. 'What the hell are you doing?' Cheshire asked. 'Sticking my neck out for you types,' replied Martin who was strafing a night-fighter airfield!

*S/L Harold 'Micky' Martin DSO, DFC (right) of Dambusters fame, pictured with W/C Freddie Lambert, CO of 515 Squadron, at Little Snoring. Martin was supposed to be 'resting' with the Mosquito squadron but flew many ops and destroyed an unidentified enemy aircraft on 26 April 1944, and a Me 410 at Knocke, Belgium on 25/26 July, both with F/O J. W. Smith as his navigator. (Tom Cushing Collection)*

On 25/26 July, Martin, with F/O J. W. Smith as his navigator, flew a night *Ranger* to Stuttgart and Boblingen. He arrived over the area shortly after midnight and stooged around 'for as long as possible' but the patrol was uneventful and he headed home. Just after crossing the Belgian coast at Knocke at 03:50 hours in very hazy conditions, an aircraft was seen about 1 mile to port flying very fast. Martin swung the Mosquito around to dead astern and below the illuminated aircraft at a height of about 3,000 ft. He closed to 50 yards and identified it as a Me 410. Martin gave the Hornisse a burst of cannon fire from astern and slightly below at 70 yards. He was so

*S/L Taylor of 23 Squadron pictured in front of a Mosquito Mk II (some Mk IIs were initially used for training) with W/C Sammy Hoare's spaniel, Pound, at his feet. There were a number of mascots at Snoring, including a pig, which used to line up at NAAFI break, until one day it finally became part of crews' bacon-and-egg breakfasts! (Tom Cushing Collection)*

*Line up of 515 Squadron Mosquitoes at Winkleigh, Devon prior to an escort mission for Lancasters attacking Bordeaux on the night of 11/12 August 1944. The second Mosquito from the left is one flown by Mick Martin. (Tom Cushing Collection)*

*Aircrew at Little Snoring.* Left to right: *Frank Bocock, P/O A. Harvey (both 515 Squadron); F/L Bill Gregory (23 Squadron); S/L Tweedale. (Frank Bocock)*

*F/Sgt 'Snogger' Rogers of 515 Squadron* (centre) *got his nickname because although he did not swear, drink or smoke, he did enjoy the ladies. (Tom Cushing Collection)*

close the tail light of the Me 410 literally blotted out the spot on his ring sight. Martin recorded:

This inconvenience was adjusted with no trouble at all, and, with the ringsight moved to the Hun's starboard engine, a short second burst of cannon set the engine well alight. This obviously shook the Hun, and he speedily dived to port, but an almost simultaneous short second burst of cannon, directed on the port wing, blew the wing off, and the enemy aircraft, burning well, went down in a screaming dive. The 410 was seen to crash on the sea, and continued burning.

Also on 25/26 July, F/L D. J. Griffiths and F/Sgt S. F. Smith of 23 Squadron recorded the Squadron's first air-to-air victory since returning from the Mediterranean, with an unidentified enemy aircraft at Laon Pouvron. The following night, 26/27 July, Sticky Murphy and Jock Reid, one of six Mosquito crews of 23 Squadron aloft from Snoring, damaged a Ju 88 during their patrol to Châteaudun/Orleans airfield. Flying Officer K. Eastwood and Flight Lieutenant G. T. Rogers bombed Clastres airfield and shot up railway trucks and a factory building. On 4 August, 13 Mosquitoes of 23 Squadron led by Sticky Murphy and 10 of 515 Squadron led by Station Commander Sammy Hoare flew to Winkleigh in Devon to escort Lancasters attacking Bordeaux in daylight. When the Mosquitoes arrived over the target, smoke from bombs dropped by the Lancs was at

11,000 ft. They flew back over Vannes and Paimpol covering the bombers and landed at Winkleigh for the night. Next day at lunch time, all the Mosquito crews returned to Snoring in great spirits.

The previous day's operation was to be run again. Twelve crews in 23 Squadron, including Sammy Hoare, flying with F/L W. Gregory as his navigator, and 17 in 515 Squadron flew out and met the Lancasters returning from Bordeaux. Unluckily, Hoare had to abort with a jammed elevator after 2 hours and landed at Colerne where all crews returned safely by 21:30 hours. Everyone returned to Snoring on 6 August at lunch time and were rewarded with a 'stand down'. On 12 August, eight Mosquitoes of 515 Squadron flew to Winkleigh to provide escort for Lancasters of 5 Group raiding Bordeaux again.

Flying their first op, in *X-X-Ray*, were F/O G. M. 'Frank' Bocock and F/Sgt Alf 'Snogger' Rogers (a member of a temperance society who didn't smoke, drink or swear, but who had a reputation for the ladies). Frank Bocock recalls:

I was one of those stupid people who liked flying at night and here we were, on our first op, at 18,000–23,000 ft in broad daylight on a Saturday afternoon! We rendezvoused with the Lancasters over the Channel. It was a long boring flight (4 hours 20 minutes). We flew out over the Bay of Biscay. The previous flight had flown over Brittany and were shot at by American troops. This time all our Mosquitoes had invasion stripes painted

*P/O Chris Harrison (far left) and his navigator F/Sgt Mike Adams, (left) one of the crews who took part in the successful recovery of a ditched crew in the North Sea on 28 April 1944. (Tom Cushing Collection)*

under the wings.

In two fingers of four, the Mosquitoes patrolled up and down the sides of the bomber force. Frank Bocock's gunsight went u/s and he was forced to use extra engine boost to keep up after his gill shutters would not close. He landed back at Winkleigh very low on fuel and rejoined the other seven Mosquitoes at Snoring later.

Frank Bocock and Snogger Rogers flew their first *Intruder* on 18/19 August to the Fw 190 airfield at Leeuwarden. Frank Bocock recalls:

W/C Lambert told us to keep weaving. That's what I did. We stooged around over Holland at 1,500 ft. Suddenly, four searchlights coned us right in the middle. Gorgeous red, green and orange tracers arced towards us. It looked beautiful but it was even nicer when it missed us! I stuck the nose down. Our tail was damaged and our W/T went dead. We ripped off our helmets and shouted at each other. I told Alf to add a minute to the next leg but as we came back over the airfield, bang, the flak opened up again. The Germans' prediction was terrific, their radar exceptional. Fortunately, I had chopped my height. If I had been flying straight and level, we'd have got the chop.

On 27 August, F/L M. W. 'Joe' Huggins and his navigator, F/Sgt Joe Cooper, took off from Snoring at 22:10 hours for a night *Ranger* over the continent. They were returning over the Dutch coast when at 00:27 hours one of their propellers ran away. Chris Harrison, a pilot on the squadron recalls:

This problem apparently occurred on several aircraft and we were told to put the pitch lever to full fine should it happen, as this apparently would stop the oil bleeding away – we were told! The engine packed up and caught fire and Huggins told his navigator to bail out, expecting to follow him. However, as he found he could control the slowly descending aircraft, he carried on, calling Mayday, and finally bailed out within sight of the English coast, from which his approaching fire was under observation. He was picked up from a calm sea in a relatively short time, and taken to sick bay for check up. [P/O G. H. Spencer of 23 Squadron came back behind them and put up a good show in staying with them. He made six runs at less than 100 ft and saw Cooper in his dinghy].

The next morning F/L S. 'Josh' Hoskins with F/O Jonah Jones and myself, with F/Sgt Mike Adams took one of the early stints and proceeded to just off the Dutch coast, where by now the weather was heavily overcast, and an approximately 8 ft confused sea was running. We searched for quite some time when suddenly Jonah sighted Cooper's dinghy and Josh called on the R/T and got into a left-hand orbit centred on Cooper. I fell into the circle but because of the sea state it was some minutes before we sighted Joe. We orbited for some time, then decided we would return to base with the good news, but how to know where to find the dinghy when we came back? I noticed a tall chimney on the Dutch coast, so I went inland and made a run back over the centre of Josh's orbit and took a course and time from the chimney, so by flying the same vector would have a reasonable pinpoint on where Joe had been when we left, so off back to Snoring.

We arranged for an ASR Walrus, and also a back-up launch to go and pick up Cooper (the sea was considered probably too heavy for the Walrus to land and take off) and to keep Joe company while this was being organized, Josh and I went out again, this time accompanied by S/L Henry Morley. I duly went inland at the Dutch coast, then flew out my time and direction, and we started to look for Joe but just could not find him. We had more or less decided he had been snatched by the Germans, who would earlier have been able to observe us orbiting and guess what was on, when once again Jonah spotted him, and again the follow-the-leader orbiting. After 15 minutes or so, eyes fixed on the dinghy, this became very unpleasant, with feelings of dizziness. Just closing your eyes for a few seconds made sighting Joe a great task due to the state of the sea, and we took it in turns to break out of the circle and relax for 10 minutes, then back in, and several minutes search to sight the dinghy. It is my recollection that Henry Morley and his navigator reported they never did sight the dinghy. After a long period of this, under about a 1,000 ft cloudbase what we at first thought was a 109 dropped out of the clouds just north of us, and hooray, its half a dozen Church Fenton Polish Mustangs, with the funny old but wonderful-looking Walrus. A couple of passes, and he dropped a smoke float. With

this reference, you could scratch yourself and then quickly pick up Joe again, so in went the Walrus, and landed in a great cloud of spray.

While the Walrus was making his circuit, I went in and took camera-gun of Joe in his dinghy, and during the several efforts the Walrus made to take off, when the wing floats kept digging into the seas, and spinning it around, I also literally between the silent prayers, flashed over and recorded this on my camera-gun. Eventually, the Walrus got off, and we decided to head for home and a celebration, and halfway across the North Sea, broken cloud and calm water, we met the back-up launch heading for the Dutch coast. This was obviously futile, so what to do? Several passes overhead frantically pointing back to England had no effect, and our VHF was useless, so we

*23 Squadron past and present gathering at Little Snoring in June 1944.* Back row, left to right: *F/L Eastwood; Bruce Martin; Anderson RCAF; George Twitt; David Atherton; u/k; u/k; Al Yates; u/k; Berry; George Stewart; u/k; Grimwood; P/O G. H. Spencer.* Middle row, left to right: *P/O G. H. Spencer; Kit Cotter RNZAF; Paul Beaudet RCAF; F/O F. C. H. Johns; F/L Rogers; Buddy Badley; Bunny Austin (?); S/L Griffiths; John Tracey; Bill Gregory; u/k; Norman Conquer.* Front row, left to right: *S/L Paul Rabone; Jackie Page, Arm Officer; u/k; Jock Brown; G/C Sammy Hoare; G/C Haycock, Station CO West Raynham; W/C Sticky Murphy; Jackie Curd; Bennett, Adj; Jock Reid. Eastwood, who had lost his family in a German raid on Liverpool, pursued the Germans with some ferocity. He and F/L Rogers failed to return from an Intruder on 24 July 1944. (Tom Cushing Collection)*

*S/L Henry Morley's and F/Sgt Reg Fidler's Mosquito PZ440 lies destroyed in a field at Dübendorf, Switzerland after the end of their day* Ranger *on 30 September 1944. Both men survived and were interned. (Tom Cushing Collection)*

decided that whoever was with me [would climb] up to achieve VHF range to England to get the launch called on its own frequency. But meanwhile the distance to the Dutch coast was reducing all the time, so in the best nautical tradition I fired a burst of war load 20 mm ammunition into the sea a few feet ahead of the launch, which promptly hove to. However, being a very keen type, after a few more of our futile gesticulating passes overhead, he decided this was just childish over-enthusiasm on our part, and headed for Holland again. Another burst, all recorded on my camera-gun, and he again hove to, and after some minutes the Mosquito up top came back on to Channel C and advised he had passed the message, and after some minutes the launch turned back for England and we headed for Snoring. Joe Cooper we gather, duly arrived and was promptly put into hospital to recover from the effects of 36 or so hours wet through in shocking weather

in his dinghy, and I never sighted him again.

On 6/7 September, F/L Arthur S. Callard

*F/Sgt Reg Fidler pictured in Switzerland. (Tom Cushing Collection)*

*Mosquito NS993 P3-T flown by F/L Arthur S. Callard and F/Sgt E. Dixon Townsley which was lost on the day* Ranger *on 30 September 1944 when it force-landed in Switzerland. Both men were interned. (Tom Cushing Collection)*

and F/Sgt E. Dixon Townsley flew an *Intruder* to Grove and Schleswig/Jagel, returning with claims of one Arado 196 floatplane destroyed and another damaged after sighting five moored in line just off shore at Aalborg. Shore batteries opened up with intense light flak but Callard and Townsley made it safely back to Snoring with a holed starboard outer fuel tank. Meanwhile, W/C Freddie Lambert DFC and F/O 'Whiskers' Lake AFC returned with a claim for a Bf 109 believed destroyed in the Grove–Copenhagen area.

Mickey Martin and F/O Smith had a very adventurous op to München and Wien a few weeks later, on 9/10 September. They made four circuits of Tulin airfield to make

sure the coast was clear, before strafing aircraft on the ground. One aircraft was left burning. A second strafing run was made and another 'vivid' fire was seen among the parked aircraft. In the Saltzburg area on the way home they attacked and destroyed a train which 'blew up in a terrific explosion followed by vivid blue sparks'. Martin and Smith flew on, pausing to rake installations at Cheim airfield with cannon fire before moving on to the south-east end of Lake Constance where a seaplane base was also strafed. At Mulhouse, Mickey Martin strafed the marshalling yards and had a pop at railway stations, buildings and lights. The former Dambuster reported that 'strikes were recorded in most cases'.

On 12/13 September, F/O Chris Harrison and F/Sgt Mike Adams flew an *Intruder* patrol to Hanau/Langendiebach and damaged an enemy night-fighter coming into land at the airfield. Searchlights and light flak became very active and patrol time was up so the pair decided to set course for home and comfort!

On 26/27 September, S/L Henry Morley and F/Sgt Reg Fidler took off on an *Intruder* to Zellhausen airfield, where they destroyed a twin-engined aircraft (possibly a He 111) on its approach. Three days later, they flew to the forward airfield at St Dizier with Arthur Callard and E. Dixon Townsley in *T-Tommy* for a day *Ranger* to the München–Linz–Wien area. The two Mosquitoes took off at 12 noon and headed for Holzkirchen airfield 20 miles south-south-east of München. Morley and Fidler attacked, firing a 4-second burst, damaging and probably destroying on the ground two Siebel SI 204 radio, radar and navigation trainers. Their drop tanks gone, Morley and Fidler parted company with Callard and Townsley. On the way back they strafed a number of Ju 86s parked on the perimeter of München/Neubiburg airfield. Between Konstanz and Zürich, when at 200 ft, Morley and Fidler's Mosquito was hit by 20 mm flak from a Swiss battery. Morley feathered the port propeller. Four Swiss Morane 406 fighters appeared and formated on the damaged Mosquito, which was losing height. The firing of Very cartridges and their general behaviour indicated that they wanted the Mosquito to land at Dübendorf. However, when over the airfield the Mosquito's starboard engine also quit and Morley crash-landed near Volketswil. Both men suffered only minor injuries.

The crew of *T-Tommy*, meanwhile, had continued their day Ranger with an attack on a seaplane base at Prien. Callard and Townsley attacked at 500 ft and destroyed two Do 24 floatplanes moored near the shore. Satisfied with their work, they carried on to the Salzburg area and investigated a small grass airfield at Friedburg about 20 miles north-east of Salzburg. They spotted a Bf 109G parked near a hangar and attacked it. The Messerschmitt exploded and pieces hit the low flying Mosquito. They were returning to base when, passing Prien again, wreckage of their earlier handiwork was seen floating in the water. Callard and Townsley immediately went in to attack the remaining Do 24, which was sunk by a burst of cannon from 200 ft. At about 14:35 hours, when south of München at zero feet, *T-Tommy's* starboard radiator began running hot. South-east of Lake Constance as the temperature rose and the needle went off the clock, Callard shut down the right engine and feathered the propeller. He found it difficult to gain height on the one good engine, which was worrying because of the hilly terrain.

Almost an hour later, when north of Zurich, four Swiss Bf 109 fighters slowly overtook and formated on *T-Tommy*. Two flew off the right wing and the other pair took the left wing. The Swiss made no attempt to attack and the Mosquito crew pretended to ignore their presence but the Swiss fighters closed in and indicated that they had to land. This was done safely on one engine at Dübendorf near Zürich at about 16:00 hours. Morley and Fidler were removed to hospital in Zürich and then interned along with Callard and Townsley. All four men later escaped from their captivity and got back to England.

# CHAPTER 6

# *LET TYRANTS TREMBLE*

*As I was walking up the stair*
*I met a man who wasn't there.*
*He wasn't there again today.*
*I wish, I wish he'd stay away.*

HUGH MEARNS (1875-1965)

Fighter-bomber operations made the headlines almost daily but support units, involved in radio countermeasures (RCM) and ELINT (electronic intelligence), received no mention because of the secret nature of the work. Yet, from the time of full-scale operations by 100 Group, Main Force losses were cut by 80 per cent, with one or two aircraft missing from a total Main Force strength of between 300 and 500 heavy bombers sent to a major German target becoming typical of the protection which was being given to the bomber stream. Who were these 'mystical' units, few in number but massive in their contribution? On 1 February 1944, 1473 Flight, who up to this time had been under the control of OC 80 Wing, Radlett, and whose activities in the main, consisted of signals investigation over friendly territory, were merged with 192 Squadron at Foulsham. It will be remembered that 192

had transferred to 100 Group from 3 Group on 7 December 1943. The brief was to carry out investigation of German signals from the Bay of Biscay to the Baltic, and along all bomber routes. The amalgamation brought 192's strength up to seven Wellington Mk Xs, 10 Halifaxes, seven Mosquito Mk IVs and one Anson. On 20 February, the Halifax Mk II was changed to Mk V, and later Mk IIIs were used. The Intelligence Officer at the station, S/L A. N. Banks, recalls: 'Mosquitos in 192 Squadron were used to monitor the frequencies being used by ground control of German night-fighters and also to record the verbal instructions used in night-fighter control.'

On 27 April at 03:25 hours at Foulsham, Mosquito IV DZ377 of 192 Squadron touched down in bad visibility. Behind the Mosquito was a 192 Halifax III, flown by F/Sgt H. R. Gibson whose R/T had failed, and on landing he collided with the

*On 1 May 1944, 199 Squadron, equipped with the Stirling III (like this one), joined 100 Group at North Creake from 3 Group. In April, 199 Squadron was stood down to await Mandrel jamming equipment to be installed in its Stirling IIIs.*

*Result of the collision at RAF Foulsham on 27 April 1944 when Halifax MZ564 of 192 Squadron landed on top of Mosquito DZ377 from the same squadron. (via Alan Hague)*

*The 199 Squadron operations board which was used at North Creake during the war and which is now on permanent display at the Norfolk & Suffolk Aviation Museum at Flixton, near Bungay, Suffolk. (Author)*

Mosquito. The RAF Form 1180 (Accident Record Card) recorded that the 'steady green' which was flashed to the Mosquito should not have been given and the pilot should not have been at 500 ft in the funnel or have accepted the steady green as permission to land. The Committee of Investigation concluded that the accident was due to 'juxtaposition of aircraft in the funnel. No navigation lights owing to air raid warning and Halifax's R/T being u/s. SFCO [Senior Flying Control Officer] posted and reduced – not considered competent.' Banks adds, 'They both came into land at the same time. They made a good landing and no one was injured. As a matter of fact, the crew of the Halifax were entirely unaware that their aircraft had landed on top of the Mosquito until they got out of the plane.' A second Mosquito in 192 Squadron, attacked by enemy aircraft over France and badly damaged, managed to crash-land at Friston on returning.

On 1 May 1944, 199 Squadron (motto: 'Let Tyrants Tremble') joined 100 Group at North Creake from 3 Group. Some months before, on 22 November 1943, 199 Squadron had taken part in the last Stirling raid on a major German target – Berlin. From this time an extensive programme of precision sea-mining was carried out and

attacks were also made on French rail and other military targets. Other useful work was carried out in ASR and, from February–April 1944, 199's Stirling IIIs delivered vital food and supplies to the occupied territories. In April, 199 was stood down to await *Mandrel* jamming equipment to be installed in its Stirling IIIs. They would supplement 214 Squadron's Fortresses over the Reich. In January 1944, 214 Squadron, then at Downham Market and equipped with Stirlings, had transferred from 3 Group to 100 Group at Sculthorpe. Although he was 28 years old, command weighed heavily on W/C Desmond J. McGlinn DFC, who had commanded the Squadron since January, and he looked much older. McGlinn and his men were assisted by a small American RCM detachment, under the command of Capt G. E. Paris, which arrived at Sculthorpe on 19 January to train the RAF crews in jamming using *Jostle* equipment (which began arriving in May). *Jostle* and *Window* patrols would form the bulk of 214 Squadron's work and for the 10 months preceding the end of the war, over 1,000 sorties were completed on 166 nights.

Meanwhile, on 10 February, six B-17Gs of the 96th Bomb Group of the 8th Air Force arrived from Snetterton Heath and,

*Fortress I AN520, formerly of Coastal Command at RAF Sculthorpe.* The White Ghost *was used by 214 Squadron for training. (Tom Cushing Collection)*

pending installation of *Jostle* equipment, were immediately fitted with *Airborne Cigar* (*ABC*), plus exhaust-flame dampers for night flying, and *Gee* navigation equipment. *ABC* was a device consisting of six scanning receivers and three transmitters designed to cover the VHF band of the standard German R/T sets, and to jam 30–33 MHz (*Ottokar*) and later 38–42 MHz (*Benito*, R/T and Beam).

No. 214 Squadron moved to Oulton on 16 May. This was a popular move, nearer

*A Fortress BIII of 214 (SD) Squadron at RAF Sculthorpe. (Rolly Harrison via Murray Peden)*

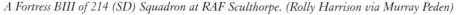

*B-17G 42-32088 pictured at RAF Sculthorpe in early 1944. On 10 February, six B-17Gs of the 96th Bomb Group, 8th Air Force arrived from Snetterton Heath and, pending installation of* Jostle *equipment, were immediately fitted with* Airborne Cigar (ABC), *plus exhaust flame dampers for night flying, and* Gee *navigation equipment. (Tom Cushing Collection)*

*Ex-USAF Fortress, now repainted in the markings of the RAF for use with 214 Squadron, with a 223 Squadron Liberator in the background. (Murray Peden via Tom Cushing)*

*Fortress BIIIs of No. 214 (SD) Squadron at Oulton in 1944. Nearest aircraft is L-London. (Ernie Frohloff)*

*A small American RCM detachment under the command of Capt G. E. Paris (seen here with Dick Gunton, 214 Squadron Engineering Officer) arrived at Sculthorpe on 19 January 1944 to train the RAF crews in jamming using* Jostle *equipment, which began arriving in May. (Tom Cushing Collection)*

to 'civilization' and in the heart of one of the most pleasant districts of East Anglia. Some of the officers were accommodated in Blickling Hall, a fine seventeenth-century mansion reputed to have associations with Anne Boleyn. The park and bathing in the lake were much enjoyed by members of the squadron. Word must have spread about the attractions because, early in May, the American 803rd Squadron, (now redesignated the 36th Bomb Squadron),

and equipped with six RCM Fortresses fitted with *Mandrel* and *Carpet*, moved to Oulton too! By the end of the month, a total of 22 crews were fully converted to Fortresses, although on 23/24 May 214 Squadron lost its first crew when P/O Hockley RAAF and his crew failed to return. On 1 June, Capt Paris, now relieved of his temporary command with the arrival of Capt C. A. Scott, took part in the first daylight operation from Oulton.

*Fortress BII BU-A SR384 of 214 Squadron was the first in the squadron to be lost, on the night of 23/24 May 1944, when P/O Hockley RAAF and crew failed to return. (Gerhard Heilig via Dr Theo Boiten)*

*Fortress BIII BU-G HB817 flown by F/O Ken Kemmett and crew of 214 Squadron at RAF Oulton. 'Lofty' Baumfield, the RNZAF bomb-aimer and second navigator, is holding the propeller. (Ted Baumfield via Dr Theo Boiten)*

During June, 100 Group began its work of deceiving the enemy, using the airborne *Mandrel* screen and *Window* feint forces. The *Serrate* Mosquitos and the low-level *Intruders* were also given a part to play in the deception. *Serrate* aircraft accompanied the diversionary forces in order to give the feint more realism and also to be in a position to intercept enemy fighters airborne in reaction to the feint. *Serrate* aircraft and low-level *Intruders* were also on occasions sent to patrol areas well away from the main attack in an attempt to deceive the enemy as to the area in which the attack could be expected.

On 5/6 June, a *Mandrel* screen was formed to cover the approach of the Normandy invasion fleet, and from subsequent information received, it appeared that considerable confusion was caused to the German early warning system. Sixteen Stirlings of 199 Squadron and four Fortresses of the American 803rd established a *Mandrel* screen in a line from Littlehampton to Portland Bill. Five Fortresses of 214 Squadron flown by W/C McGlinn, and S/L Bill Day and S/L Jefferies, the A and B Flight Commanders respectively, and F/L Murray Peden RCAF and F/O Cam Lye RNZAF, also operated in support of the D-Day operation in their *ABC* role. A protective patrol lasting over 5 hours was flown at 27,000 ft starting just north and east of Dieppe and running almost perpendicular to the coastline carrying out jamming and *Window* dropping in conjunction with 24 Lancasters of 101 Squadron of 1 Group. One Lancaster was shot down. Overall though, the patrol was outstandingly

*S/L Bill Jeffries, McGlinn's R/O on 5/6 June, Bill Doy and George Wright of 214 Squadron at Oulton 1944. Jeffries and Doy flew the ABC operation in support of D-Day on 5/6 June 1944. (Tom Cushing Collection)*

successful and earned a personal congratulation to all concerned by Arthur Harris, to whom he pointed out that 'the work carried out was of paramount importance in connection with the Invasion Forces'. A Me 410 had the misfortune to choose McGlinn's aircraft which had Eric Phillips, the Squadron Gunnery Leader, manning the tail turret, and he shot it down!

D-Day saw 192 Squadron in a new operational role. A constant patrol was maintained between Cap Gris Nez and the Cherbourg area to see if the enemy was using the centimetric band for radar, all the known enemy radars being effectively jammed. No positive results were obtained but centimetric investigations continued right up until the end of the war. At a later date, it was confirmed by the Y-Service that the enemy was indeed using centimetric radar and it was believed that it was in fact, captured 'friendly' equipment. No. 192 Squadron used sound recorders, both on film and on wire on investigations into the enemy's radar secrets. It had always played an important part in the interception of enemy VHF R/T and W/T traffic, both air-to-air, and air-to-ground. Its value was doubly increased from D-Day onwards due to the old question of optical range and such transmissions being outside the normal interception of a Y-Service ground listening station.

A sound recorder also played a very important part in establishing the use by the enemy of the *Bernardine Geräte*, this being a complicated system, ground-to-air, involving the transmission of *Hellschreiber* traffic, operative only for about 10 seconds a minute. Without a sound recorder this particular type of transmission could not have been broken down. Sound recordings were also of considerable assistance in assessing the efficiency of friendly RCM. Sound recordings made of RAF countermeasures, with the actual signal as it was being jammed in the background, meant that the efficiency of the jammers could be assessed accordingly. Cameras such as Leica, Contax, Kodak Cine and Bell and Howell, were also used. The duration of certain enemy transmissions being so short, it was not always possible for a detailed analysis of a signal to be made by the special operator, but in many instances the duration of the signal did permit a photographic record to be made, enabling further information to be obtained. Cine cameras played a very important part in establishing the polar diagrams of enemy radar transmitters. Some very good results were obtained on the *Jagdschloss* type of transmitter.

*W/C Desmond McGlinn, CO 214 Squadron* (left) *with S/L Bill Day A Flight Commander* (right) *at Oulton. Both men flew the* ABC *support operation on D-Day. (Tom Cushing Collection)*

During June, P/O Don Earl, a Londoner, and his crew, all fresh from 12 OTU at Chipping Warden where they had trained on Wellingtons, arrived at Foulsham for operations with 192 Squadron on the Wimpy. Earl, and the rest of the crew, all flight sergeants – Jimmy Jones, navigator, Frank 'Doc' Elliott, the signaller, bomb-aimer Walter 'Buck' Rogers, a Canadian, and Jack Short, tail gunner – had expected to be posted to a HCU and Lancasters. They had never heard of Foulsham or 100 Group. Before the war, Shorty Short had been a child prodigy of impresario Carroll Levis. He recalls:

On arrival crews were thoroughly briefed about the importance of total secrecy. We didn't expect to fly ops in a 'Welly', stooging around for 5 hr or more. Our allotted Wellington X was christened *B-Bambi* by kind permission from the Walt Disney office

in London who supplied suitable stencils. Our first op was flown on 23 June, to Brest–Cherbourg. Most aircraft were fitted with two banks of oscilloscopes with a special operator (ours was F/Sgt Robert Webster), using a 35 mm German Leica camera (which amused us no end), to record the incoming German signals data for subsequent interpretation. Externally the aircraft carried an array of different aerials which were the subject of much attention when landing away from base, particularly as it called for a guard to be mounted.

On one occasion, a 192 Squadron Halifax diverted to Manston after a raid accompanying 3 Group Stirlings. The captain of the aircraft was so pressed by the Stirling aircrew to disclose the function of his aircraft that he made up a code-name to fend off the interest. He whispered – 'in the strictest confidence' – that his was a 100

*On 16/17 June 1944, Stirling EX-N LJ531 of 199 Squadron failed to return to North Creake. P/O T. Dale, RNZAF, his six crew, and W/O F. Lofthouse, the special wireless operator, all perished. This painting of the aircraft adorned a wall at North Creake until it was skilfully removed intact by the Fenland Aircraft Preservation Society and is now on permanent display at RAF Hendon. (Author)*

Group 'Clothes Line' aircraft and that in consequence the 3 Group loss rate would be minimal, and truly, that night it had been! Through the post-raid intelligence debriefing, information emerged about 'Clothes Line'. This resulted in a request from 3 Group HQ to 100 Group HQ for the attendance of another aircraft similarly equipped for the next operation. Tracing action quickly identified the pilot as F/L Hayter-Preston, a pre-war Fleet Street journalist, who was using his acquired skill with words and for which he was appropriately admonished by W/C flying. He had previously used this off-the-cuff ability when landing at an OTU by stating that the squadron dropped bags of flour across the Continent to leave a dotted white line to the target for the Pathfinder force to follow!

Throughout June, *Mandrel* screens were flown on a number of nights, sometimes as cover for Main Force bombers, and on a few occasions as a diversion to alert the enemy defences unnecessarily. At this early stage, it was necessary to make experiments in order that the best uses of the *Mandrel* screen might be determined. It was found that to a considerable extent, in practice, more was achieved than the theoreticians had dared hope for. A consideration which also arose immediately was that, owing to lack of aircraft, only a small screen could be put up. It was, of course, necessary to fly RAF aircraft in pairs to give full coverage. The American aircraft flew singly, but did not cover so wide a frequency band. A very high standard of flying by the pilot, and of dead reckoning on the part of the navigator, was essential, for the Stirlings flew always at their maximum operational height, often in cloud conditions. Some *Gee* chains were

*214 Squadron personnel at Oulton.* Left to right: *Dick Dixon; Murray Peden RCAF; Dick Gunton; George Mackie; Tommy Crow; Tony Bayliss and Jackie Furner. On 21/22 June, F/L Murray Peden brought F-Fox back from Gelsenkirchen with one engine still on fire and crash-landed at Woodbridge where he made a spectacular arrival on two good and one partially serviceable engines before cutting a Lancaster in two. (Tom Cushing Collection)*

jammed by the *Mandrel* itself, and thus there was no means of wind finding once the racecourse pattern had started. As the aircraft were not fitted with AFIs, even a good direction finding (DR) position could not be established from the last found wind velocity once jamming commenced. (Many of these problems were overcome with the changeover to Halifaxes, but this was not completed until March 1945.)

June 1944 was not without loss. On 16/17 June, Bomber Command lost 31 bombers from 321 dispatched to the synthetic oil plant at Sterkrade Holten in Germany. Six B-17s of the 36th Bomb Squadron joined 16 Stirling IIIs of 199 Squadron in routine *Mandrel* sorties to cover the attack. Stirling EX-N LJ531 of 199 Squadron failed to return to North Creake. Pilot Officer T. Dale RNZAF, his six crew, and Warrant Officer F. Lofthouse, the special wireless operator, all perished. On 21/22 June, 214 Squadron was detailed to cover an attack on the Nordstern oil plant at Gelsenkirchen. Flight Lieutenant Murray Peden and his crew took off in *F-Fox*. Peden, a Canadian, saw in the darkening sky the spire of Norwich cathedral looming in the distance as he swung on to an easterly heading and made for the coast and the unfriendly stretches beyond.

I never saw it without thinking of that wonderful brave woman, Edith Cavell, sleeping in its shadow. We had read about her as kids when we were at school, and I always had the greatest admiration for her courage. I read more about her as I grew up, and used to remember, too, that she had spent many summer holidays at the coast at Cromer. And many times Cromer was our point of departure into England on operations.

At a point approximately 15 minutes from the target area, *F-Fox* was attacked by a Me 410. In the ensuing combat, the Fortress was seriously damaged, the starboard inner engine was set on fire, and the intercom system was put out of action. Both F/Sgt Alfred 'Stan' Stanley, the wireless operator, and the special operator were wounded in the attack, and F/O J. B. Waters, the air bomber, gave them some timely first aid. Waters also helped to restore the intercom. A few minutes later, the Fortress was attacked by a Ju 88 but coolness and good shooting on the part of F/Sgt Johnny Walker, the air gunner, drove off the night-fighter. Strikes were obtained on both enemy machines.

With one engine still on fire, Murray Peden set course for home and, displaying great ability, successfully reached the long emergency airfield at Woodbridge. He made a spectacular arrival on two good and one partially serviceable engines, and came straight in. He was unable to acknowledge instructions because of the damaged equipment which rendered the instructions almost unintelligible. The Fortress put down but burst a tyre, causing it to swing violently off the runway towards a Lancaster of 61 Squadron which had just landed without hydraulics after an encounter with night-fighters. Fortunately, the Lancaster crew and the maintenance personnel milling around were able to get clear before the Fortress cut the bomber in two. Murray Peden recollects:

Years later, when I tracked down Dennis Copson, the only survivor of Butch Passant's crew, he gave me a laugh. You have to understand that he had been wounded that night near Gelsenkirchen, and had to be more or less chopped out of the turret when Passant landed. He had just been assisted out of the turret by a groundcrew man named Cpl Francis, who had been wielding the emergency axe from the aircraft to help free him. They somehow managed to leave the scene at a handsome pace a few seconds before we arrived on the scene at a rate of knots and cut the Lancaster in half.

Four crashes occurred in all, in the space of 13 minutes. There were no injuries from any of them. Later, Peden was told that the Lanc had a 12,000 lb bomb on board! Murray Peden, Waters and Walker were commended for their actions and Stanley was awarded the DFM for continuing to carry out his duties after being wounded. Murray Peden concludes:

Stan still remembers, as his clearest recollection of the crash landing at Woodbridge, his skipper coming over for a look at him on the grass, in a rather breathless state, and offering the Mayo Clinic medical opinion: 'Oh . . . the poor bastard . . . he's had it.' He was still conscious when this encouraging prognosis was announced and now we have a good laugh about it every time we get together and I point out that I didn't actually put a time limit on the occurrence!

This story is one of many related in full in Murray Peden's autobiographical classic, *A Thousand Shall Fall*.

Another Fortress, flown by F/O Johnny Cassan, failed to return from the Gelsenkirchen operation. The bomb-aimer, W/O Doug Jennings, was the only survivor. He eventually returned to Oulton during August after first being signalled as "killed", reclassified as a PoW and again reclassified as 'now in the UK'.

July 1944 saw the operational birth of two new and important countermeasures, *Jostle* and the special *Window* Force. The former made its first appearance on 4/5 July and the latter on 14/15 July when all available spare aircraft from 100 Group's heavy squadrons were used. The *Mandrel* screen was used on 16 nights in August, on several occasions over south-east England, giving coverage to bomber attacks on V-1 sites in the Pas de Calais.

On 14 August, the 36th Bomb Squadron's 11 B-24H/J Liberators and two B-17s left Oulton for Cheddington, where

*A Jostle R/T jamming transmitter on a special transporter at Oulton ready for insertion into the ball turret opening beneath a B-24 Liberator of 223 Squadron. (IWM)*

they continued to operate in 100 Group, principally on daylight missions, until January 1945. (In August, 199 Squadron was increased to three flights to give added cover at night.) The greatest success achieved by a Spoof Force to date occurred following the Main Force attacks on Kiel and Stettin on 16/17 August. On 17/18 August, no major bomber attack took place, but a *Window* Force, strengthened in numbers by a *Bullseye*, and covered by a *Mandrel* screen, headed towards north Germany. The windowers kept on almost to the Schleswig coast, and created in the enemy mind a complete impression that the previous night's attack was to be repeated. No less than 12 Staffeln were sent up against the bomber stream. An even more important after-effect of this *Spoof*

took place on 18/19 August when a Main Force actually did go to Bremen, on a route similar to that of the Spoof Force. The German defenders, thoroughly confused, took this attack to be another Spoof, and left it entirely unopposed by fighters.

On 23 August, 223 Squadron took the Americans' place at Oulton, formed initially with a handful of B-24H/J Liberator aircraft from the 8th AF for operations using *Jostle* jamming equipment. The B-24 was capable of carrying up to as many as 30 jamming sets. This and its long range capability made it a much more ideal aircraft for the task than the Fortress, which equipped 214 Squadron. Unfortunately, 223 Squadron's B-24s, some of which had accumulated as many as 350 flying hours in 8th AF service,

*Ground and flight crews of Wellington X HE472 B-Bambi of 192 Squadron, RAF Foulsham. Aircrew back row, left to right: F/Sgt Jim Jones; P/O Jack Short, tail gunner; P/O Don Earl, pilot; Frank 'Doc' Elliott; F/Sgt Bob Webster, special wireless operator; F/Sgt Walter 'Buck' Rogers RCAF. B-Bambi survived the war and was reallocated to No. 11 Air Gunners School at RAF Andreas, Isle of Man. (G/C Jack Short)*

*P/O Jack Short, tail gunner of* B-Bambi. *(G/C Jack Short)*

had seen far better days. During August, W/C McGlinn left 214 Squadron after 14 months' tenure, to be replaced by W/C D. D. Rogers, and for a short period commanded 223 Squadron. Although 223 Squadron was originally formed as the second *Jostle* unit, its role was set to change when in mid-July 1944 the wreckage of a German rocket, thought to be a V-2, was flown to England for scrutiny at RAE Farnborough. The missile had landed in Sweden after a test firing from the German research station at Peenemünde. Immediately, urgent steps were taken to develop a countermeasure and *Jostle* equipment was subsequently modified to the Big Ben configuration. However, the wreckage in the hands of the RAE Farnborough belonged not to the V-2 but the *Wasserfall* anti-aircraft missile, although this was not realized until after the war.

With the advent of the V-1 and V-2, 192 Squadron was prepared in as much as Mosquito, Halifax and Wellington aircraft were suitably equipped and kept on stand-by for immediate take off in order to investigate the possibility of some

form of radio control being used with weapons. In the initial stages of the V-2, a 24-hour patrol was maintained by the squadron. Shorty Short, tail gunner of *B-Bambi*, recalls:

While on a North Sea patrol, Robert Webster, the special signals operator, had

*On 16 August 1944, Wellington X LP345 D-Dog, piloted by P/O Don Earl of 192 Squadron, crashed at Foulsham shortly after take off. The explosion was caught on film by the station photographer. All the crew had a narrow escape. (G/C Jack Short)*

*The burned-out skeletal remains of the geodetics of* D-Dog *the morning after the crash at Foulsham on 16 August 1944. (G/C Jack Short)*

*Starboard engine of* D-Dog *which caught fire just after take off on the night of 16 August and which forced Don Earl to crash-land with devastating results. (G/C Jack Short)*

picked up on one of his oscilloscopes some unusual returns emanating from the area of the Hague. Having photographed these signals and logged the relevant data an immediate return to base was initiated. Unfortunately, the weather made a recovery to Foulsham impossible and the aircraft diverted to Methwold. The usual guard was placed on the aircraft and the 'spec-sigs' crewman with his secret information was rushed off by staff car to 100 Group HQ for urgent analysis. Not long after this occurrence, a major 'gas explosion' which had demolished a row of houses in London, was reported on the front page[s] of national newspapers. This was generally accepted by the populace as there had been no air raid in progress. A few days later there was a similar explosion, again without warning. Hitler's random terror weapon directed against the civilian population. It was a good day's work by Bob Webster, special operator!

At midday on 16 August, *B-Bambi* was taken aloft for an air test but failed it after just 15 minutes. For the night's operation to the Frisian Islands, Don Earl was given *D-Dog*. 'No one was ever happy about a change of aircraft,' recalls Shorty Short, the tail gunner, 'it meant a change of luck.'

We took off at full throttle. At 100 ft the starboard engine backfired and began to run rough. Don did a full circuit at 200 ft and came in for an emergency landing. Downwind the signaller fired off a red flare and the pilot shouted his intentions over the R/T. He made the bomb-aimer flash 'SOS' on the nose light. So we were shouting, flashing and firing! I was dead worried. To me it seemed we were still at nominal flying speed. The controller's caravan went 'pumpff' as we passed it at 140 mph instead of drifting gently past. We only had a 2,000-yard runway. I knew either we were going to go off the end or shed rubber. We did the latter. I'd turned the turret right 90° and unlocked the doors as we clobbered the runway hard – the oleos penetrated the wings. The tyres burst and sparks from metal on concrete set the ruptured bomb-bay overload fuel tanks alight. Flames came back along the fuselage. I had my bum out of the turret and my fingers on the rim. If the wing dug in I'd be flung out like a tennis ball. The undercarriage crumpled and we went off the runway. Flames immediately roared up through the fuselage. I literally fell out backwards on to the grass. I tried to run but after two paces I found I was still plugged into the aircraft intercom! I went back and unplugged and sprinted. Everybody scrambled clear in 11 seconds (practice paid off!), although Jim Jones grabbed hold of the already hot astrodome rim to get out and burned his hands to the sinews. We all scattered. Ammo soon began exploding.

Left to right: *Bill Doy, (McGlinn's WOP); W/C Desmond McGlinn, CO 214 Squadron; Dick Gunton, 214 Squadron Engineering Officer; John Sharp, Gunnery Leader, pose in front of the lake on the Blickling estate. (Tom Cushing Collection)*

# CHAPTER 7

# DARE TO DISCOVER

*We are the heavy bombers, we try to do our bit,*
*We fly through concentrations of flak with sky all lit . . .*

'**W**hen asked to design a crest and motto for 100 Group,' recalls Jack Short, 'one wag produced a drawing of an aircrew officer peering through the keyhole of a bathroom [ostensibly at a young lady in a tub] with the motto, "We snoop to conquer"! As things turned out not too far removed from the *Chester Herald* approved version of

"Bricklayer's Arms"

"Dare to Discover" and a bright-eyed owl over a signals motif.'

In the investigation for signals in connection with the V-2, assistance was given by the 8th Air Force which had already detached a flight of four P-38J Lightnings to Foulsham, arriving on 24 August under the command of Capt Kasch. (In July 1944, an ELINT P-38 of the 7th Photographic Group (Reconnaissance) arrived at Foulsham to operate alongside 192 Squadron.) A total of four P-38s was eventually based at Foulsham for daytime *Ferret* sorties. (One P-38, crewed by Capt Fred B. Brink Jr and 2/Lt Francis Kunze, was lost on 26 October 1944, and in March 1945, when the 36th Bomb Squadron assumed all RCM tasks for the 8th AF, the three surviving Lightnings were relocated to Alconbury.) Although V-2 jamming proved impossible, during August, 192 Squadron had some success when it found and established the

*'We Snoop To Conquer', a humorous cartoon version of the 192 Squadron crest! (via G/C Jack Short)*

*192 Squadron's official crest. (G/C Jack Short)*

identity of an enemy radar transmission on 36.2 MHz. By means of a Fuge 16 homing loop, which was fitted to one of the Wellingtons, homing runs were made, and its site on the coast of north-west Holland established.

By the end of August, 214 Squadron, which shared the 24-hour watch on the V-2 rocket launchings with 192 and 223 Squadrons, had completed 305 successful operational sorties as a countermeasure squadron with the loss of only three crews. It had achieved a record of no flying accidents for six months. Oulton took on a flurry of activity. By early September, 223 Squadron was up to nearly full strength. Training was begun and two American Liberator pilots helped to check out the captains. Five Liberators were allotted for this and other training. On 19 September, F/L A. J. Carrington DFC carried out the first *Big Ben* patrol for 223 Squadron. The patrols were of 4 hours duration and at 20,000 ft (a new experience for many Coastal Command crews). On 23 September, W/C H. H. Burnell AFC arrived to take command of 223 Squadron from W/C

McGlinn. The new commander continued with the training programme and operated those crews judged fit for patrol duty. Later, the squadron was left solely on this task and all crews were placed on the work. It served as a useful start for squadron crews, for these 4-hour patrols entailed full briefing, de-briefing and

*Miss Ann, one of two P-38 Lightnings of the Intruder Detachment at Little Snoring, which became operational on the night of 24/25 March 1944 when Maj Gates flew a P-51 Mustang to Berlin. The unit worked closely with 515 Squadron Mosquitoes but was disbanded in April after sorties had revealed that American single-seat fighters were unsuitable for intruder operations. (Tom Cushing Collection)*

careful maintenance of flight plan.

Very few of the groundcrew at Oulton had any experience of American aircraft, no perfect tool kits, and because of the urgency of provisioning, the Liberator aircraft were far from new. Yet they never lost heart and although the east of England turned out some of its most bitter winter weather they kept on trying and did exceptional things. Ernie Frohloff, a Canadian radar mechanic in 214 Squadron at Oulton, recalls:

Life for the groundcrews was a daily routine of getting a maximum number of aircraft serviceable for the next op. Leisure time was spent at the 'large, modern NAAFI in Norwich'; 'lunches of fresh crab on the cliffside at Sheringham and Cromer,' where we played golf but were warned never to try and retrieve a ball from the beach, as they were mined! After the day's work we went to our favourite pubs; the Bird in Hand opposite the main gate at Oulton; the White Hart at Marsham and the Buckinghamshire Arms adjacent to Blickling Hall, for a few quiet pints, a few games of darts, or shove-halfpenny, or just to talk. At Christmas 1944 we augmented our food parcels from home with a large goose, purchased from a local farmer and cooked by the landlady of our favourite pub in North Creake. No one instructed us in how to pluck a goose, with the result that the Radar Hut, and surrounding countryside, was white with goose feathers for weeks after!

Fellow Canadian Murray Peden recalls:

Blickling was our home in effect. Our Officers Mess was only about 100–150 yards clear of the box hedges of Blickling Hall, and our Nissen hut billets only another 200 yards further on. When we went into Aylsham, or into Norwich, or went away on leave, the

*The Buckinghamshire Arms adjacent to Blickling Hall. Another favourite was the White Hart at Marsham where RAF men spent the evening playing darts and shove-halfpenny. The Bird pub at Oulton was not frequented too often because it was close to the station guardhouse, 'which always was considered a place to stay as far away from as possible'. (Ernie Frohloff)*

*Digging a radar van out of the snow at Oulton in the winter of 1944–45. (Ernie Frohloff)*

place to which we were always returning to lay our heads on the pillow was the billets hard by Blickling Hall. When we wanted to have a bath, we walked over to Blickling Hall and up to the top floor of the old mansion where we got a cold (make that, frigid) bath. Oulton, on the other hand, was the place we returned to when we'd been airborne for a while. To go to work every morning, we left our 'homes' at Blickling and rode by bus up to the Flights at Oulton. Sometimes during the morning or afternoon, if things were slack, we'd walk off the station, out past the guard-room and just across to the opposite side of the road to the Post Office there, where we would buy a cup of tea and a muffin or scone.

Such had been the urgency to get 223 Squadron operational that crews, drawn from Coastal Command Liberator OTUs, became operational after only 15 hours' flying training. Sergeant Don Prutton, a flight engineer, was among the first to join the Special Duties squadron at Oulton.

In the early hours of 3 September 1944 myself and a party of sergeant flight engineers fresh from technical school at St Athan, arrived slightly puzzled at Norwich railway station. We gathered that 100 Group, to which the newly formed 223 Squadron belonged, was a 'Special' Group; we would be on 'Special Duties' and would be joined by 'special operators'.

They were not the only ones on a Norwich railway station in August 1944 who were slightly puzzled. The 32-year-old S/L John Crotch and his crew, who had flown 20 operations in Halifax BIII, MZ706, *V-Victor*, in 76 Squadron at Holme-on-Spalding Moor, had had enough of 'life' at the bleak Yorkshire air station. It had not taken too much urging on the part of their skipper to consider a posting to 100 Group, which he assured them, 'would be good because it was near Norwich.' (John Crotch has been a practising solicitor in the city since 1935.) They were duly given a posting to 192

*F/O Steve Nesser, special wireless operator, and Murray Peden RCAF (behind) enjoying themselves on a motorcycle at Oulton. Nesser, born in Yugoslavia of German parents, Canadian by naturalization, flew 17 trips in 100 Group in American aircraft, bombing his ancestral origins! While recovering from an ear, nose and throat operation his first crew were shot down in the circuit at Oulton on 3/4 March 1945. On 15/16 April Nesser was injured when the Fortress he was in crash landed in Belgium after being shot up over Schwandorf. (Murray Peden via Tom Cushing)*

*Halifax* V-Victory *which was flown by S/L John Crotch DFC and his crew in 192 Squadron at RAF Foulsham. (John Crotch)*

Squadron at Foulsham, which was equipped with the Halifax. When their train steamed into Norwich, Crotch went home for the night and told his crew to stay at the Bell Hotel with instructions to meet him at the station at 10:00 the next morning. They did. So far so good, but the Midland & Great Northern route (otherwise known as the 'Muddle and Go Nowhere' line) involved many stops and they did not get to Guestwick station near Foulsham, until 3.00 in the afternoon! John

*S/L John Crotch DFC and his crew. Back row left to right: Tony Leonard, rear gunner; D. H. Moore, WOP-AG; J. Lysaught, mid-upper gunner; A. H. Martin, flight engineer. Front row, left to right: W/O V. Worsley, bomb-aimer; John Crotch DFC, pilot; C. W. Ashworth, navigator. (John Crotch)*

Crotch never lived it down. 'My crew said, "Hey Skip, we thought we were going to a base near Norwich!' John Crotch recalls:

There were lots of boffins at Foulsham. Our job was to fly Halifax IIIs over enemy territory in the bomber stream and monitor German fighter frequencies with a bank of a dozen radar sets in the back of the aircraft. An operator would establish the frequencies and then photograph the radar displays, which were lit by Anglepoise lamps. The photographs would be developed and next night the frequencies would be jammed with engine noise. It would take the Germans a week to change their frequencies. My boys felt it a waste of time not to carry bombs so I got six American 500-pounders, had them put in the wings, and we dropped them on occasion. On nights when there were no

Main Force operations we flew what were called 'Foulsham Follies'. Two Halifaxes would be sent on shallow penetration over the continent, dropping *Window* (long strips of metal foil) all the way to simulate raids by 50+ aircraft. Each Halifax then dropped flares over its target to raise 150 fighters. It was reckoned that at least 10 would crash on take off or landing so it was more effective than *Intruder* operations.

On 28/29 August we flew a 8 hr 4 min round trip to Stettin in Poland. We flew over Sweden, received a few warning shots of ack-ack, and carried out ELINT support for the main force. The next day I led five Halifaxes to Lossiemouth to take part in an ELINT operation against the *Tirpitz*, at anchor in Altenfiord in Norway. This meant a 1,500-mile, 9 hr 45 min round trip; all of it over water. Two Halifaxes were sent back to

*Halifax BIII Matthews & Co. Express Delivery Service of 192 Squadron flown by F/L Matthews RAAF, 4th from left, at Foulsham. W/C David Donaldson, CO, is to his left and S/L John Crotch, is 3rd from right. (John Crotch)*

Foulsham with faulty radar and the three of us set out at 19:00 hrs that evening. One returned early with engine trouble. We flew in at 200 ft to avoid enemy radar. Near the Arctic Circle it is difficult to judge your height above sea level because there are no white caps and the water gives an 'oily' appearance because it is half frozen. We monitored the *Tirpitz* radar frequencies and found blank spots for the Lancasters to come in on. [On 15 September, Lancasters of Nos 9 and 617 Squadrons, operating from Yagodnik airfield, Russia, attacked the *Tirpitz*, scoring one hit. The warship was finally sunk in Tromsöfiord by 12,000 lb Tallboy bombs dropped by 617 Dambusters Squadron Lancasters, on 12 November 1944.]

On 13 September S/L John Crotch and his crew flew one of 24 aircraft which stooged around Holland, escorted by Spitfires, waiting for the V-2s which were normally fired at around 17:00 hours, to get the supposed frequency. Starting on 9 September, 214 Squadron Fortresses, equipped with a special modification to the *Jostle* apparatus, had also started *Big Ben* patrols. Extensive modifications were made in the Liberators belonging to 223 Squadron and the crew was reduced by one

as the front gunner was unnecessary. A large floor space in the rear bomb cell was provided for *Window* storage and the whole of the navigator's position was enlarged and improved. Additional jammers were installed and the squadron was ready to begin *Window* patrols.

Sgt Don Prutton did his first operational flight in a Liberator on 2 October 1944 in *B-Baker*.

We patrolled in daylight off the Dutch coast at about 20,000 ft, hoping to spot a V-2 on its way up from its launching pad. We carried two special operators who were doing mysterious things with radar-jamming devices but security was so good that even the rest of the crew did not have the slightest idea of what they were up to.

All this was in vain – the V-2 could not be jammed. In November 1944, *Big Ben* was deleted and replaced with *Carpet* and *Dina* jamming devices.

Meanwhile, with operations against the enemy reaching a climax, it was decided by the Air Ministry to supplement the already powerful Bomber Support force by forming 171 Squadron on 7 September 1944 at North Creake within 100 Group. Initially, the Squadron, commanded by W/C M. W.

*F/L Geoff Liles' Fortress M-Mike in 214 Squadron, showing to good advantage Piperack (Dina II) American-developed radar-jamming device which replaced the Monica tail warning installation when it was found that German night-fighters were able to home in on Monica transmissions from up to 45 miles away. Behind can be seen another BIII with plastic H2S nose radome (fitted to all 214 Squadron aircraft during June–August 1944 to aid navigation). (Geoff Liles via Murray Peden)*

Renaun DFC, was formed with Stirling Mk III aircraft and crews, pending the allocation of 20 Halifax IIIs. In order to get the new unit operational, one flight of 199 Squadron was posted in. No. 171 Squadron's first operation took place on 15 September, when two Stirlings took off on a special mission which was completed successfully. Shortly after, 14 Halifax crews were posted in from squadrons under the operational control of 4 Group HQ but they were unable to operate as 171's Halifaxes were held at St Athan undergoing installation of *Mandrel* and *Window* chute equipment. (Stirlings would continue to be used until 21 November.) Finally, on 21 October, 171 Squadron Halifaxes took off on a windowing operation. While *en route*, the operation was cancelled and the aircraft recalled. However, one aircraft failed to receive the signal and pressed on to the target where it was plotted as 'a force of some 30 heavy bombers', a successful, if unintentional start for the squadron!

Meanwhile, on 5 October, Mosquito Mk IVs of 192 Squadron flew over enemy territory in an attempt to pick up FuG 200 transmissions and, the following night, checked on the density and characteristics of German AI on 90 MHz while another Mosquito crew carried out *Jostle* jamming of enemy VHF signals. On 19 October, a Mosquito of 192 Squadron flew to Stuttgart to try and discover low frequency Würzburg signals and on 30 October another Mosquito was dispatched to Berlin to determine if FuG 216 or FuG 217 could be intercepted. On 2/3 November, five Mosquitoes of 192 Squadron listened in on German radio communications. On 4 December, a Mosquito flew to Karlsruhe to determine whether coastal observation units were being used on inland flak control.

During October 1944, meanwhile, daily 'Intention of 100 Group Operations' were sent to all groups in the Main Force in order to keep everyone in closer touch with each other's activities and also show just how much protection and assistance they were getting. On 7/8 October, in riposte to the enemy R/T communications used in its *Zahme Sau* operations, Lancasters of 101 Squadron, fitted with *Airborne Cigar* carried out jamming of the enemy R/T frequencies. These special Lancasters also carried a specially trained German-speaking operator. This night the order 'All butterflies go home' was broadcast on the German night-fighter frequency, resulting in many enemy night-fighter pilots returning to their airfields! The most outstanding *Window* success of the month

*Halifax Mk III MZ971 6Y-E I'm Easy! (E-Easy) of 171 Squadron pictured at North Creake flown by W/O Jamieson RAAF. (Bill Tiltman via Dr Theo Boiten)*

was perhaps on 14/15 October when 1,013 heavies went to Duisburg and 200 to Brunswick. It was anticipated that the Duisburg raid, by low approach, radar silence and shallow penetration, would get through with little trouble, but that the Brunswick force might be strongly opposed. A *Window* Force was therefore routed to break off from the Brunswick route and strike at Mannheim. This had success beyond all expectations, for the Brunswick attack was almost ignored because the Mannhein area was anticipated as the main target. Only 14 bombers were lost this night. Pilot Officer Morris and his crew from 223 Squadron, which completed its first *Window* patrol this night, was hit by flak and the navigator was badly wounded.

October also saw the introduction of *Dina*, the jammer used against SN-2. *Dina* was installed in the *Jostle*-fitted Fortresses of 214 Squadron. This was frequently used in the *Window* force, as were *Jostle*, *H2S* and *Carpet*, thereby more effectively giving the simulation of a bombing force. A further realistic effect, also born in October, was created through the co-operation of PFF, which, on several occasions *Oboe*-marked and bombed the *Spoof* target. (The *Window* Force itself had not yet arrived at the bomb-carrying stage.) The noise of *Oboe*, which had until that time always preceded real attacks only, was thought to give still more confusion to the enemy controller, who, as the 100 Group diarist put it 'was already thinking furiously about many other forms of deceit'. It was also found in October that *Window* Forces could only be increased by deductions from the *Mandrel* screen and jamming forces. It was a point to be considered very seriously, for there was every indication that the enemy was trying to see through the screen, thus making it very likely that more aircraft might shortly be needed to increase the screen effort. So, after the daylight patrols by 223 Squadron came to an end on 25 October, crews began their 'real work' which involved night operations with the rest of Bomber Command. Don Prutton recalls:

These operations were of two distinct types. In the first, two or three of our aircraft would accompany the main bomber stream and then circle above the target; the special operators used their transmitters, in particular, *Jostle* to jam the German radar defences while the Lancasters and Halifaxes unloaded their bombs. Then everyone headed for home. Our friends in 214 Squadron seemed to do more of these target operations than 223 Squadron. My own crew did a small number of these but the majority of our operations were of the second type, the *Window Spoofs*. The object of these *Window* raids was to confuse the enemy as to the intended target. There was a radar screen created by other aircraft patrolling in a line roughly north to south over the North Sea and France. A group of us, perhaps eight aircraft, would emerge through this screen scattering *Window* to give the impression to the German radar operators that a large bomber force was heading for say, Hamburg. Then, when the Germans were concentrating their night-fighters in that area, the real bomber force would appear through the screen and bomb a totally different target, perhaps Düsseldorf. After several nights, when the Germans had become used to regarding the first group of aircraft as a dummy raid, the drill was reversed; the genuine bombers would appear first and with luck be ignored by the German defences, who would instead concentrate on the second bunch, which was of course our *Window Spoof*. So we rang the changes, sometimes going in first, sometimes last, in an attempt to cause maximum confusion to the enemy, dissipation of his resources and reduction in our own bomber losses.

The *Window* was carried in the rear half of the bomb-bay which was floored and separated from the rest of the aircraft so it was impossible to have a low light on. The rear bomb doors were fixed shut, unlike the front ones which were still operational and were the means of getting into and out of the aircraft. The *Window* was wrapped in brown paper bundles about a foot long and perhaps 2 or 3 inches across. Each bundle had a string loop and the idea was that as you pushed the bundle down the specially installed chute near the floor of the compartment you held on to the string loop. This ripped the brown paper wrapper and as the bundle was drawn out by the slipstream the contents were scattered on the night air.

It was normally a two-man job, usually the flight engineer and one of the beam gunners, and was quite hard work bearing in mind we were in bulky flying suits, helmets and oxygen masks. At the pre-flight briefing the rate of discharge was stipulated; it was to start at, say, 40 bundles a minute and then as we approached our 'target' it must increase to perhaps 60 a minute! In practice we knelt or sat on the floor surrounded by the mountain of bundles and when the navigator gave the word the plane started weaving gently and we started pushing the stuff out fast. When the time came to increase the rate we just went even faster but whether it was correct or not we never knew.

We normally used Type 'A'. We also carried a few bundles of Type 'C' and always made sure we knew where these were because Type 'C' was for our own protection. If the anti-aircraft fire started getting too close for comfort we would sling out some Type 'C' and miraculously the flak would drop behind us. I believe our *Window* operations were reasonably successful; certainly our bomber losses were greatly reduced in the last months of the war. I think we also helped the Germans use up their aviation fuel. [During the latter months of 1944, a machine to eliminate entirely manual launching of *Window* was designed by F/L Merryfull A.F.R.Ae.S. of 199 Squadron at North Creake. During February 1945, it was decided to form a Window Research Section under Merryfull's command at Swanton Morley. Sadly, Merryfull was killed on 8 July 1945.]

*F/L C. J. Merryfull* (back row, centre) *and other ranks pictured at North Creake. Merryfull established the BSDU at Foulsham and later at Swanton Morley. (RAF Swanton Morley)*

On 9 November, F/O Briscoe and his crew completed a *Window* and VHF *Jostle* patrol in the face of the worst weather, including snow, and a personal message of commendation on RAF Station Oulton's effort was sent from the AOC, AVM Addy Addison. November 1944 produced a new and rather different use of the *Window* Force. With the frequent repetition of Heavy attacks on the Ruhr, the enemy adopted a policy of keeping his fighters there, regardless of attempts to draw them away by *Spoofs*. The *Window* Force was therefore used on several occasions to infest the whole Ruhr area with vast quantities of *Window* immediately prior to the arrival of the Main Force from behind the covering influence of the *Mandrel* screen. It was assumed that the enemy fully expected attacks on the Ruhr area, and could not be persuaded otherwise. Therefore, the *Window* Force's achievement, which seemed highly successful, was to confuse the enemy so he could not distinguish the bomber track in the maze of *Window* echoes. Still further was he confused when once or twice this tactic was employed and there was no bomber force. Always, however, the *Mandrel* screen was present if the weather allowed, to keep the Nachtjagdgeschwader crews in their cockpits, and the controllers at their desks, just in case the bombers were en route. Don Prutton cites an example of this:

On 10/11 February 1945 there were 12 of us against the Luftwaffe. We had a briefing in the afternoon but weather was clamping down all over Britain and the bombing plans were later 'scrubbed'. However, two crews each from 214 and 223 Squadrons were put on standby. At 9 p.m. we had another briefing and learned that as East Anglia seemed likely to remain clear it had been decided that 100 Group should deny the German forces a night off. So just after midnight a dozen assorted aircraft from the group took off on a *Window* raid to Krefeld in the Ruhr. It was

bright moonlight above the clouds; the occasional searchlight filtered through and at one stage a fighter tailed us for a few minutes but other than this we saw no enemy activity and all returned safely. In all we felt the trip was probably a waste of time, but when we landed at about 5 a.m. we were greeted by our commanding officer, W/C Burnell, with the news that 'half the German air force' had been up looking for us. We later had a message from the AOC confirming that the operation had been 'an unqualified success and in every manner achieved its object.

(On 2 May 1945, a *Window Spoof* over Kiel by four Fortresses and five Liberators was the last operation of 223 Squadron as a heavy Bomber Support squadron operating with the Main Force of Bomber Command in Europe.) Flying Officer Jackson's crew in 214 Squadron went one – one being the operative word – better! Jackson took off from Oulton to join a *Window* Force from Manston which failed to materialize owing to a last minute recall. They continued to 'press on' to the Ruhr, blissfully unaware of their isolation. They returned safely and were greeted with the news that the German defences had plotted them as a force of 50 aircraft!

Meanwhile, on 14 January 1945, 223 Squadron lost its first aircraft when B-24 'R' piloted by F/L Noseworthy RCAF was hit by an enemy fighter and crashed near Antwerp. Noseworthy and one gunner had miraculous escapes but the rest of the crew were killed. On 20 February, F/O J. Thompson RCAF was shot down by a night-fighter. The third Liberator to be lost was 'T' flown by F/O N. S. Ayres. The only survivor was one of the special operators who escaped after the aircraft was hit and plunged into a pine forest. When this special operator recovered consciousness, which as he said 'was a shock that nearly killed him', he found the *Jostle* weighing over 600 lb lying on him. He later recovered from multiple injuries in an English hospital.

Don Prutton recalls:

Our own losses were comparatively light. Of the six flight engineers I arrived with, four survived, but in the squadron as a whole the survival rate was probably slighter higher than this. It used to be said sometimes that we were in more danger from the unserviceability of the aircraft than from enemy action. By the late stages of the war we had become somewhat blasé. Due to the shortage of fuel, German fighter activity was severely restricted; we no longer did a detour via Gravesend, but flew straight back to base across the North Sea and our gunners unloaded their guns as soon as we crossed the Dutch coast.

During March 1945, 223 Squadron learned that it would be converting to the Flying Fortress. The changeover went on apace and on 15 April the first successful operation in a Fortress was completed by Don Prutton's pilot, F/L Gordon Bremness.

Like 223 Squadron, 214 Squadron had its bad times as well as good at Oulton. On 16 November, one of its B-17s crashed near Foulsham while landing and all the crew were killed. Murray Peden recalls, on another occasion, coming down to breakfast one morning and hearing that Johnny Wynne had flown his Fortress home the night before, *alone*.

It was the talk of the mess. It turned out that, like us, Johnny had a fire in an engine. It got so bad that he'd ordered the crew to bail out, and intended doing the same himself. His chute accidentally opened inside the aircraft, and left him with no choice but to try to bring his Fortress home. He had a hell of a time but Johnny made it

*Crew of* W-William *in 223 Squadron at Oulton. Left to right: F/Sgt Benn Buff, beam gunner; F/O Joe Doolin, WOP; Sgt Murdo McIver, beam gunner; F/L Gordon Bremness, pilot; F/O Hal Booth, navigator; Sgt Sam Leach, tail gunner; Sgt Roy Storr, mid-upper gunner; Sgt Don Prutton, flight engineer. Note the sealed Emerson nose turret painted over black and the* Window *chute protruding from the bomb bay below the flame damper under the nacelle. (Don Prutton)*

to Bassingbourn. The tragic side of the story was what happened to his crew. Five of them were murdered by the Germans. At a war crimes trial after the war, three or four of the perpetrators had an appointment with the hangman.

Unfortunately, murders of RAF aircrew, were not uncommon. On 21/22 November, five days after Johnny Wynne's crew had been murdered, two men in a Halifax III of 192 Squadron, flown by W/O B. H. Harrison, suffered the same fate after the aircraft was shot down by fighter attack during an operating to the marshalling yards at Aschaffenberg, Germany. The navigator, Sgt Stan Wharton, recalls:

We flew at 14,000 ft and we lost *Gee* as we crossed the Dutch coast due to German radar jamming. But I had calculated an accurate wind speed and direction at that height which took us within pinpoint precision to the target. I was 25 seconds early.

As we did not carry bombs, we were told at the briefing to 'skirt' the target. I

instructed the pilot to turn to port, did a 180° turn south-east of the target and came on to my 'Return to Base Course'. On both sides of the track were German air flares, lighting up the return course like a main road. I instructed the pilot to increase to maximum speed, nose down, and after a few minutes in this attitude I heard the rear gunner shout: 'Fighter attacking. Corkscrew starboard skipper!' Tracer bullets passed between my feet and the two starboard engines were on fire. As there was no response from the pilot I gave the order to bale out, jetisonning the escape hatch in the foreward part of the aircraft. I pressed the 'destroy' buttons for all the secret equipment and went though the hatch. In my haste, I had forgotten to unfasten my oxygen supply and found myself dangling under the crashing aircraft. I felt a boot on the top of my head which I think belonged to Sgt Bloomfield, the bomb aimer, which snapped the oxygen connection, and I lost consciousness.

Stan Wharton and Jack G. Smith RAAF, the wireless operator, were made PoW. Harrison was killed in the crash. Sergeant R. B. Hales, the flight engineer, and Bloomfield, after first being apprehended by villagers, were handed over to the police. Later, the two fliers were taken under guard by a guard by a party of Volkssturm (Home Guard) who, *en route* to Erbach, murdered them in cold blood. Two of the perpetrators died in a car crash three weeks later, one committed suicide and four more were later given sentences of 15, 12, 7 and 5 years.

Between 8 February and 22 March 1945, seven other 214 Squadron crews failed to return to Oulton. The captains of these crews were P/O Robertson, F/O Shortle,

*F/L Johnny Wynne of 214 Squadron in the cockpit of E-Easy at Oulton. Wynne once brought E-Easy back minus his crew who were ordered to bail out after an engine fire (Wynne's parachute accidentally opened inside the aircraft). Five crew were beaten to death by German civilians. (Les Bostock)*

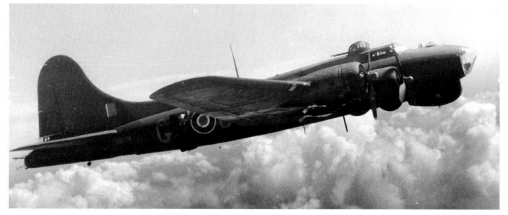

*Boeing Fortress BIII of 214 Squadron. Note the prominent* Jostle *transmission mast behind the radio room, H2S scanner nose radome and rear-mounted* Airborne Grocer *and* Dina *aerials. (via Martin Staunton)*

F/O Stewart, F/L Rix (all of these crews were reported to be PoW), F/O Anderson (all except two of his crew were reported safe), F/O Kingdon and F/L Allies. Air gunners destroyed two Ju 88s, one in July 1944 and another in February 1945, plus two probables. Nine enemy aircraft damaged were claimed.

Towards the end of February, when the heavies in 100 Group had started carrying bombs as well as *Window*, it was obvious to the squadrons from events on the continent that a still greater air effort was going to be demanded. This was made quite clear by the Air Staff branch at Bylaugh Hall, when information was received that the only stand-downs would be through adverse weather conditions that rendered operational flying impossible.

As well as the heavies in 100 Group, for the last few months of the war, controllers in Fliegerkorps XII and their plotters at their *Seeburg* tables also had to contend with an increasing numbers of *Intruder* aircraft in the circuit over the night-fighter bases. Over the Reich airwaves triumphant German battle-cries of a few months previously had now given way to 'Achtung Moskito': the 'bed of heavenly bliss' had become a bed of nails.

*Boeing Fortress BIII BU-W of 214 Squadron. In March 1945 223 Squadron also converted to the Fortress. (via Martin Staunton)*

# CHAPTER 8

# *'DUTCH'*

*Press on regardless – never mind the weather*
*Press on regardless – it's a piece of cake*
*Press on regardless – we'll all press on together*
*Cos you're bound to see the Dummer or the Steinhuder Lake*

(TO THE TUNE OF 'POOR JOEY')

---

Leslie 'Dutch' Holland had flown 5 hours short of a thousand when he first joined 515 Squadron on offensive operations. This late baptism of fire came nearly two years after having done about six months on home defence night-fighters. In the period between, a year spent instructing pilots destined for night-fighters and on a refresher course at an Operational Training Unit, had nurtured a gradual build-up of confidence, capability and a certain amount of fatalism.

At Cranfield one evening in August 1944, the OTU Beaufighters were lined up on the spare runway with engines running in readiness for the night's training exercises, when a V-1 came blathering along over our aircraft. All of us fully armed and unable to do a thing about it. Unfortunately, a Czech pilot with an Australian navigator broke the rules and went down to London looking for them only to run into balloon cables instead.

On arriving at an operational station one is naturally eager and perhaps a little anxious about the task soon to be undertaken and above all keen to make a decent showing. But the welcome from the CO, W/C 'Cordite' Lambert made two things clear. In his own words, 'Your name's on the squadron status board are in chalk and it is easy to erase. This will be done for one of two reasons. First, if you have an accident and put an aircraft out of service, in which case you will be immediately posted: second, if you allow yourself to succumb to enemy action. Either event is referred to as "wastage". See to it that neither of these occurs.'

Air operations have always been a matter of teamwork. The aircraft; the groundcrew; the flight crew. In each of these aspects I was extremely fortunate. Groundcrew – fitter and rigger – worked all hours to keep aircraft on the top line. Always cheerful, never

*No. 31 Course, No. 51 OTU Cranfield, summer 1944.* Back row, left to right: *Flt/O. R. D. S. Gregor; F/Sgt. Habgood, A. G; F/Sgt. Reynolds, S. G; Sgt. Fawcett, G. R; Sgt. Thurgood, C. M; P/O K. W. Munro; Sgt. MacNicol, D. K. I; P/O F. J. Brooker.* 2nd row, left to right: *Sgt. Kinnear, R. A; Sgt. Cooper, J. G; Sgt. Broomfiield, E. J. A; Sgt. Young, R; Sgt. Griffiths, H. S; Sgt. Fidler, R. A; Sgt. Frost, W. D. G.* 3rd row, left to right: *Sgt. Letten, P. J; Sgt. Walker, R. S; F/O W. R. Barber; P/O A. M. Grant; P/O L. C. Lucas; F/O V. W. J. Evans; P/O J. A. Webster; W/O Fisher, J. D; Sgt. Harwood, G.* 4th row, left to right: *P/O J. R. Walters; W/O Holland, L. G.; F/O J. E. Mannering; F/O J. E. Harper; F/O J. J. Bambury; F/O S. W. L. Richins; F/O R. E. Smith; F/O A. Talevi; F/O J. C. Barton; P/O R. A. Henley; P/O M. R. Colhoun.* Front row, left to right: *F/Lt. H. A. Lightbody; F/O M. W. Huggins; F/O D. C. Paterson; F/O W. V. Wilkin; F/Lt. J. V. Thatcher; F/Lt. A. J. Smitz; S/Ldr. H. F. Morley; F/O W. L. Ruffley; F/O B. E. Plumer; F/Lt. I. A. MacTavish; F/Lt. G. M. Barrowman. (Tom Cushing Collection)*

complaining, although like so many of their unsung brethren, constantly working in the open, often in atrocious weather, at hours of the day or night intended for comfortable repose, and waiting faithfully and patiently for our return.

The aircraft – Mosquito FB Mk VI. In 1944, 515's aircraft carried no air interception radar (still referred by us as AI) but did have *Gee* as a navigational aid, helpful for course-checking on approach to the enemy coast but little use beyond that. For armament they carried the full complement of four .303 in Brownings and four 20 mm Hispano cannon. A 63-gallon

fuselage fuel tank could be removed and two 250 lb bombs or incendiaries or flares carried instead. Wing 'stores' carriers would take a 250 lb bomb each or a 50-gallon drop tank. On one op, the last of the war in Europe, a primitive form of napalm tank was carried. These bare facts tell nothing of the character of the Mossie and the Mk VI in particular in which a crew could have complete confidence under all circumstances and equally, in the Merlin engine and the DH propellers.

And the long suffering bloke in the right hand seat, the navigator on whom one depends for more than finding the way in

*A Pat Rooney caricature of 'Dutch' Holland, pilot in 515 Squadron at Little Snoring. (Tom Cushing Collection)*

*Mosquito FBVI PZ187 YP-E of 23 Squadron flown by George Stewart RCAF. It was kept in store after the war and sold to France in September 1947. (Tom Cushing Collection)*

*Mosquito FB Mk VI NT193 in flight. (Hawker Siddeley)*

the dark. I was particularly lucky to have teamed up with a very down-to-earth Geordie – one Robert Young, ex of the 43rd and 52nd of Foot, the Oxfordshire and Buckinghamshire Light Infantry, transferred to the RAF for which I remain always humbly grateful. It does help to have someone as phlegmatic as Bob in the other seat when things are getting hot. 'What colour's blood?' was his only comment if he thought we might be exceeding our duty.

[The] 28th October 1944 being Bob's birthday was a very appropriate occasion for our 'Freshman Operation'. This consisted of a very easy trip as far as the Zuider Zee without any hanging about. We were only airborne 2 hours and it was uneventful except for some useful exercise in dodging searchlights. Blacked-out Holland looked very much the same as blacked-out Norfolk. Somewhat to our surprise, next morning 'Charlie', our F/Sgt in charge of groundcrew, informed us that there was a bullet hole in

one wing. Somehow this seemed like a lucky omen.

After this trip the squadron received a Mosquito Mk XIX fitted with Mk X AI (SCR 720) and which Bob and I flew twice only before taking it back to Swannington where it probably lived with 85 Squadron. We never had another Mk XIX at Little Snoring.

Up to late 1944, day *Rangers* had been flown occasionally but usually by more than one aircraft. W/C Lambert was particularly keen on these and S/L Walter Gibb, the Bristol Aircraft Company test pilot who was on 515 until shortly after I joined them, described to me a somewhat hairy run down to Brest or Bordeaux, a region in which one was bound to run into a great deal of trouble. I believe it was in the course of this effort that, legend has it, Lambert shot the wheels off a Storch because it didn't seem right to blast such a small aircraft out of the sky.

*F/L T. L'Amie with his original navigator, P/O S. H. 'Frank' Lindsay in front of PZ344 E in which L'Amie and F/O J. W. Smith destroyed a Fw 190 and a Ju 34 in the air and a Bf 109 in the process of taking off and three 109s on the ground on 29 October 1944. (Tom Cushing Collection)*

*The two 515 Squadron intruder crews refuel at the forward base at St Dizier on 29 October before they wreaked havoc on the Continent. F/L J. W. Smith, F/L T. L'Amie's navigator (left foreground) and F/Sgt Dockeray (right foreground), P/O Terry Groves' navigator. Groves is on the wing of his Mosquito, PZ217, with an American refueller. He destroyed a Bf 110 in the air and six Bf 109s on the ground. Note the German bomb and fin. (Tom Cushing Collection)*

A day *Ranger* was flown by 515 on 29 October 1944 by two aircraft when they were still without radar: F/L F. T. L'Amie with F/O J. W. Smith and P/O Terry A. Groves DFC with F/Sgt R. B. Dockeray DFM. Between them, they left a trail of destruction across Bavaria and on to Prague. Both crews took off at 14:20 hours from St Dizier and crossed liberated territory south of Nancy at 8,000 ft. Allied ack-ack fired at them as they sped overhead but no lasting damage was sustained. At zero feet at Hechingen, 30 miles south-south-west of Stuttgart, a Fw 190 was spotted to port on a reciprocal course. L'Amie and Smith did a climbing turn and came behind the Fw 190. They attacked below and astern, with L'Amie giving the enemy machine a 1-second burst of cannon fire from about 100 yards. The Fw 190 immediately burst into flames and disintegrated. At Ingolstadt just over 20 minutes later, a Bf 110 was seen at about 500 ft. This time it was the turn of Terry Groves and 'Doc' Dockeray. They got astern and fired three bursts of cannon fire from 100 yards. Pieces fell off and the Messerschmitt crashed to the ground and continued burning.

The two Mosquitoes continued on their patrol. At Straubing at 16:32 hours a Ju 34 crossed from starboard to port at a height of about 1,000 ft. The pilot spotted the Mosquitoes and took evasive action but L'Amie and Smith got into position and made a starboard quarter attack from 50 yards range. L'Amie gave the Junkers a 1-second burst of cannon and it exploded in flames. Then the starboard wing blew off and the rest of the transport aircraft disintegrated. L'Amie and Smith flew through the burning oil and petrol which

severely scorched the fuselage and rudder surfaces of the Mosquito. Flying debris from the Ju 34 punched a small hole in the tail plane but the Mosquito remained airworthy and L'Amie and Smith were ready for more. Just over a quarter of an hour later, they attacked a Bf 109 taking off from a grass airfield in the Beroun area. The Bf 109 stopped and swerved to port and although a number of strikes were seen all around the enemy aircraft they could not confirm its destruction.

About a dozen Bf 109s were seen parked on the grass airfield and both Mosquito crews went in to attack. Altogether, four strafing runs were made on the enemy field and they left nine burning fiercely with three damaged. A hangar was set alight by the fires and burst into flames. L'Amie and Smith claimed three Bf 109s destroyed and two damaged. Terry Groves and Dockeray also claimed three Bf 109s destroyed and two damaged. There was no opposition, save for a lone machine-gunner who put a

*Obergefreiter Helmut Siemon mans an early warning radar receiver. Siemon was bombed repeatedly by Mosquitoes in France and was finally captured on Jersey and made a PoW in England where he settled after the war. (Helmet Siemon via Tom Cushing)*

hole in Groves' starboard engine cowling. Terry Groves and 'Doc' Dockeray landed at Juvincourt at 19:05 hours and L'Amie and Smith put down at Amiens/Glisy 30 minutes later, both crews well satisfied with their work. (L'Amie and F/O Smith were killed on 21 November 1944.)

Dutch Holland and Bob Young's first 'op in earnest' was to Kitzingen, which says Holland,

lies about 25 miles south of Schweinfurt, and between Würzburg and Nürnberg. That makes it nearly 500 miles from base. *Intruder* sorties were flown at low altitude, generally around 2,000 ft above ground, and a straight course was not usually held for more than about half a minute at a time as no area could be regarded as entirely 'safe'. A more-or-less continuous weave about the required

course was adopted so as not to let the opposition have it all their own way. I never was especially good at flying straight courses.

All navigation after crossing the coast was by contact flying, or if the ground was obscured, by dead reckoning. Contact flying means simply map reading and endeavouring to anticipate prominent ground features. It is an art which improves with experience but I had been fortunate in having been on a two-week course in 1942 at No. 2 School of Air Navigation at Cranage which specialized in low-level pilot navigation. It taught how to look ahead for the next line features; how to assess, reasonably correctly, the size of area features like woods and lakes and built-up areas and how to work out course corrections in one's head. That was in daylight. At low level at night it's a different story but that

*F/Sgt Dockeray DFM and P/O Terry Groves DFC of 515 Squadron who destroyed a Bf 110 and destroyed and damaged several Bf 109s on the ground on their day* Ranger *with L'Amie and Smith on 29 October 1944. (Tom Cushing Collection)*

course provided an invaluable grounding.

On the run to Kitzingen, a half moon gave us good sightings of rivers, canals, lakes and railway lines. As a result, we arrived on target within 2 minutes of scheduled time. An hour's patrol was normal, calculated to cover either the approach of the main force to their target or return. Sometimes a follow-up patrol was laid on, but it was not usual. The object was to cause as much disruption as possible to German night-fighter operations. As this was a fairly deep penetration requiring the fuselage fuel tank, no bombs were carried but the 20 mm guns could be used whenever there were signs of activity on the airfield. Intelligence sources led us to believe that Me 163 rocket-propelled fighters were based at this airfield but we saw no sign of them. A mild strafe of the airfield produced only a half-hearted reaction from ground defences and there was no evidence of any air activity.

It was also a part of the briefing for all *Intruders* to attack transport of all kinds. However, this was not entirely a one-sided activity. Many trains carried light flak batteries which made it foolhardy to make the simpler lengthways attack. It is very much easier to aim the length of a train and much more difficult to get elevation and range in a crossing attack, even in daylight. In addition, night trains were more likely to be carrying some very explosive loads. All fuel for V-2 rockets was taken to launch sites by rail. Activity of this type occurred on most sorties and only occasionally got a mention in our logbooks if really positive results were observed.

While on patrol at an airfield, light flak was usually encountered, and at some airfields various devices were kept in readiness for the protection of aircraft landing or taking off. These included flak screens on the final approach path which probably accounted for several *Intruders* who went missing. We were repeatedly reminded at briefing to be wary of following an aircraft into the runway threshold and to refrain from continuing an attack below 200 ft. But at such times the eyes are not on the altimeter but at the gunsight, and it is easy to misjudge height, especially on a dark night with ground details not too clear. Discretion gets elbowed aside.

A 5-hour flight without much activity on the patrol and 2 hours each way out and back tends to get a bit tedious strapped to the seat the whole time but the need to stay alert and keep a look out does not cease until the wheels are firmly on the ground. Some months later the aircraft were fitted with *Monica*, a rearward looking radar which was intended to indicate the presence of an aircraft behind, but it gave so many false alarms that it became a normal practice to try a couple of turns to see if the pursuer followed exactly. If it did, it was pretty safe to assume that it was a spurious 'ghost'. There will always be the one occasion when the cry 'wolf' is not to be ignored. There were also rumours of balloons on lengths of wire and I am bound to say that some of the 'ghosts' behaved very much as if they were just that.

There followed several sorties of a similar nature to patrol night-fighter airfields; Marx and Varel, near Wilhelmshaven; Vechta and Quakenbrück, north of Osnabrück and near the Dummer Lake; Hanau; Lippestadt; Erfurt and one to Schwabisch Hall. This last was a departure from the norm in that we had a partner, our great buddies 'Bunny' Adams and Frank Widdicombe. As this was after the aircraft had been equipped with a radar of very limited capability, we spent most of the patrol time intercepting and identifying each other – a dreadful waste of time. I do not remember that this rather frustrating pairing was repeated.

The Dummer Lake was one of a pair in north-west Germany which were easily identified landmarks. In impromptu sessions round the piano in the mess 'Press on regardless – never mind the weather' a little ditty commemorating the fact was a regular favourite. Among other things which we saw in our comings and goings there were of course several sightings of flying bombs. Although the jet flame could be seen from a long way off in clear conditions, it was extremely difficult to assess the actual distance. On more than one occasion we witnessed the launch of a V-1 in the middle of the North Sea but a bit of simple trig' will show that apart from failing to make our own target on time, it would be an impossibility to make an interception of an object travelling on its own vector at around 400 mph.

I did go down to Lowestoft one evening and while I was waiting for my date who was on duty at the Fire Brigade HQ, went up to the clifftop at Sparrow's Nest to see if there was any 'trade'. There was a layer of cloud at about 2,000 ft but otherwise clear and dark. Sure enough a small gaggle of them could be heard throbbing their way westwards and two flickering orange flames increased in brightness. [The] 40 mm guns opened up but only when they were less than half a mile out. Suddenly, a great orange ball bathed the sea in glare and 2 seconds after, an almighty BLAM and blast wave was shortly followed by a repeat performance. But there was still the same fluttering drone above the clouds. An unseen battery of 'heavies' suddenly blasted off and a further explosion lit the clouds from above. When my ears had recovered they could detect one solitary 'bug' droning its way inland.

One sortie brought us back on a course to pass north-westwards, well clear to the east of Antwerp. This was at the time when it was the principle supply port for the Allied armies. We picked up a V-1 and set off after it but it was too low for us to range it in the ground returns on the ASH. However, it ought to be possible to tell if one was within about 400 yards, or so one would think. A

*A 515 Squadron Mosquito crew waves off another squadron Mosquito as it taxis out from Little Snoring for a night operation. (Tom Cushing Collection)*

handy patch of moonlight suddenly revealed that we were going along a heavily wooded valley at treetop height. This was not the spot to generate a cataclysmic explosion even if one could be sure of doing so and it was deemed prudent to delay the attack until circumstances were more propitious. Further progress in our stalk was made inadvisable by the rise of a wall of tracer ahead. We had crossed it clear into the Antwerp *Diver* defences and our only option was a very steep turn out of it. All *Diver* defences were ordered to shoot at everything – but everything – flying below a certain height unless specifically ordered (for which on a later occasion I had reason to be thankful).

At Little Snoring at this time, morale wasn't good – it was excellent. And one of the chief reasons was that the Station Commander was none other than the redoubtable 'Sammy' B. R. O'Brien Hoare,

with multiple DSOs and DFCs. A legend in his own time, he had done heaven knows how many *Intruder* sorties both day and night from as early as 1941 during which he had destroyed some 10 aircraft in the air, probably destroyed and damaged 8 more, and left a trail of wrecked German aircraft on airfields in Germany and occupied territories. Most, if not all of this was achieved with only one eye and without radar. After we had a small anti-surface-vessel radar (AN/APS4) fitted to our aircraft, my own being out of service for an inspection, he did me the great honour of letting me have his personal aircraft with the comment, 'You will find that my aircraft does not have radar; I don't need it!' Needless to say, I was also requested not to bend it.

By late 1944, many of the veterans of earlier years were less directly in contact

*Prelude to a night* Intruder *at Little Snoring. In front of PZ338, left to right: W/C Freddie Lambert, S/L Ginger Farrell, F/O 'Whiskers' Lake (Lambert's navigator) and P/O Terry Groves. (Tom Cushing Collection)*

*A 515 Squadron Mosquito returns over Little Snoring after an* Intruder *operation. (Leslie Holland)*

with operations. Sammy Hoare was still flying occasional sorties and showed no signs of losing any enthusiasm. Briefings were sometimes a bit daunting when particularly 'dicey' jobs were 'on' but Sammy's attitude of courtly chivalry never waned. Stroking his immensely long moustache (you could see both ends at once from behind), he would conclude with; 'Let us sally forth and do battle with the Hun', or, on one memorable occasion, a quote which should be engraved in stone: 'Gentlemen, there will be flak; almost certainly quite heavy flak. If you cannot go over, you will go under. If you cannot go under, you will go through!'

Sadly, this reference to a very gallant character has to end with the recollection that after surviving the war he went missing on a flight in a Mosquito.

S/L 'Ginger' Farrell, whom I had previously known for a brief spell on 85 Squadron, was our Flight Commander. On a unit like 515 naturally one could not be nursed along by the flight commander during the actual op as one was on day fighters but he could and did in his own very pleasant fashion give us all the tips we needed and the feeling that he was 'with us'. Life at the squadron dispersal was somewhat informal. A good-natured camaraderie served in place of subservience to rank without prejudice to respect for commanders or obedience to orders. After our somewhat late arrival in the mornings, the first thing to interest us was the schedule of crews for the night's ops. If you were 'You're ON' the day would then be occupied with going over the aircraft with the groundcrew, perusing intelligence reports and aerial photographs of enemy airfields, and conscientious air testing of the aircraft which was done before every sortie.

Air tests, always referred to as night-flying tests or NFT, consisted of a full check of systems and engine performance as far as could be done in about 30 minutes and without going much above 2,000 ft, our normal operating height. Being near the sea gave us the chance to test the guns and a ship stranded on Brancaster sands provided an excellent target for practice. Naturally it was too large an object for precise aiming, so we concentrated on trying to be the one to fell the funnel. It was like a cheese-grater before it finally went. Other units used the same target and there was no control as on target ranges so that a very sharp look-out was required and this added to the value of this exercise. Other aircraft firing at the ship were not too hard to spot but on one occasion a Swordfish appeared to be trying to convey a message by frantically waggling its wings. The intent of this gesture became clear when a fountain of smoke and sand erupted alongside the hull. Clearly, RAF and RN were not on the same frequency.

It will be appreciated that night-fighter crews put in a lot of effort to keep up to scratch in aircraft recognition. Many hours were spent in a very specialized approach to this art. In a totally dark room, a special projector threw a silhouette on to a screen. It showed accurately the shapes of all types of aircraft which we were likely to encounter, friend or foe, from all angles, but mostly different aspects from astern, including the exhaust glow. The silhouettes were only just visible against a dark background but with progressive reduction of the exposure, it proved to be possible to get correct identification in as little as a fifth of a second.

Before November was out we took part in a couple of *Spoof* raids on Bonn and Wiesbaden. The object was to come out through the front of a screen of *Window*, representing a major raid and to drop a couple of 250 lb bombs to give the

*Two armourers bomb up a Mosquito Intruder at Little Snoring. The ammo belts around their necks are at the request of the cameraman. (Tom Cushing Collection)*

impression that an actual raid was developing. The defences took it very seriously and made good but not perfect practice on the one blip showing clearly on their radar. Heavy (large bore) flak was not something we frequently encountered but on these occasions saw plenty and actually encountered it too. The Mosquito VI of course, had no bombsight, and bomb aiming entailed no more than letting go once the target had disappeared under the nose regardless of altitude or attitude, but we did attempt to aim at pinpoints such as junctions in a railway siding or airfield buildings. Both Bob and I had experienced too much on the receiving end of haphazard bombing from the Luftwaffe to be particularly worried where our bombs went but also believed that they could be more usefully employed on targets of some tactical or strategic significance rather than on the populace at large. Probably because we did our usual best not to present too easy a target, our aircraft suffered no damage despite almost continuous illumination by radar-controlled searchlights. These would suddenly and very accurately swat the aircraft with a blinding blue light, whereupon several lesser minions would latch on and follow any frantic effort to evade until out of range. Fortunately, I had heeded the injunction never to look at the lights but keep eyes glued to the instruments.

At this stage in the proceedings, the aircraft of 515 Squadron began to be equipped with the AN/APS4 radar (ASH). This was a small torpedo-shaped installation more often seen on Fleet Air Arm Fireflies. Originally intended for searching for surface vessels and reading coastlines, it had the tiniest plan position indicator (PPI) of all airborne radars, measuring about 3 in by 1½ in, and was proportionally efficient for air interception. During the re-equipping some practice in its use was carried out on Ansons with the 'bomb' slung under the nose. After a week or two of this, and almost before we had digested our Christmas dinner, a very

different sort of task awaited us for which the newly fitted ASH was of very little consequence.

At the end of December, German troops were being moved from Norway, presumably to reinforce the Ardennes front. Consequently, it was required that mines be laid in the intervening waters, especially in Oslo Fiord. This task was to be performed by Lancasters and 515 was to do its best to divert the attention of local anti-aircraft defences. The briefing was extremely exact. First, the timing had to be spot on otherwise the defences would either be alerted too early – this meant not more than 1 minute before the arrival of the mine-layers – and secondly, attention must be directed to those batteries whose exact position, calibre and number was described in considerable detail. The underground intelligence service must have been very active.

So we set out on the 2½-hour flog across the North Sea, taking a final fix and wind check with *Gee* about 100 miles out. After that it was necessary to start losing height, flying the last 100 miles at about 50 ft in fair visibility but only a little starlight. Using the new wind and corrected course from the *Gee* fix, it was dead reckoning the rest of the way, aiming to avoid the radar on the Danish coast. How much it was luck would be hard to say but, all credit to Bob, we arrived within our time slot and, helped by the enticing lights of a Swedish coastal town (should be able to make that on one engine), were able to identify Moss, about 20 miles south of Oslo opposite Jelo [Jeløy] Island. Our ASH would have been no use for coast reading at that height and would only have betrayed our presence. The channel between the mainland and this island was one of those to be mined.

A few dimly discerned features were enough to tell us roughly where the supposed batteries were situated and we had only just taken up a position about half a mile inland when a stream of tracer curved

23 and 515 Squadron score
boards that hang in the church
at Little Snoring, close to the
former WW2 intruder station.
(Author)

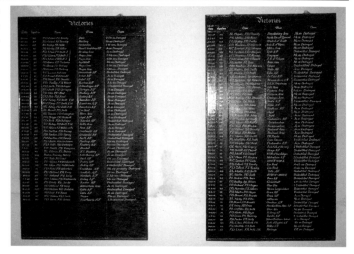

seaward nicely pinpointing for us the exact location. From about 500 ft, a shallow dive brought the sights nicely to bear on its source and a burst of 20 mm must have caused some consternation. A tight turn brought us round for another attack across their line of fire. Part of the battery had picked us up and returned fire. By this time flak and air-to-ground fire was lacing the fiord in all directions, particularly on the opposite side of the fiord, and the operation was evidently in full swing.

The brief had been to draw fire away from the mine-layers so the next attack was made from the landward side. The annoyance of the gunners became apparent when all their guns opened up in our direction. It was like driving into snow with headlights on. There appeared to be several 20 mm and possibly 40 mm, judging from the different colours and rounds per burst. By this time the party seemed to be over so we were happy to break off and not continue the confrontation. As it was we used all our 400 rounds. The fireworks over the water transpired later to have been largely due to the late arrival of a cruiser which fact caused F/L Lawrence, who was dealing with that particular patch, to remark when he was informed in debriefing afterwards that there did seem to be a bit

more reaction than he had been led to expect.

Then it was straight down on to the water and set a course for home. Fortunately, no searchlights followed us but reaction from fighters remained a distinct possibility at the start of the long sea crossing. Setting the radio altimeter to 20 ft made the indicator lights flash continually red, amber, green, amber, red, due to the wave height, and it proved easier to judge height visually by what could be seen of the wave tops.

After about half an hour we came up a bit to ease the strain. The constant drone of the engines and the visible swish, swish, swish of the sea below become hypnotic after a while and the mind drifts off into hallucinations which turn the instruments into jazz pianists with big white teeth and suchlike. Worse, one starts to nod. Bob stirs uneasily in his harness when bank begins to exceed 30° and I do my best to pretend I was doing a little turn as a normal precaution. Neither of us refers to the lost 50 ft. It is with a warm feeling of relief that we touch down and taxi in with our minds firmly fixed on the prospect of one fried egg, one rather small rasher of streaky bacon and a few greasy chips, then to flop out on a three-biscuit mattress with damp sheets and blankets which smell like they have been on a horse all day.

# CHAPTER 9

# *FLUCTUATING FORTUNES*

*Tighter and tighter turned the fighter*
*Till he blacked out P/O Paine,*
*Then he gave max boost and revs*
*And turned just half as tight again*

During the month of November 1944 there was not one single *Serrate* contact during the month's operations on any one of the three *Serrate* Mosquito Squadrons, 141, 169 and 239. The situation had been getting worse since the summer of 1944. Although 141 Squadron had successfully destroyed three enemy aircraft in air-to-air combat on *Serrate* operations in October, these were all through AI contacts and not *Serrate*. It was a poor month for all three *Serrate* squadrons, with only five enemy aircraft being destroyed, three by 141 and two by 239 Squadron. The former had only one *Serrate* contact all month, and 169 and 239 had only four between them.

For the reasons, one must go back to May 1944. In the early months of 1944 the Luftwaffe had begun to bring into service the new SN-2 AI radar which was not affected by *Window* and the *Serrate* homer fitted to the Mosquitoes was calibrated to the frequencies of the old *Lichtenstein* AI sets. For some time, *Serrate* crews had noticed on operations that the enemy

night-fighters quickly took evasive action when picked up on AI radar. By May, the majority of German night-fighters had been fitted with SN-2 sets. SN-2 rendered the *Serrate* sets practically useless and the Luftwaffe had also introduced backward-looking warning devices. During June–July 1944, the number of *Serrate* contacts obtained during operations had noticeably started to tail off. All *Serrate* Mosquito crews could do was rely on their old Mk IV AI radar for interceptions. These were few and far between. The few *Serrate* contacts that were made were almost all found to radiate from ground stations. In July, only one in 10 sorties on average reported a *Serrate* contact – in May it had been one per sortie, and in the early part of the year each sortie was reporting a large number of contacts.

When the frequency band of the SN-2 was discovered in June, work was at once started to develop a homer, later called *Serrate* Mk IV. An aural presentation was decided upon with dots and dashes, similar to the *Lorenz* beam system. Considerable trouble was experienced due to the interference caused by *Freyas* on the same frequency band, but eventually a satisfactory filter was devised. (*Serrate* Mk IV would not be used operationally until January 1945.) The development of another homing device, *Perfectos*, was started in June 1944. It was known that the *Egon* system was one of the main methods the enemy used for controlling his fighters. In this system, the *Freyas* interrogated an IFF (Fuge 25A) in the fighter, and so were able to direction find and range on them. There was no reason why the Bomber Support fighters should not do the same as the ground stations, and *Perfectos* was to interrogate the enemy IFF and then direction finding and ranging on the return signal. *Perfectos* would clearly have one advantage over the *Serrate* type of homing since ranging would be given. However, it

was not found possible to provide the *Perfectos* equipment with the elevation planning. (The first *Perfectos* operations would not be carried out until November.) One further homing device, *Benito*, was under development for a considerable time but was never used operationally. It was intended that that this equipment should allow homing on to the 38–42 megahertz transmissions from the enemy fighters when they were being controlled from the ground under the *Benito* system. However, it was never found possible to devise an aerial system which could be carried satisfactorily on a Mosquito and eventually, the project was dropped.

Meanwhile, another German prize fell into the RAF's lap when Obergefreiter John Maeckle landed his Ju 88G-1 night-fighter 4R+UR of III./NJG 2 at RAF Woodbridge on 13 July. The crew had taken off from their base at Twenthe at 23:05 and had

*Captured Ju 88 at Great Massingham, part of 1426 Enemy Aircraft Flight at Duxford, which was used to evaluate enemy aircraft and display the Circus at operational stations. Obgfr John Maeckle landed his Ju 88G-1 night-fighter 4R+UR of III./NJG 2 at RAF Woodbridge on 13 July and was allowed to sit unmolested for 20 minutes while they burned classified material and demolished radar equipment. The Ju 88 carried FuG 220 Lichtenstein SN-2, FuG 227/1 and FuG 350 Z Naxos radars, the last two types being previously unknown to the RAF. Note the Hirschgeweih (antler) aerials of the FuG 220 radar. (Tom Cushing Collection)*

become lost in thick cloud which had a ceiling of about 14,000 ft. For 45 minutes, the Bordfunker tried to establish radio contact but without success. After 4 hours in the air and very low on fuel, Maeckle told his crew they might have to bail out. However, the flight engineer informed him that he had not packed his parachute. Maeckle decided to get the Ju 88 down. He wrote:

Fuel gauges showing empty and descending at 6 ft per second, we broke through the clouds at 600 ft and miraculously discovered we were coming down right on top of an airfield. I did not waste any time landing the aircraft. When I saw the big white flashing light on the control tower and all the four-engined airplanes, I had no doubts where we were. After we touched down, the plane rolled to a complete stop in the middle of the runway with both engines dead. While bright

spotlights aimed at our plane, we sat there for 20 minutes or longer before we were finally approached by an armoured vehicle and thus had plenty of time to burn classified material and demolish valuable instruments. We were happy to be alive and well, especially the flight engineer.

Scientists from TRE investigated the Ju 88's FuG 220 *Lichtenstein* SN-2, FuG 227/1 and FuG 350 Z *Naxos* radars, the last two types being previously unknown to the RAF. They confirmed *Serrate*'s ineffectiveness and discovered that the Luftwaffe was using the FuG 227/1 equipment to home on to *Monica* tail-mounted warning device, and the FuG 350 Z *Naxos* to home on to *H2S* radar bombsight transmissions. RAF bombers were ordered immediately to restrict the use of *H2S* while *Monica* sets were removed from the Lancasters and Halifaxes. *Window* was modified to jam the new *Lichtenstein* radar.

*Messerschmitt Bf 110G-4 fitted with* Lichtenstein *FuG 220B SN-2 and FuG 212 C-1. SN2 was not affected by* Window *and the* Serrate *homer fitted to the Mosquitoes. C-1 was often used in conjunction with SN-2 because of the latter's poor resolution at close range. (via Hans-Peter Dabrowski)*

In June, almost all the contacts obtained over enemy territory had been by the Mosquitoes' AI radar with its limited range. This was due to the success of beacon patrols. It became clear in June that the enemy was making more and more use of his assembly beacons in France. The area of these beacons proved to be the most profitable type of patrolling for the *Serrate* Squadrons. Many of the Mosquitoes' successes at the beacons were obtained before the enemy fighters had attempted to intercept the bombers.

On 28/29 June, P/O Harry 'Shorty' Reed and F/O Stuart Watts of 169 Squadron picked up an AI contact 2 minutes after their arrival at Beacon Mücke. Reed turned hard to starboard in an attempt to get behind the enemy aircraft. After losing the contact twice through fading and interference, it was eventually picked up again at a range of 15,000 ft dead ahead and just below, after two hard orbits and some weaving. Harry Reed closed to about 5,000 ft after some difficulty due to unreliable elevation signals. The Mosquito's height was now 12,000 ft. A visual was obtained at 3,000 ft and the enemy aircraft continued weaving. Harry Reed called 'bogey bogey wiggle wings' but there was no reply. It had to be an enemy aircraft. Then it fired off four star red cartridges. Range was reduced to about 150 ft when the enemy aircraft was recognised as a Bf 110 with external wing tanks. Harry Reed fired two 2-second bursts and the Bf 110 exploded. The Mosquito's AI and *Serrate* failed immediately after the guns were fired. The Bf 110 was seen to go down in flames until it entered cloud at 4,000 ft. A bright flash followed on the ground. With their radar now u/s, Harry Reed and Stuart Watts turned for home.

June seemed to offer much for the *Serrate* squadrons. For instance, 239 Squadron reported 89.7 per cent of sorties completed (compared to only 62.5 per cent in January) and registered 11 victories. But 141 and 169 had shared only eight evenly between them. July would be the same for the *Serrate* Mosquitoes. Both 141 and 169 notched six victories, while 239 Squadron racked up seven, without any operational losses. On 4/5 July, S/L N. A. Reeves DSO, DFC with P/O A. A. O'Leary destroyed a Bf 110 north-west of Paris, and F/L J. D. Peterkin and F/O R. Murphy of 141 Squadron bagged a Me 410 near Orleans. Flight Lieutenant J. S. Fifield and Flying Officer F. Staziker of 169 Squadron added a Bf 110 at Villeneuve. Near Paris on 5/6 July, S/L N. E. Reeves and W/O A. A. O'Leary of 239 Squadron destroyed a Bf 110, and F/O P. G. Bailey and F/O J. O. Murphy of 169 Squadron destroyed a Ju 88. Four of 239 Squadron's seven victories in July came on the night of 7/8 July. A Fw 190 was destroyed by W/C P. M. J. Evans and F/L Tommy Carpenter in the Pas de Calais and F/L V. Bridges DFC and F/Sgt D. G. Webb DFM shot down a Bf 110 near Chaleroi. Their Mosquito went into a violent spin which tore the rear hatch off and damaged the wing tip and elevator. Bridges feathered the starboard propeller and the door was jettisoned. They landed at

| | May | June | July | Aug | Sept |
|---|---|---|---|---|---|
| Average No. of *Serrate* contacts per sortie completed | 1.1 | 0.2 | 0.1 | 0.02 | 0.005 |
| Average No. of AI contacts (without initial *Serrate*) per sortie completed | 0.3 | 0.5 | 0.8 | 0.5 | 0.3 |
| AI contacts per successful combat | 9 | 9 | 10 | 16 | 60 |

Comparison of *Serrate* with AI contacts May–September 1944

Woodbridge safely. Two Bf 110s were destroyed at Paris S/L Jackson Booth DFC* and F/O K. Dear DFC.

Booth celebrated his double victory by performing a slow roll over West Raynham's No. 4 hangar at 1 a.m. He explained later that he didn't think his action was at all dangerous as he had practised several times on the way back. His moustache grew at least an inch longer overnight and he blushed modestly as he introduced himself to newcomers by saying, 'Just call me ace!' Rivals, 141 Squadron, salvaged some pride when S/L G. J. Rice and F/O J. G. Rogerson destroyed a Bf 110 north-west of Amiens and on 28/29 July parity was almost restored when 141 destroyed three aircraft in one night. In the Metz–Neufchateau area, P/O I. D. Gregory and P/O D. H. Stephens destroyed a Ju 88 and none other than F/L H. E. White DFC* and F/L M. S. Allen DFC* emulated Booth's and Dear's feat, getting two Ju 88s.

A famous night for 169 Squadron, now established at Great Massingham, occurred on 20/21 July with the destruction of '100 Group's 100th Hun'. Harry Reed and Stuart Watts got a Ju 88 in the Homburg area while W/C Neil B. R. Bromley OBE, DFC, the CO, destroyed a Bf 110 near Courtrai. The squadron were presented with a coveted silver tankard inscribed, 'To the hungry hun hunters of 169 Squadron . . .' a reference to the Squadron's motto 'Hunt and Destroy' on its proud crest, designed by S/L Joe Cooper. The former 4th Hussars' trooper cleverly featured a hunting horn, signifying the intruder role, against a midnight-blue hurt, representing the night.

When 239 Squadron was told, at the end of July, that it was to be called upon for greater efforts in order to offset a shortage of trained crews and a lack of serviceable aircraft in the two sister squadrons, the general opinion was that nothing better could happen. At the beginning of August,

*169 Squadron receives its crest (motto 'Hunt and Destroy') in front of a hangar at Great Massingham near where 1692 BSTU was located, in July 1944. The Mosquito is a standard Mk VI. (Joe Cooper)*

however, German-originated radar, which had begun to bother crews in June, became rapidly more troublesome, and the next four months the maximum detection range of 10,000 ft became a rarity. Even the most experienced and successful crews returned from sortie after sortie with reports of jamming so intense that, as one navigator remarked, it was flooding the tubes and spilling over the cockpit.

In August, 331 *Serrate*/AI Mk IV sorties yielded just eight successful combats. No. 141 Squadron claimed just one, while 239 Squadron, which completed 93 per cent of all sorties it dispatched, destroyed only three but lost two crews, one killed in landing, the other disappearing without trace on a non-operational night flight. No. 169 Squadron destroyed four. Tim Woodman and Patrick Kemmis destroyed a Fw 190 near Abbeville on 9/10 August when the heavies attacked V-1 sites in the Pas de Calais. On 26/27 September, W/O Les Turner and F/Sgt Freddie Francis destroyed a Ju 88 near Bremen to add to the Bf 109 they had shot down on 14/15 July. The two other 169 Squadron victories in August went to F/O Andy Miller DFC and F/O Freddie Bone DFC. Their Bf 109 over Dijon on 10/11 August was their tenth victory of the war. Their eleventh, scored the following night, was not confirmed until after the war for Andy Miller and Freddie Bone failed to return from a patrol near Heligoland. Andy Miller recalls:

Freddie picked up a contact crossing slightly 'at quite a lick'. We eventually caught up with it. Vertically above it I identified it as a He 219. I dropped back to about 150 yards and gave it four 2-second bursts. We were hit by debris and lost coolant in both our engines. I glided in over the coast of Holland and Freddie bailed out at 1,200 ft and I followed, at 800–900 ft.

Freddie Bone was captured early next morning and later sent to Stalag Luft III.

Andy Miller evaded. For four weeks he was sent along the Dutch Underground. Then the network was betrayed. He was among evaders captured at Antwerp and handed over to the Gestapo. At Dulag Luft he was confronted by the pilot of the He 219 he had shot down in August! 'He wasn't too pleased and his arm was in a sling.' Andy Miller was sent to Stalag Luft I. Freddie Bone DFC* returned to the police force after the war and was promptly put back on the beat!

In September, three Mosquitoes were lost. On the 6th, Neil Bromley and Philip Truscott were killed by flak near Oldenburg during a night bomber support operation to Hamburg. (W/C T. A. Heath assumed command of the Squadron on Bromley's death.) Meanwhile, 239 Squadron lost Bill Breithaupt DFC and F/O J. A. Kennedy DFC on 12/13 September, shot down by the Bf 110 they brought down, and F/O W. Osborne and F/Sgt Acheson were also lost. Despite 93 per cent of all sorties being completed, 239 Squadron had nothing to show. In fact, the 240 sorties flown during the month by the *Serrate* squadrons bore little fruit – on the 7th, F/L Paul Mellows and F/L S. L. 'Dickie' Drew of 169 Squadron had damaged a Ju 88 15 miles south of Wilhelmshaven – and produced only one successful combat. On 11/12 September, F/L Peter Bates and P/O William Cadman of 141 Squadron destroyed a Bf 110 south of Mannheim. Despite these successes there were obvious signs that the German defences were countering the Mosquitoes' *Serrate* radar. On 26 September, S/L Tim Woodman, who had taken over B Flight in 169 Squadron from Joe Cooper, found there were 'plenty of Huns airborne' during a *Serrate* sortie near Frankfurt, but found that his 'radar [was] completely jammed'.

Group obviously took notice of the changing fortunes, for that month the *Serrate* squadrons began much practice (more hours of practice flying were actually recorded than on operations in August) and low flying in anticipation of a new role that was to be found for them. In September, the three *Serrate* squadrons joined 85 and 157 Squadrons which had returned to the fold at the end of August following their anti-*Diver* patrols at West Malling, on low-level strafing and *Intruder* attacks over enemy territory. No. 85 Squadron, which had destroyed 33 V-1s, and 157 Squadron's Mosquitoes retained the modifications they had received for anti-*Diver* operations except the stub exhausts which were replaced again with shroud exhausts. Both Mk X Squadrons were also used on high-level patrols and the results for both kinds of operation were very encouraging. From 167 Mk X high-level patrols, 47 suspicious AI contacts were reported leading to 12 successful combats. Ben Benson and Brandy Brandon, who had destroyed six V-1s, opened the scoring for 157 Squadron

since returning to Swannington by destroying two Ju 88s on 11/12 September. A Bf 110 was knocked down on the 13/14 September by S/L 'Dolly' Doleman and F/L 'Bunny' Bunch, and F/L Vincent and F/O Monoy destroyed a Me 410 Hornisse on 29/30 September. In 85 Squadron, Branse Burbridge and Bill Skelton destroyed a Ju 188 on 11/12 September, the first squadron victory since returning to Swannington.

Another six enemy aircraft were destroyed by 85 Squadron by the time the month was out, including two Bf 110s which fell to the guns of Ginger Owen on 17/18 September, and a Ju 188 which was destroyed by F/L Micky Phillips and F/L Derek Smith on 28/29 September. (Phillips and Smith failed to return on 6/7 November after a British bomber fired on them, setting one engine ablaze and were then shot down by a He 219. Phillips and

*85 Squadron line up for the camera.* Back row, left to right: *F/O Symon; F/O Cleaver; F/L Molony, Adjutant, F/O Bill Skelton; F/L Branse Burbridge, S/L Gonsalves; S/L Davison; W/C John Cunningham; Capt Weisteen; u/k; u/k; F/O Ginger Farrell; F/O Thomas.* Front row, left to right: *F/O Custance; u/k; u/k; S/L Rawnsley; u/k.*

Smith bailed out. Captured, they spent the remainder of the war in Stalag Luft I.)

Besides patrols in the target areas after bombing and around the assembly beacon, escorting the stream was tried with the Mk X-equipped Mosquitoes of 85 and 157 Squadrons flying at 10 to 15 miles from the mean track. A number of contacts were also obtained on the rearward-looking *Monica* equipment carried by the AI Mk X high-level *Intruders*. It was found that these contacts could generally be evaded fairly easily but that it was often difficult to convert them to forward AI Mk X contacts – only about a quarter of the *Monica* contacts reported were converted. Thus it appeared that the main value of *Monica* was the prevention of surprise attack from the rear rather than as an additional interception aid. The Mosquitoes of 85 and 157 Squadrons did not, in general, find much activity at the airfields to which they were sent. They did, however, achieve three successful combats from 13 AI contacts.

A few weeks earlier, 141 Squadron had at last begun receiving Mosquito Mk VIs; 169 Squadron had had them since June, and 239 had received them in December 1943. The Mk VI was standard *Intruder* equipment in 100 Group and 2nd TAF. Meanwhile, a modified *Serrate* Mk IV was being tested and flown operationally by the BSDU. There was also increased German jamming and interference of the old Mk IV AI sets and although frequencies were changed from 193 MHz to 188 MHz, it was not a success and introduced complications in interrogating IFF and beacons.

On 2 September, W/C Winnie Winn had held an aircrew conference at West Raynham, giving a lecture on the operational aspect of low flying. Another was given two days later, although the first victory of the month on 141 Squadron was the result of an AI contact on a *Serrate* patrol on 11/12 September when Bomber Command visited Darmstadt. A head-on AI contact was obtained by F/L Peter A.

*Mosquito NF Mk XIX of 157 (SD) Squadron at its dispersal near St Peter's Church, Haveringland on whose land part of RAF Swannington airfield was sited.*

*Bomber Support Development Unit which was formed at West Raynham on 10 April 1944 to develop, test and produce a wide variety of radar and radio equipment for 100 Group. BSDU moved to Foulsham and finally, in December 1944, to Swanton Morley where this photo was taken. Front row, 8th and 9th from left: F/O F. W. Sticky Clay, navigator; F/L D. R. Podge Howard, pilot. They destroyed a Fw 190 while with 239 Squadron on 14/15 October 1944. S/L N. A. Reeves and F/O Phillips of BSDU destroyed a Bf 110 west of Giessen on 6/7 December 1944. S/L B. Gledhill (front row, 11th from left) W/C R. F. H. Clerke DFC, the CO, (front row, 12th from left). Clerke flew the first operational sortie, on 4 July 1944, when he and F/L Wheldon investigated V-1s. (RAF Swanton Morley)*

Bates and P/O William G. Cadman 10 miles north-west of Frankfurt at 23:50 hours at 18,000 ft. Both aircraft went into a dogfight lasting some 20 minutes with neither aircraft getting anywhere. Canary was tried without result but eventually the contact made off to the north-west. A chase lasting 5 minutes ensued but the contact eluded them.

Bates and Cadman returned to the target area, and as the bombing had ended, decided to fly slowly westward in the hope of deceiving enemy fighters that it was a straggling bomber. Twenty miles west of Darmstadt, a backward AI contact was picked up 12,000 ft behind crossing starboard to port. Bates turned and followed. For almost 20 minutes the Mosquito tailed the enemy machine through twists and turns towards Darmstadt. Eventually, Bates closed to 900 ft range and a visual was obtained on two exhausts. Bates and Cadman dropped back but the visual was lost. Closing again a pale bluish-white light was seen underneath the dim silhouette of an

aircraft. At that moment, the enemy aircraft opened up from the upper gun position and tracer hit the Mosquito's starboard drop tank. Bates pulled up, visual was regained on the exhausts and he gave the enemy aircraft a burst of 2–3 seconds of cannon fire from 600 ft range. The enemy's starboard engine exploded and Bates had to pull up to avoid a collision as it passed underneath. It was then that they could see in the light of the explosion that it was a Bf 110. Cadman watched the contact going down on his AI set before the Bf 110 hit the ground and exploded. Five other victories that month can be attributed to Mosquitoes of 85 Squadron. During the month, *Intruder* and escort operations for the four-engined bombers in 100 Group were the order of the day, or rather the night.

On 16/17 September, Bomber Command's operations were in support of the Allied airborne landings at Arnhem and Nijmegen in Holland. Six Mosquitoes of 239 Squadron supported attacks on German airfields in Holland and Germany during the night and 141 took part at dawn on the 17th. Winnie Winn and five other Mosquito crews carried out a low-level attack on Steenwijk, one of three airfields bombed during the night. Four Mosquitoes were damaged by flak. Winnie Winn damaged a twin-engined Junkers on the ground, and buildings and personnel were strafed. Trains were attacked on the way home. Six more Mosquitoes from 239 Squadron kept up the momentum, with support raids on the airfields again the following night. At last light on 18 September, two Mosquitoes of 141 Squadron flew protective patrols for nine Fortresses of 214 and 223 Squadrons supplying a *Mandrel* screen off the Dutch coast and the action was repeated again at first light on the 19th. The Fortresses were covered by two 141 Squadron Mosquitoes again at last light on the 22nd. By the end of September, the score for the two *Serrate* squadrons at West Raynham stood at 38 destroyed by 239 Squadron and 25 destroyed by 141 Squadron. Despite the problems with *Serrate*, these sorties still predominated, 141 Squadron, for instance, flying 62 *Serrate* sorties on 11 nights and 14 *Intruder* sorties.

October saw a great decrease in the effectiveness of the enemy opposition to the night bomber. This was a combined result of the Allied advance into the continent and the technical and tactical countermeasures employed. The enemy warning and inland plotting systems were thrown into confusion and the low-level and high-level *Intruder* played no small part by causing the enemy to plot hostile aircraft over very wide areas as well as forcing him to broadcast

frequent warnings of the presence of hostile aircraft to his own fighters. In fact, the 100 Group fighters made a very important contribution to Bomber Support. The fighters also took part in the *Window* feints, flying with them to add to the effect of the deception and then fanning out to take advantage of enemy reaction.

In October the *Serrate* Squadrons led the rest of the field, with six enemy aircraft destroyed to the Mk X Mosquito Squadrons' five. No. 141 Squadron shot down three enemy aircraft, although these were accomplished using AI and not *Serrate*. No. 239 also scored three. No. 169 Squadron, which damaged three enemy aircraft that month, was already having nine of its *Serrate* homers replaced by *Perfectos*, a homer which gave a bearing on the enemy night-fighter's IFF set and had a range of 40 miles. Stopgap arrangements were made to fit some of 141 Squadron's Mosquitoes with ASH (Air-Surface H), a centimetric radar originally developed in the USA as an ASV (air-to-surface-vessel) radar for US Navy aircraft and the Fleet Air Arm. ASH was a wing mounted radar but could not be fitted to the Mosquito wing so it was installed in a 'thimble' radome in the nose.

The first of the victories by 141 Squadron occurred on 6/7 October when F/L A. C. Gallacher with P/O G. McLean destroyed a Ju 88 during a *Serrate* patrol to Dortmund and Bremen. On 19/20 October, when 853 bombers raided Stuttgart and Nuremberg, 141 and 239 Squadrons dispatched a total of 26 Mosquitoes. Warrant Officer Falconer and Flight Sergeant Armour of 239

| | Sept | Oct | Nov | Dec | Jan | Feb | Mar | Apr |
|---|---|---|---|---|---|---|---|---|
| Average No. of AI contacts per sortie | 0.28 | 0.24 | 0.38 | 0.34 | 0.25 | 0.18 | 0.18 | 0.11 |
| Average No. of AI contacts per successful combat | 3.9 | 5.6 | 3.5 | 2.4 | 3.4 | 4.6 | 5.2 | 5.3 |

AI contacts made by 100 Group Mosquitoes September 1944 – April 1945

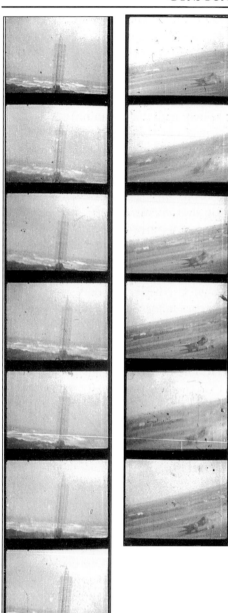

*Far left: Camera-gun film from George Stewart's Mosquito of 23 Squadron intruder strafing a FuMG Jagdschloss Michael (Hunting Castle Michael) early warning radar site on the Danish coast near Ringkjobing Lake on 26 September 1944. 23 Squadron flew a day Ranger to Grove aerodrome in Denmark. One of the Mosquitoes was flown by Bud Badley, and the other by F/O George Stewart with Paul Beaudet, both Canadians. Stewart attacked a radar site and stirred up a real hornet's nest. His Mosquito took a bullet in a feathering button. (Tom Cushing Collection)*

*Left: George Stewart of 23 Squadron strafing Grove airfield, Denmark on 26 September 1944. Also a soldier armed with a hand-held machine-gun put out one of Buddy Badley's engines and damaged an elevator so that Badley could only climb using his trim tab. Badley ordered his navigator to bail out but his parachute spilled out in the cockpit. Badley landed the Mosquito at Woodbridge safely on one engine and with no rudder control. He received the DFC. Badley's Mosquito was almost a write-off. After this incident they stuck to straight intruding and night targets! (Tom Cushing Collection)*

Squadron shot down an enemy aircraft and two Ju 88s fell to the guns of 141 Squadron. A Ju 88 claimed by F/O J. C. Barton and F/Sgt R. A. Kinnear as 'damaged', which they attacked on three separate occasions 10–15 miles north of Nürnberg, was confirmed as a victory upon their return to West Raynham by S/L Goodrich whose inspection revealed the leading edge of the Mosquito's starboard spinner and starboard mainplane were extensively covered in oil from their victim while several indentations in the aircraft were found to be caused by flying debris.

The second Ju 88 was destroyed by F/L G. D. 'Charlie' Bates and F/O D. W. Field approximately 10 miles south-east of Karlsruhe after a 10-minute chase. Charlie Bates gave the Ju 88 a 2-second burst of cannon fire from 300 ft dead astern. After what seemed like 'hours', the enemy aircraft's starboard engine burst into flames and the Ju 88 pulled up in a hard starboard turn. Bates turned hard port and came in to deliver a second attack. However, the Junkers was by now well alight and after firing red and white Very lights, went into a steep dive into cloud. Two seconds later, two explosions of great force were seen below, the second one lighting up the whole cloud. The Ju 88 split into three pieces, which were picked up on AI, scattering themselves into the night.

Four aircraft were destroyed by 85 Squadron and 157 Squadron scored one victory, a Bf 110 which fell to the guns of F/L Jimmy Matthews on 7/8 October. On 14/15 October and 19/20 October, Branse Burbridge and Bill Skelton destroyed a Ju 88 both nights, and Dolly Doleman shot down another. The other victory was on 15/16 October when F/L C. K. Nowell and W/O Randall bagged a Bf 110. A number of day and night *Intruder* operations were carried out by the *Serrate* Mosquitoes during the month. On 17 October, Tim Woodman flew a daylight *Intruder* sortie to north-east Germany. He recalls:

S/L Mike O'Brien DFC, a pilot from 23 Squadron, came as my observer and F/O Pierre Dils DFC (Belgian) as my No. 2. Fifty miles off the Danish coast Dils saw two men in a dinghy. They did not wave and looked like 'krauts'. I sent him back to call up and radio their position. The Germans were informed as they were too far out for our rescue services. We pressed on alone, crossing into the Baltic without any trouble. Flew past German airfield at Eggebec which looked deserted. Low-level flak with tracer had me doing ducks and drakes at 50 ft to avoid it. Crossed into the main coast at Barth. What I thought was a forest fire look-

out platform in the conifers proved to be a sentry post at Barth Stalag. (Paddy Barthropp was a prisoner there and a test pilot with me at Boscombe Down after the war. He said I had flown right over the camp at midday.) Some 50 miles inland I shot up a long train of tanker wagons (empty) plus the loco. On the way out I shot up the Heinkel factory at Barth. No aircraft on the airfield or in the air. Was able to put some cannon shells into a converted M/Y which had shot at me on the way in. Crossing Schleswig-Holstein there was a small passenger train entering a small station. I shot up the engine. Passengers got out and started to run across a field. I dived down on them as they stared terror-struck at me. 'Don't shoot,' Paddy O'Brien said. 'They're nice people up here.' I had no intention of doing so, only giving them something to tell their grandchildren about. Machine-gun bullets in our starboard engine when we got back. Probably from a sentry on one of those platforms at Barth.

On the 23rd S/L Tim Woodman flew another daylight *Intruder* to north-east Germany.

S/L Mike O'Brien was again my observer; another volunteer crew – a black West Indian F/O pilot – as my No. 2. I let them lead the way across the North Sea, doing the *Gee* navigation. They brought me right up the main street of Westerland, the Luftwaffe fighter base on Sylt, 40 miles from where I had intended to cross in! I flew down the coast with white Very lights being fired by shore stations. Surprise factor was essential and we had lost that. Suddenly all hell broke loose as a number of Oerlikon cannons fired at us from Eggebec, no longer deserted. Total blue skies too, no cloud cover. I decided to abandon. Told the West Indian to break to starboard, hit the deck and pour on the coal to the North Sea. Took me 20 miles to catch him up. He looked like he intended to make it all the way to Barbados. Some hits on my Mosquito from machine-gun bullets.

S/L O'Brien, with his navigator, F/L P. A. Disney, who had flown with Woodman on 6 October, were killed on their 23 Squadron *Intruder* op on 22 March 1945.

On 28/29 October, six crews in 239 Squadron made low-level *Intruder* patrols over north-west Germany and left a trail of destruction, including nine trains, a lorry and a marshalling yard. 'Podge' Howard and 'Sticky' Clay destroyed a Heinkel 111, which exploded with such force that it was probably carrying a V-1 flying bomb. Gallacher and McLean of 141 Squadron were gratified to see clouds of steam as 'their' train stopped with seven wagons damaged. On 29/30 October, 11 out of 12 No. 239 Squadron crews completed sorties in support of a heavy raid on Köln. Squadron Leader D. L. Hughes and Flight Lieutenant R. H. Perks returned with bullet holes through the tail unit and both

wings, including one through the port wing tank, while F/L F. Wimbush and F/O Fraser 'tangled' for 35 minutes with a German fighter.

November saw the same pattern of operations with bomber support and night and day *Intruder* and *Ranger* patrols. No. 85 Squadron continued its run of success with a superb individual effort during a night *Intruder* on 4/5 November when Bomber Command's main thrust was against Bochum with smaller raids on the Dortmund–Ems Canal and on Hannover. Branse Burbridge and Bill Skelton were airborne from Swannington at 17:31 hours on a high-level *Intruder* patrol south-east of Köln. They crossed the enemy coast and headed into Germany. Burbridge wrote later:

We were returning to our patrol point

*On 4/5 November 1944, S/L Branse Burbridge DSO\*, DFC\* and F/L Bill Skelton DSO\*, DFC\* shot down three Ju 88s, and this Bf 110 of II./NJG1 north of Hangelar airfield. It crashed into the River Rhine at 21:50 hours. Oblt Ernst Runze, pilot, was killed; Ogefr Karl-Heinz Bendfeld, radar operator, and air gunner bailed out safely. Burbridge and Skelton finished the war as the top scoring night-fighter team in the RAF.*

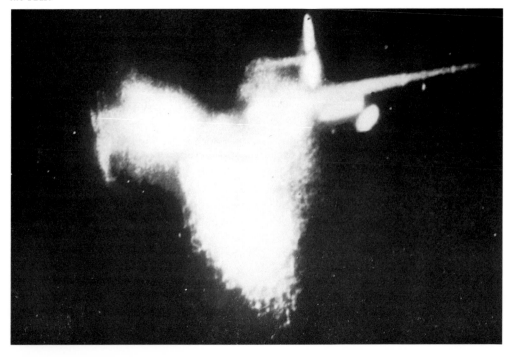

from Limburg at 15,000 ft, on a north-westerly course, when Bill reported contact at 19:04 hours, range 4 miles, crossing starboard to port at about our level. We turned in behind it, flying west, looking vainly for Type F response while closing in. I obtained a visual at 1,500 ft range. At 1,000 ft, I believed it to be a Ju 88, and using night binoculars Bill identified it as a Ju 88C. I fired a short burst from 500 ft, producing strikes on the port engine. A dull flame appeared. A second short burst gave the same result, and a fire slowly developed in the engine as the enemy aircraft lost height. Soon it began to dive steeply, exploding on the ground at 19:09 hours.

By the time we had climbed up again to our patrol point, the markers were beginning to appear in the target area, so we set course towards it. On returning to a reciprocal brief investigation of further flares south-west of us were fruitless, but at 19:53 hours Bill reported contact at 4 miles range. We dived after it and found that it was taking regular evasive action by losing height at high speed, weaving up to 45° in either direction. After about 5 minutes we had lost height to 7,000 ft, and I obtained a visual at about 1,200 ft range. Again no Type F response or exhausts were seen. We closed in and identified the target with binoculars as a Ju 88. At 500 ft range, having finger trouble, I pressed the camera button by mistake, but the absence of thunder, and the mocking buzz of the camera on the R/T put me right. A short burst (cannon) gave strikes and a flash from the port engine and fuselage, but owing to the dive I lost the visual against the darkness of the ground. Bill regained contact, and although the evasion of the enemy aircraft had increased and became irregular, we closed in again to visual range of about 1,200 ft after a further 5 minutes, our height now being 3,000 ft. Another short burst at 20:02 hours at the same engine produced the same results, and once again the visual was lost below the horizon. We searched around, but were unable to pick him up again; our

position was roughly 5 miles SE of what we took to be the dummy flarepath of Bonn. At 20:05 hours, an aircraft exploded on the ground some distance ahead of us. Two minutes later I saw what I believed to be another crash on the ground.

We now proceeded to regain a bit of height, and when at 8,000 ft, set course from the last named position to join the bomber homeward route near Düren, which point we reached at 20:20 hours. It was our intention to fly on the reciprocal of the route, towards the target, and to intercept contacts coming head on: these would most likely be hostiles attempting late route interceptions, as the bombers should all have been clear. After 2 minutes flying on p50°, my attention was attracted by a recognition cartridge (red and white) fired about 25 miles east of us. We hurried in its direction losing height on the way, and shortly the red perimeter lights of an airfield appeared. Then I saw the landing light of an aircraft touching down east to west at 20:28 hours.

A minute later we had a snap contact and fleeting visual of an aircraft above us, but were unable to pursue it. On commencing a right-hand circuit of the airfield, however, Bill obtained a contact (on the north side of the aerodrome) at 2 miles range and at our height, which was about 1,000 ft above the ground. Following round the south side, we closed in to identify a Me 110. He must have throttled back rather smartly when east of the airfield for we suddenly found ourselves overtaking rapidly, horn blaring in our ears, and finished up immediately below him about 80 ft away. Very gradually we began to drop back and pulling up to dead astern at 400 ft range, I fired a very short burst. The whole fuselage was a mass of flames, and the Me 110 went down burning furiously, to crash in a river about 5 miles north of the airfield, which we presumed to be Bonn/Hangelar. The time was 20:32 hours.

We flew away to the north for a few minutes, and then turned to approach the airfield again. As we did so Bill produced yet another contact at 2 miles range, 80° starboard. When we got in behind him he appeared to be doing a close left-hand orbit of the airfield. Again we followed round the west and south sides, and as he seemed to be preparing to land, I selected 10° of flap. I obtained a visual at 1,500 ft range; no u/c was visible, so I took the flap off again. We identified the target as a Ju 88 and a very short burst from dead astern, 400 ft range, caused the fuselage to burst into flames. The cockpit broke away, and we pulled up sharply to avoid debris. Crosses were clearly visible in the light of the fire, and the Ju 88 dived towards the airfield. He finally turned over to starboard and exploded in a ploughed field just north of the aerodrome at 20:40 hours.

We could see intruder warnings being fired from aerodromes in every direction by this time, and although we tried to investigate one further recognition signal some distance from us, we obtained no joy, and presumed that we had outstayed our welcome.

Burbridge and Skelton landed back at Swannington at 22:23 hours and submitted claims for one Bf 110, one Ju 88 and one Ju 88G destroyed and one Ju 88 probably destroyed. James Lansdale Hodson, a newspaper reporter, visited Swannington and in his subsequent article attributed the reasons for Burbridge's and Skelton's great success to 'intelligence'.

They knew before they set out precisely where they will be at a certain time. They carry a picture in their head of the whole night's operation . . . the various bomber streams, times, targets. They try to read the enemy mind . . . they visualise at what time he will discover what is happening, how far he will be misled, what he will do, what airfields he will use, what times he will rise, whether he will fly, what his tactics will be. They act accordingly. If one expectation fails, they know which next to try. After they had shot down three on the night they shot

down four, Burbridge said, "Time we were starting for home, Bill." To which Skelton replied: "Well if you like, but I've got another Hun for you." They went round after him and destroyed him too. Then they had a further look round, "But," says Burbridge's combat report, "we found no joy and presumed we had outstayed our welcome."

The popular press dubbed Branse and Bill the 'Night Hawk Partners'. Such was the need for morale-boosting headlines. Less happy reading was that although 100 Group Mosquitoes claimed six enemy aircraft this night it had been a sorry 24 hours for Bomber Command. Despite the actions of the Mosquito crews (239 Squadron and 157 Squadrons also destroyed an enemy aircraft apiece) and a *Window Spoof* by 100 Group, out of a combined 1,081 sorties during the day (to Solingen) and night, 31 bombers were lost, the highest for some time.

Two nights later, on 6/7 November, the bombers attacked the Mittelland Canal at Gravenhorst. It was one of the worst night's weather Tim Woodman, who had also bagged a Bf 110 on 4/5 November, had ever flown in.

We left the target area and flew into a cold front of exceptional violence. We were thrown all over the place, ice quickly froze on the windscreen and static electricity began to spark about the cockpit. We would drop like a stone and I feared my wing tips would come off. Down at 800 ft the ice cleared but it was too dangerous so close to the sea so I went back up to 2,000 ft. F/O Witt had his straps loose in order to operate the *Gee* set but after he had hit the top of the cockpit for the third time I told him to lock his straps and I would fly due west until we reached better weather. I listened out on the radio. Other crews were obviously in dire trouble from the nature of their calls. Outside the propellers were whirling discs

S/L Tim Woodman (back row, 2nd right) *pictured while with 96 Squadron at Honiley, equipped with Beaufighters. F/O Arthur Witt (front row, 2nd from left) accompanied him as navigator on the operation to the Koblenz–Dortmund–Ems Canal on 6 November 1944. Witt was killed two weeks later flying with another pilot. (Tim Woodman)*

of violet fire, the aerials on the wings glowed violet like neon tubes. The inside of the windscreen was a lattice of static and, as I leant forward concentrating on the instruments, the static struck across like pinpricks on my face. We dropped out of the sky in another violent air disturbance, the instruments went spinning and we waited to hit the sea. Arthur Witt then said, quite calmly, 'Another one like that . . . why not let the controls go. Then it will all be over. I am quite easy about dying.' We made it after some more dicey episodes. But poor Arthur was killed a fortnight later flying with another pilot. Eleven aircraft were lost due to the weather, including two 100 Group Mosquitoes.

When the fitting of AI Mk X into 100 Group Mosquitoes began there were not sufficient equipments available for the whole force. Tim Woodman recalls:

Although 85 and 157 Squadrons had been attached to 100 Group since May 1944 with 10 cm AI, we considered they were not

*Swannington 'Score Board' showing the kills attributed to both 85 and 157 Squadrons. 157 achieved its highest night score of four German aircraft destroyed on Christmas Eve 1944. In total, 85 Squadron claimed 43 kills and 157 Squadron claimed 28 by the end of the war. (Author)*

shooting down the numbers of Hun night-fighters they should have. Our Mk IV radar was completely jammed over Germany. Only half a dozen crews of 85 and 157 were getting scores: two or three doing quite well. I challenged the SASO, A/Cdre Rory Chisholm, to let two of 169 crews have the use of 85 Squadron's aircraft for five ops each, guaranteeing to shoot down a Hun apiece. We went over to Swannington, myself to fly with F/O Simpkin, an 85 Squadron observer, plus Mellows and Drew from 169. What a delight to have 10 cm radar which could range up to 8 miles ahead and no jamming. Mellows proved my challenge by shooting down a Heinkel 219 on the second of his five ops. I failed but nearly got a Ju 88 on my fifth op on 2 January. Chased three Huns but had partial radar failure. Shot at Ju 88 as it entered cloud. Followed him down through, shooting blind on radar. Clear below cloud. A light on the ground and another pilot said he saw an aircraft crash. Made no claim, however, and climbed back up as unsure of the height of the ground.

This was Tim Woodman's fifty-first op, and his last with 169 (85). He was assessed as a 'Bomber Support Pilot: Exceptional'.

He received a commendation from 100 Group's AOC for meritorious service and appointed to be operational test pilot at the BSDU at Swanton Morley. At BSDU Woodman, S/L Gledhill, F/L Neville and F/L Carpenter, specialist radar observers, checked out ASH, *Perfectos*, *Piperack*, centimetric homer and other electronic devices, and flew eight more operations.

ASH was not so elaborate an AI as the Mk X, and was expected to be much better than Mk IV for bomber support operations. It was decided to equip 23, 515 and 141 Squadrons with it. On 8 November, Mr Willis of Western Electric and Mr Glen Turner, the US technical representative, visited West Raynham. The reason for their call was to inspect the ASH Mk XV AI installation which had been fitted to an Anson (and an Oxford) for testing by 141 Squadron. Some weeks later, on 21 November, F/L R. A. W. Scott DFC and F/O W. G. Cadman DFC, flew in the Anson on ASH training and obtained excellent results, especially at minimum range. Two days later, aircrew at West Raynham were shown a 2-hour film on ASH. ASH required a very high degree of skill for successful operation. With a very highly skilled operator, 100 Group hoped

*Cartoon of a Mosquito being serviced at the BSDU at RAF Swanton Morley.*

*23 Squadron at Little Snoring on 26 November 1944. George Stewart on top of his Mosquito. Left to right: W/C Sticky Murphy; F/Lt Curd; F/O Joynson; F/L Griffiths; S/L Philip Russell; F/O Cocky Cockayne; F/L Tommy Smith; F/O Lewis Heath; W/O Rann; F/L Jock Reid; F/L Bill Gregory; Lt Christie; P/O George Sutcliffe; F/O Atherton; F/Sgt Freddie Howes; F/O Paul Beaudet RCAF; P/O Neil; F/Sgt Chessel; F/O Berry; F/Sgt Alex Wilson; F/Sgt Don Francis; F/L Buddy Badley; F/Sgt Tommy Barr; F/O Kit Cotter; F/Sgt Thompson; F/Sgt Jock Devlin; F/Sgt Jimmy Weston; F/O Spetch; F/L Tommy Ramsay; F/Sgt 'Benny' Goodman; F/Sgt Jimmy Gawthorne; F/Sgt Sid Smith. Joynson and Spetch went missing on 28 October. (Tom Cushing Collection)*

that it might become a really valuable weapon in bomber support.

On 25 November, two Mosquitoes of 141 Squadron carried out low-level night *Intruder* sorties to enemy airfields in Germany. One crew returned early after failing to find Sachsenheim airfield, but F/O R. D. S. Gregor USAAF with his navigator/radar operator, F/Sgt F. S. Baker attacked vehicles *en route* to Hailfingen and Eutingen. The latter was all lit up but there was no sign of any aircraft so they blew up some more vehicles before returning to Norfolk. Low-level and high-level *Intruders* continued to be flown during the month and, starting on 25 November, two 500 lb MC bombs were carried by 141 Squadron Mosquitoes for the first time on attacks on German airfields. Alternatively, eight

40 lb bombs could be carried. The small 40 lb bombs caused little damage but helped disrupt the German night-fighter airfields. Also, high-level bombing sorties were flown, using *Gee* navigation fixes to pinpoint targets, to help foster the impression that the 100 Group *Spoof Window*-dropping aircraft were, in fact, a bombing force and so divert German night-fighters from the main attack by the heavies and by Mosquitoes of 8 Group.

On 30 November, when 141 Squadron dispatched eight *Intruders*, P/O E. A. Lampkin and P/O Bernard J. Wallnutt were shot down during their patrol to Diepholz airfield. Lampkin was last heard transmitting 'Winball 20 pranging in Holland'. Wallnutt was killed and Lampkin was made PoW. Eight day *Intruder* sorties and 35 night *Intruders/*

*Mk XXX Mosquitoes of 85 Squadron at Swannington in the winter of 1944. (IWM)*

*Rangers* and night bomber/-*Intruder* sorties were flown during November by 141 Squadron. On 2/3 December, two Mosquitoes in 141 Squadron carried out the last *Serrate* patrols of the war, having been the first to fly *Serrate* sorties on 14 June 1943 from Wittering. No. 239 would continue with *Serrate* patrols for a little longer during December 1944 and, starting on 7 January, some of their Mk VIs were transferred to 141 Squadron as 239 received new Mk XXXs. Some patrols using Mk IV *Serrate* were carried out by 169 Squadron at Great Massingham right up until the end of the war. Mosquitoes from 141 Squadron would start ASH operations in December, thus joining sister squadrons 23 and 515 at Little Snoring. Since late 1944, both squadrons had begun training with ASH for low level raids on German airfields. For many months with and without ASH, these two squadrons had been long established in this deadly, incisive form of airborne warfare. No. 23 Squadron was led by W/C Sticky Murphy whose panache and aggressive leadership had created a fresh *élan* which boded ill for the Reich's Nachtjagdgeschwader gruppen.

# CHAPTER 10

# *DECEMBER DAYS*

*Here both men and maidens tended
To the harsh and warlike needs,
Of men who through the dark hours
Flew their man-made steeds.
The sky at night their hunting ground
In which they sought their prey,
Returning only when the night
Gave way to breaking day.*

S. F. RUFFLE

Jock Reid was uneasy. Sticky Murphy's trusty navigator had flown on almost all of his commanding officer's sorties from Malta, Sardinia and Little Snoring but the period between ops was becoming longer and longer. It was 2 December and their previous operation together had been on 26 November, 26 days before. Jock Reid explains.

The reason for so long a gap between ops was to lengthen his stay as CO of 23 Squadron. Sticky was a swashbuckling character, proud of the fact that his identity card carried the description 'Colour of eyes: bloodshot blue'. Only one other I knew had this mark of identification, 'Micky' Martin, one of the Dambusters, who came to 515 for a rest!

Jock was the perfect foil of practical navigational skill to complement Sticky's audacity and exceptional experience. A rather dour Scot, Jock saved his unexpected glimpses of humour for special occasions. Saturday 2 December was not one of them. He met the CO going into the mess for lunch. '"We're flying tonight [an *Intruder* trip to Gütersloh]," he said. I then told him I was grounded for a few days because I had seen the MO that morning. "That's OK – we'll just scrub it," Murphy said.' Murphy however, took off from Little Snoring at 20:18 hours, his eighty-sixth op. All told, 16 crews (eight from 23 Squadron and eight from 515) flew *Intruder* patrols over airfields in Germany, Denmark and Norway while 504 bombers attacked Hagan. The 21-year-old F/Sgt Douglas

Darbon had gone with Murphy. The route to and from Gütersloh had offered an ideal opportunity for the experienced leader to blood young Darbon in the art of 'Nacht Zuster' (Night Nurse) tactics. (Most towns and cities in Holland had their Night Nurse. The Dutch were glad to hear any aircraft of the RAF and USAAF flying. It gave them a lift.) Darbon most probably noticed that his W/C had inexplicably shaved off his prized handlebar moustache. (Murphy had once clipped a quarter of an inch off each end of his moustache so that it did not 'outrank' Sammy Hoare's, which was six inches, 'wing tip to wing tip'.)

Earlier in the day Sticky had called to see his friends the Andersons at a farm near the base where he shot pheasant, but they were out. Caretaker Eric Myhill had watched as Murphy rocked up and down on his heels in front of the log fire roaring in the grate. He noticed that the W/C was wearing his favourite American brown flying boots. 'Tell Mr and Mrs Anderson I'll be back tomorrow,' Murphy had told Myhill. 'I'm on ops tonight.' Sticky's wife Jean, whom he had met when she a WAAF officer while he was instructing at an OTU in Scotland in 1941, has fond memories of him: 'rough

shooting through the corn stubble for rabbits and any game – Sticky was an excellent shot with a .22.'

When 23 Squadron had moved to Snoring Jean had moved to Norfolk from Berkshire with their daughter Gail (born three days before Sticky returned from Sardinia) and had lodged at a farm some distance from the airfield. (Crews were not permitted to 'live out'.) Living there was Spartan and cold, and Jean became ill. She moved to a more congenial farm house at Tuddenham, where the farmer was also a butcher, so they lived well! Illness persisted, however, and Jean had to spend several weeks in the Norfolk and Norwich hospital where Sticky visited whenever possible. After her spell in hospital, Jean had moved with Gail to lodgings in a terraced house in Fakenham where they saw much more of Sticky. On 2 December, he visited and told Jean he was flying that night. She argued, 'Surely you've done enough, Sticky?'

'Don't worry,' he said. 'It's a wing commander's moon tonight.'

It was Sunday morning at 10 o'clock before Jock Reid knew Sticky had gone flying and who had gone with him. 'When I met some of the boys who were at church, they said, "Oh, so you got back". I replied that I hadn't been anywhere. I didn't even know the F/Sgt who was his navigator that night.' This was not the first time that something like this happened. 'In Pomiglicino d' Ario (Naples) after a rowdy party, he went off with a friend. I was asleep but got up and waited for 3½ hours till he returned. They had attacked boats in a harbour (suicide). It all came as a shock to me on the morning of 3 December.' Two crews took off early on ASR patrols to search the North Sea but they met with no success. Intermittent rain with much low cloud and gale-force southerly winds made the task even more difficult. The only

*W/C Sticky Murphy, CO of 23 Squadron, as he is always remembered. (Tom Cushing Collection)*

*High jinks at the home of local farmer Kedric Thistleton-Smith near Little Snoring where weekend Pimms parties were a favourite of Mosquito crews. As usual Sticky Murphy* (left) *and Sammy Hoare* (pointing) *led the way. S/L Johnny Booth DFC\* of 239 Squadron, who with F/O K. Dear DFC, shot down two Bf 110s on 7/8 July, stands above all the rest. (Jean Bunting)*

information that came through, quite early in the morning was that the Squadron would be stood down for the night. Jock Reid recalls, 'There was no mourning, spirits were kept up. In fact that Sunday night there was a party at North Creake, to which 23 Squadron were invited. It went ahead as usual.'

The flight to and from the target had passed without incident but approaching the Zuider Zee on the return, Murphy's aircraft was hit by flak. Murphy had been Squadron Commander for almost a year and a flight commander for some months before. On 4 December, Sgt Pieter de Jong of the military police at Wezep, and two labourers, went to the scene of the crashed Mosquito. Close by the two bodies of Sticky

*Jock Reid (left), Sticky Murphy's navigator, who missed the fateful 2 December Intruder trip to Gütersloh, F/Sgt Darbon (right) went in his place. (Tom Cushing Collection)*

Murphy and Douglas Darbon, de Jong found a silver cigarette case, twisted by the inferno, with the words 'A. M. Murphy RAF' engraved on it. (It was later sent to the Air Ministry in London with other effects.) The labourers laid the bodies into two coffins and took them to the cemetery at Oldebroek. Sammy Hoare broke the news to Jean. On 10 December, a postagram was received from ACM Arthur T. Harris, which was forwarded to Jean. Four days earlier Sticky had been awarded a Bar to his DSO.

Squadron Leader Philip Russell was promoted wing commander and with the promotion the task of assuming Murphy's mantle. Philip Russell had suffered the after-effects of untreated diphtheria contracted in Sardinia but after treatment at the RAF rehabilitation unit at Loughborough College he had returned to the Squadron on 7 October completely recovered. Returning to the squadron had been a bit of a wrench as he admits.

The rehabilitation unit was run by Dan Maskell of subsequent tennis fame. I had to learn to walk again, helped with lots of massage from attractive nurses and swimming lessons with even more attractive ones. At the end of September I went for an RAF medical examination and (and here I have to admit rather shamefacedly) to my mild disappointment I was passed fit for flying duties. The European picture had changed considerably since we had left the UK and our targets were now principally in Germany and all rather heavily defended. In December we were fitted with radar and I took on a new radar operator, Hugh Boland, who was as mad as a hatter and totally without a trace of fear. As we were crossing the enemy coast amid curtains of flak, he would laugh out loud and say, 'Gosh, isn't that pretty?' and he meant it!

He also carried a flute stuck in his flying jacket and would play happily to himself until I told him to belt up and find out where we were. His hobby on the ground was making up anything explosive such as bombs and rockets. He made a sort of Very pistol, and on the way home from a rather wild night in Norwich, during which we had stormed the Castle, he sat on the back step of the aircrew bus firing Very lights along the road at following traffic. Judging by their evasive action, it must have been quite upsetting, seeing these coloured lights bouncing along the road towards them. To be frank, in the aircraft I would sooner have had a navigator who was as frightened as I was but he did enjoy it so much.

Philip Russell would prove a very inspiring leader in the long tradition of 23 Squadron COs. He used to attend the daily briefings at 100 Group HQ at Bylaugh Hall near Swanton Morley, which was also home for the Mosquito Servicing Section and, conveniently, for aircraft of 100 Group Communications Flight. At the briefings, Russell recalls:

*W/C Philip Russell who assumed command of 23 Squadron at Little Snoring on the death of Sticky Murphy. (Philip Russell via Tom Cushing)*

It was fascinating to watch the plot being hatched out, and then, on the next day to be able to see what results had been achieved. It all worked out very well and the losses in Bomber Command fell dramatically. The Germans very much resented our efforts to prevent their night-fighters becoming airborne. The airfield flak was increased heavily and we lost rather a lot of crews. We were quite often within sight of the mainstream bomber attack and a big raid was a most dramatic sight.

A big raid was indeed an impressive sight, probably even the Germans thought so on their *Würzburg* radar scopes. Of course, for reasons of great secrecy, the vast majority in 100 Group were not privy to the over-all picture. Crews, unaware of the important role they were playing, could easily become disillusioned. Many resented being used as 'bait' night after night. Being restricted to dropping nothing more volatile than *Window* did little for their psyches. Planning for 100 Group operations took place at Bylaugh Hall, a beautiful mansion in secluded woodland near RAF Swanton Morley where AVM Addison and his staff approved the night's complex RCM and *Spoof* operations. Battle summaries for the previous night's work went each day to 52 different recipients in 12 groups and nine OTUs, as well as to the Air Ministry, the HQs of Fighter and Bomber Commands, and 25 stations and squadrons within 100 Group itself. Even Section 22, its opposite number in the South-West Pacific, was kept appraised of the role 100 Group was playing.

Throughout 1944, the Fortresses of 214 Squadron and the Liberators of 223 Squadron had been 'Jostling' for every major bombing raid. By December, all were of still greater assistance, being fully equipped with *Carpet* (anti-*Würzburg*)) and *Piperack* (anti-SN-2) besides *Jostle* (anti-HF and anti-VHF). Mosquitoes began operating this month as jammers. Their role was a dual one. They flew to target areas on routes which took them well

*Throughout 1944, the Fortresses of 214 Squadron (BIII BU-W is pictured) and Liberators of 223 Squadron had been 'Jostling' for every major bombing raid. By December, these aircraft were fully equipped with Carpet (anti-*Würzburg*) and Piperack (anti-SN-2) besides Jostle (anti-HF and anti-VHF).*

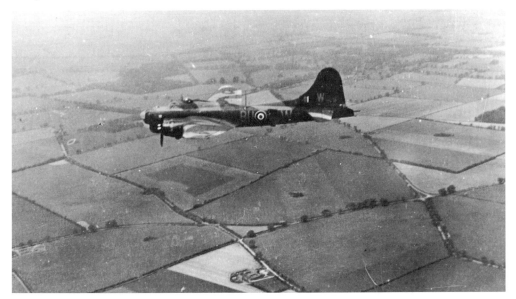

clear of the Main Force and on the way they made 'Y' recordings of enemy R/T traffic. Arriving at the target area, they jammed the enemy AI with *Piperack* and they stayed there until well after the attack was over, thus covering the withdrawal of stragglers. It was intended to increase and prolong the AI jamming in the target areas to which the enemy fighters would ultimately gravitate. During December, the Mandrel screen and *Window* Forces also kept up the good work of confusion and diversion. The Ruhr was still the favourite target, and *Window* flooding continued to be used with success. Even though 141, 169 and 239 Squadrons would not shoot down any enemy aircraft during the month, their part in the overall scheme of things was of great importance. This started on 1/2 December when a *Spoof Window* attack on the Ruhr by 49 aircraft of 100 Group with no losses among the 81 heavies that attacked Karlsruhe, Duisburg and Hallendorf, was supported by *Intruder* and high-level patrols by the *Serrate* Squadrons. They would continue this type of operation throughout the month.

The following night, 2/3 December, was again judged successful, with only two aircraft missing from the 504 dispatched to Hagen and Giessen. The operation was supported by 110 aircraft of 100 Group, losing one aircraft (Murphy), and claiming two aircraft destroyed in the air. Low-level *Intruder* squadrons bombed enemy airfields and strafed rolling stock. On patrol at Fassburg airfield, F/O F. X. A. Huls and F/O Joe Kinet of 515 Squadron saw four twin-engined aircraft on the ground and attacked them. Two He 177s were set on fire and claimed as destroyed. A Ju 88 was destroyed by F/L Taylor of 157 Squadron a little to the east of Stagen at 21:36 hours. Capt Tarald Weisteen, a Norwegian serving in 85 Squadron, obtained a contact at 5 miles going west across the target area. Range was closed to 4,000–5,000 ft, and at 2,000 ft it was identified as a Bf 110. Weisteen opened fire at 200 yards and

portions of the aircraft broke off and the starboard engine caught fire before the Bf 110 spun down. The explosion could be seen through the cloud half a minute later. A 223 Squadron Liberator rear gunner obtained a visual on an aircraft carrying an orange light on the starboard quarter which closed very fast at 2,000 yards. He ordered the pilot to corkscrew starboard and nothing more was seen. It was presumed to be a German jet.

There were no 100 Group operations on 3/4 December. An outstanding piece of spoofery was on 4/5 December when 892 heavies set out for Karlsruhe, Heilbron, Hagen and Hamm in the north and south of the Ruhr. The *Window* Force (altogether 112 aircraft of 100 Group were aloft, including a Liberator of 223 Squadron, captained by F/L Haslie on the Squadron's first target patrol at Karlsruhe) went straight into 'Happy Valley', supported by PFF marking, and held not less than 90–100 fighters in the area until much too late for their deployment against the heavies. Losses to the Main Force were kept to 15 aircraft, or 1.5 per cent of the force. The Mk IV AI Squadrons obtained numerous contacts in the Ruhr area, but AI was mainly unworkable due to heavy interference from *Window*. Contacts in the south showed great superiority in speed and in all cases drew away from the aircraft. Low-level *Intruder* squadrons, meanwhile, bombed airfields but results were unobserved due to adverse weather conditions. Victories were recorded by the Mk X AI Squadrons. A contact was obtained by F/L Taylor of 157 Squadron in the Frankfurt area at 4½ miles range. He chased it for 10 minutes, the enemy all the time taking violent evasive action. Taylor closed to 1,500 ft and identified it as a Bf 110. At 250 yards he gave it a 2-second burst from dead astern. The Bf 110 burst into flames, dived and exploded on the ground near Limburg. His colleague, F/L Mathews, obtained a contact in the Ruhr area at 5 miles range and chased it for 40 minutes before he identified it as a Ju 88. Taylor dispatched it near Dortmund.

The 23-year-old F/L Richard 'Dicky' Goucher and 33-year-old F/L C. H. 'Tiny' Bullock of 85 Squadron completed their patrol and set course for Swannington. These men had crewed up in North Africa in 1943 and they would remain together until the end of the war, being posted to 151 Squadron at Hunsdon on 18 January 1945. Thoughts of home were abandoned when a *Monica* contact was obtained. Tiny Bullock successfully converted it to a forward contact at 8,000 ft range. The enemy aircraft was going in the direction of Karlsruhe at 2,000 ft. In the light of flames from Karlsruhe, Dickie Goucher identified it as a Bf 110. He gave it two bursts without apparent result but a third put out the port engine. The fourth caused the aircraft to explode and it crashed in the vicinity of Germersheim close to a red beacon. Almost immediately another contact was obtained at 4 miles range.

After several orbits around the beacon a visual was obtained on a Bf 110 at 2,000 ft. Two short bursts caused the enemy aircraft to explode and crash in approximately the same place as the first one. Goucher and Bullock's Mosquito was struck by flying debris but returned to Swannington safely.

The German night-fighter force was run ragged by 85 Squadron. At 10,000 ft, Capt Sven Heglund obtained a contact 6 miles ahead and well below – an aircraft doing a mild corkscrew. He chased down to 2,500 ft and overshot but obtained a visual on a Bf 110. Contact was maintained and finally a visual was obtained at 400 ft and held. The Norwegian gave the Bf 110 a 1-second burst which caused the Messerschmitt to catch fire and side-slip into the ground near Rothenburg where it exploded. Flying Officer Ginger Owen and Flying Officer J. S.V. McAllister got an AI contact in the Ruhr area at 4½ miles range and chased it for 26 minutes before a visual on a Ju 88 was obtained before shooting it down. It was 85

*157 Squadron gathered on the steps of the Officers' Mess at Swannington. Front row, left to right: F/L J. R. V. Smythe; Stevens; Chisholm; W/C H. D. U. Dennison (CO, March– June 1944); Towser; F/L J. O. Mathews DFC; S/L J. G. 'Ben' Benson; S/L Dolly Doleman. Others identified are Wylde (back row, 3rd from right); to his right is F/L Lewis Brandon; Smythe's navigator, F/O Waters, (2nd from far right). (Richard Doleman via Dr Theo Boiten)*

Squadron's 100th enemy aircraft at night.

Flight Lieutenant Edward Hedgecoe finished an uneventful patrol except for chases and visuals on other Mosquitoes before setting course for home. However, a minute later, a contact at 4 miles head on was obtained. The 34-year-old former accountant officer had remustered to aircrew and joined 85 Squadron where he crewed up with F/L Norman Bamford. On 24/25 March they had a narrow escape when their Mosquito, *O-Orange*, had been severely scorched with the rudder fabric being burned away following their shooting down of a Ju 188 at 300 ft range off the south coast. Hedgecoe had nursed *O-Orange* back to base where a piece of debris from the Ju 188 was removed from the port

wing. He and Bamford both received the DFC after this encounter. This harrowing experience appears to have had an effect on Hedgecoe who now employed a more judicious approach on the bogey behind which he turned and gave chase for 8 minutes. Over Detmold airfield at range of 1,000 ft at 6,000 ft the unmistakable outline of a Ju 88 was made out. Its identity was confirmed at 300 ft. Dropping back to 150 yards, Hedgecoe gave it three short bursts and saw strikes all over the aircraft. Burning debris flew in all directions. Hedgecoe overshot and was unable to regain contact before a shortage of petrol forced him to set course for Brussels/Melsbroek to refuel. He put in a claim for a Ju 88 probably destroyed.

*F/L E. R. Hedgecoe and F/Sgt J. R. Whitham of 85 Squadron shot down three Bf 110s in December 1944, including two west of Münster on the night of the 6/7th, all in O-Orange. Hedgecoe pressed home his attacks from close in, risking the kind of damage seen here which almost claimed his Mosquito NF XII which was very badly damaged during the destruction of a Ju 188 on 24/25 March 1944. This kind of damage was experienced by victorious Mosquito crews in 100 Group, including Denis Welfare and Derek Bellis on 11/12 June 1944. (via Philip Birtles)*

On 5/6 December, 553 aircraft attacked Soest, Duisburg, Nürnberg and Mannheim. Some 76 aircraft of 100 Group supported the operation which cost one heavy bomber. Reports indicated: 'there was probably no fighter reaction. Only a few contacts were obtained. This was probably due to adverse weather conditions over enemy airfields.' A very severe ground frost heralded a bright and clear morning on 6 December, and all anticipation was for a maximum effort. Low-level *Intruders* bombed and strafed enemy airfields but the weather conditions were not good for this type of operation. That night, 1,291 aircraft attacked Bergesburg, Osnabrück, Giessen, Berlin, Schwerte and Hanau. Some 89 aircraft of 100 Group supported the operations and lost one aircraft. The heavies lost 21 of their number, or 1.7 per cent of the force. Squadron Leader Neil Reeves DSO DFC and Flying Officer Phillips, attached to the BSDU, were carrying out a *Perfectos* patrol when they obtained a contact west of Giessen at 12 miles range. They followed and eventually got a visual on a Bf 110. After a long chase

they shot it down. It was the first victory to *Perfectos*.

Bad weather did not prevent crews of 157 and 85 Squadrons from running up the score. A contact was obtained at 5 miles range by F/L Jimmy Mathews of 157 Squadron, which he chased for 13 minutes through several orbits and changes of height. A visual was gained at 1,000 ft range on a Bf 110 with long-range tanks. He closed to just 50 yards and gave it a 1-second burst, scoring strikes all over the fuselage. The Bf 110 burst into flames and crashed at Limburg. A second contact at 5 miles led to a visual on a Ju 88 at 1,500 ft range. Mathews gave it a short burst from close range and the enemy aircraft broke its back and crashed 15 miles south-west of Giessen. Squadron Leader Dolly Doleman dived to 11,000 ft on the bomber route home, closed in and identified a Bf 110 which he then shot down in the Kitzingen area.

Flight Lieutenant Edward Hedgecoe and Flying Officer Norman Bamford of the Fighter Interception Unit at Ford were attached to 85 Squadron at Swannington

*Mosquito Mk VI with W/C N. A. Reeves DSO, DFC, who commanded 169 Squadron at Great Massingham January 1945 – August 1945, in the cockpit. On 6/7 December 1944, flying with the BSDU, S/L Reeves and F/O Phillips shot down a Bf 110 west of Giessen. (Tom Cushing Collection)*

for a 10-day period. Hedgecoe took off in *O-Orange*, a 85 Squadron Mosquito XXX, with F/Sgt J. R. Witham as his radar operator. They obtained several contacts at 15,000 ft. One was selected and chased westwards for 10 minutes. A visual was obtained at 800 ft on a Bf 110. It was being flown by Hptm Helmut Bergmann of 8/NJG4. Hedgecoe gave it a 1-second burst between the exhaust flames. It crashed and exploded on the ground 25 miles west of Münster. Several more contacts were obtained in the target area. One at 4 miles coming towards the Mosquito was selected. After a 5-minute chase, a visual was obtained on another Bf 110. A 1-second burst produced strikes and a flash on the port engine. Visual was lost. When it was regained, the Bf 110 was going very slowly with its port engine feathered. Hedgecoe closed in again but overshot due to ice on the windscreen. He tried a second time but the Mosquito stalled and the enemy aircraft was lost. He claimed it as a 'damaged'. (A Ju 88 was also claimed as a 'damaged' by Fortress gunner, F/O Corke of 214 Squadron, while on a *Jostle* patrol.)

For two nights following, no operations were flown by 100 Group. Then on 9/10 December, when 79 aircraft of 8 Group attacked Duisburg, Koblenz, and Berlin, 100 Group dispatched 68 aircraft. One of their number, a Halifax of 171 Squadron, piloted by W/O Powe RAAF, failed to return from windowing Koblenz. All Mosquito patrols were 'completely uneventful', probably due to adverse weather conditions over Germany. No operations were flown the following night for the same reason. The morning of 11 December was much milder and warmer in contrast to the previous day's sleet and rain but that night's operations were also scrubbed. Late that evening, the Met gave crews the 'gen' that it was to be 'a lovely day tomorrow', but then it broke dull and wet. That night, 12/13 December, 592 bombers attacked Essen and Osnabrück. (Six

aircraft, or 1 per cent of the force, failed to return.) Ninety-one aircraft were dispatched 100 Group. No. 192 Squadron played its first operational role as an airborne jammer when the first Mosquito fitted with two channels of *Piperack* operated. (In time, all the squadron's Mosquitoes would be fitted with *Piperack*. A dual role was played by the aircraft: signals investigation continued to and from the target; *Piperack* itself was used over the target). The Mk IV AI squadrons, meanwhile, obtained only two contacts but no combats resulted and in the main, the low-level *Intruder* squadrons were once again defeated by the weather. Not so 85 and 157 Squadrons. A contact was gained by S/L Branse Burbridge and Bill Skelton at 7,000 ft and 2½ miles. They followed it at a low air speed through port and starboard orbits. A visual at 1,000 ft confirmed the contact as a Ju 88. Burbridge gave it a 1½-second burst from 500 ft and set one of the engines on fire. The Ju 88 G-1, Wrk Nr 714530 of 6.NJG4, crashed at Gutersloh airfield. Uffz Heinrich Brue (pilot); Uffz Emil Hoffharth (radar op.) and Uffz Wolfgang Rautert (AG) were all killed.

Flying towards Essen, another contact was obtained at 4 miles and 12,000 ft. Burbridge and Skelton dashed towards the target area at high speed and climbing. Luckily, a burst of flak illuminated a Bf 110, and Burbridge closed to 400 ft for final identification. He gave the Bf 110 ½-second burst from 500 ft and the enemy aircraft exploded before spinning down in flames, the tail unit breaking off. It crashed about 2 miles west of Essen. Burbridge and Skelton finished their second tours early in 1945. Both were awarded Bars to their DSOs to go with the Bars they had already awarded to their DFCs. Burbridge with Skelton finished the war as the top-scoring night-fighter crew in the RAF with a final total of 21 victories. Bob Braham and W/C John Cunningham both destroyed 19 enemy aircraft at night. Post-war, Branse

Burbridge became a lay preacher, while Bill Skelton was ordained as a clergyman in the Church of England and became chaplain of Clare College, Cambridge.

Capt Eric Fossum and F/O S. A. Hider, another Norwegian crew on the strength of 85 Squadron, obtained a contact crossing port to starboard. A hard turn brought the contact dead ahead at a range of 4,500 ft and he closed in. At 300 ft, the silhouette was made out to be that of a Ju 88. Fossum dropped back to 600 ft and fired a short burst. Strikes on the tail unit were seen and debris flew off. A further burst produced more strikes on the fuselage and the Junkers spun to port. A few seconds later, a faint glow was seen through the clouds.

Edward Hedgecoe and F/Sgt J. R. Whitham in *O-Orange* again obtained a contact at 6 miles range, head on and below them. Violent evasive action followed before Hedgecoe was able to close to 1,000 ft and obtain a visual. He closed right in and positively identified it as a Bf 110. Hedgecoe dropped back to 75 yards and fired a short burst which caused an explosion in the fuselage. The Bf 110 dived steeply, burning furiously, and disappeared into 10/10ths cloud at 7,000–8,000 ft, 20 miles south of Hagen. A second contact was obtained at 4 miles range, slightly above them and orbiting. It eventually settled down on a course towards Essen. Hedgecoe closed the range to 2,000 ft and saw exhaust flames at 1,000 ft. Obtaining a visual, he closed right in and recognized it as a Bf 110. A 2-second burst from 100 yards caused the enemy aircraft to disintegrate and fall vertically in approximately the same area as the first one. (Later, Hedgecoe and Norman Bamford, were posted to 151 Squadron at Hunsdon where the promoted Hedgecoe was a flight commander. Both died in a crash-landing on their first flight with the squadron. Hedgecoe had shot down eight enemy aircraft and Bamford had taken part in the destruction of 10.) Wing Commander K. H. P. Beauchamp of 157 Squadron got a couple of squirts off at a Bf 110 in a port orbit over a lit airfield believed to be Ashaffenburg. Strikes were observed before visual was lost and his AI set became u/s. His radar operator/navigator could not regain contact and Beauchamp could only claim a 'damaged'.

The thirteenth day of December broke under a very heavy frost and towards mid-morning fog 'thick enough to shame any Manchester could boast about' enveloped stations in Norfolk and operations were scrubbed very early. Therefore, 100 Group did not support Bomber Command operations in north Denmark and Norway that night, or *Gardening* operations on 14/15 December. On 15/16 December, 73 aircraft were used to support operations by 409 aircraft which attacked Ludwigshaven, Osnabrück, Hannover and Duisburg. Mosquitoes from 239 Squadron led a *Spoof* raid by a small force and dropped 500-pounders and 250 lb yellow target indicators through solid cloud over the target, spoofing was adjudged successful; only two heavy bombers were lost (5 per cent of the force). Only two AI contacts leading to chases were made. The following night, 100 Group stood down again. On 17/18 December, 96 aircraft in 100 Group, including a *Spoof* raid by 239 Squadron on Mannheim, supported a massive operation by 1,174 aircraft which bombed Ulm, München, Duisburg, Hanau, Münster and Halendorf. Dickie Goucher and Tiny Bullock obtained a contact about 40 miles from Ulm. Their prey was above them and because of evasive action was at first thought to be a Mosquito. Goucher closed to 2,000 ft and got a glimpse of a green resin light. At 1,000 ft, he obtained a visual and Dickie Goucher closed to 400 ft. It was a Bf 110. A short burst set fire to the port engine and the Bf 110 pulled up and dived, hitting the ground about 8 miles from Ulm where it continued to burn.

No. 157 Squadron also reaped rich

rewards this night. About 5 miles west of Duisburg, W/O Taylor obtained a contact at 8 miles range and 13,000 ft. He chased it for 5 minutes, closing to 1,500 ft and obtained a visual on a Bf 110. Closing to 300 ft, he pumped a 2-second burst of cannon into the Bf 110's airframe and it exploded, covering the Mosquito with oil and debris. It crashed north-west of Neiss. Thirty miles north-north-east of Ulm, another Bf 110 was shot down by F/Sgt Leigh. One of the crew bailed out before it crashed in flames. A Ju 88 was damaged by S/L James Gilles Benson and F/L Lewis Brandon during a dog-fight lasting an exhausting 40 minutes after obtaining the contact near a cone of searchlights. Benson had been forced to fire blind after a 4-star cartridge burst the gloom while he was not more than 50 yards behind, completely destroying his night vision. However, when the enemy aircraft was silhouetted by the falling cartridge he again opened fire, scoring strikes behind the cockpit. A second cartridge was fired and the Mosquito was held by the searchlights. At 800 ft now, Benson could not get into a firing position again and contact was lost.

On 18/19 December, 308 bombers attacked Gdynia, Münster, Nürnberg and Danzig. Some 48 aircraft of 100 Group supported the operation. Four heavies, and a Mosquito flown by F/O Desmond T. Tull DFC and F/O Peter J. Cowgill DFC, of 85 Squadron, failed to return. Tull accidentally rammed Bf 110 G9+CC of Stab IV./NJG1 flown by Hptm Adolph Breves who was coming into land at Düsseldorf airfield at 22:30 hours. A large part of one of the wings of the 110 was torn off but Breves (who finished the war with 18 victories) managed to land the aircraft without further damage. The Bf110 was repaired and test flown on 31 December. Tull and Cowgill, who were both killed, are buried in Reichswald Forest Cemetery near Kleef.

Low-level *Intruders* reported no combats and the Mk IV AI squadrons did not operate. The one victory this night went to F/L William Taylor and F/O Jeffery N. Edwards of 157 Squadron. At first their patrol was uneventful. Having set course for base, they ran into *Window* but were able to pick up a contact at about 6 miles range. Their target was climbing steeply and orbiting. At 2,000 ft and 80° above they obtained a visual. Taylor was nearly overshooting so he dropped back and weaved gently. Another visual was obtained 30° above him. After chasing for another 5 minutes, the contact was identified as a He 219 He 219A-O Wrk Nr 190229 G9+GH of 1/NJG1. Taylor opened fire from 250

*F/O Jeffery N. Edwards, 22-year-old navigator, 157 Squadron, buried in the churchyard of St Peter's Church on the airfield at Swannington. He was killed on 22 December 1944 when a Mosquito NF XIX piloted by F/L William Taylor crashed while attempting to land after informing Flying Control over the R/T that they had no aileron control. (Author)*

yards but the Mosquito was caught in the enemy night-fighter's slipstream and his shooting was erratic. Strikes were observed and minor explosions appeared in the fuselage before the Owl turned slowly to port and peeled off. Visual was lost, but the Heinkel was followed on AI until contact was lost at 12,000 ft. A few seconds later, it exploded on the ground at Suedlohn. (Uffz. Scheuerlein (pilot) bailed out. Uffz Günther Heinze (radar op.) was KIA. Taylor and Edwards were killed on 22/23 December when they crashed while attempting to make an approach to land at Swannington after informing Flying Control over the R/T that they had no aileron control.

Bad weather interfered again before operations resumed on 21/22 December. Only 28 aircraft supported 475 heavies attacking Köln, Bonn, Politz and Schneidemuhl. Low-level *Intruders* and Mk IV AI Mosquitoes did not operate. The only contact of the night was obtained by W/C K. H. P. Beauchamp south of Bonn. He followed it for 15 minutes. North of Frankfurt, he identified it as a Ju 88 and

shot it down. Three bombers failed to return. More Ju 88 losses occurred on the following night, 22/23 December, when 45 aircraft were dispatched to cover 274 heavies attacking Koblenz and Bingen.

High-level ASH patrols were carried out but no contacts resulted. The mercurial Mk X AI squadrons worked their magic once again with a wizard prang or two. Branse Burbridge, and Dolly Doleman, both of 85 Squadron, destroyed a Bf 110 and a Ju 88 respectively while Ginger Owen went on the rampage. He shot down a Bf 110 north of Saarbrücken. Then a *Monica* contact was obtained almost immediately afterwards. It was converted to AI at 14,000 ft range. At 1200 ft, visual was obtained, and confirmed as a Ju 88 on closing dead below it. Owen gave it a 'medium' burst from 150 yards which set the port engine on fire before crashing in the same area as the Bf 110. Twenty minutes later, a third contact was obtained 4 miles ahead. Closing to 2,000 ft, a visual was obtained well above him. It was another Ju 88 and it was taking evasive action. A short deflection burst scored strikes on the port wing and pieces flew off.

*Heinkel 219A-5/R1 Owl fitted with SN2 and FuG 212 radar. F/L William Taylor and F/O Jeffery N. Edwards of 157 Squadron shot down one of these formidable fighters on the night of 18/19 December 1944 in the Osnabrück area. Taylor and Edwards were killed landing at Swannington three nights later. The 219A-7/R5 version of the Uhu was developed especially for anti-Mosquito operations being powered by two 1,900 hp Junkers Jumo 213E engines with MW-50 water-methanol injection. (Hans-Peter Dabrowski)*

The Ju 88 dived vertically and contact was lost at 7,000 ft. Four minutes later, an explosion occurred on the ground. Flight Lieutenant Hannowin obtained a visual on a Ju 88 but contact was lost because of violent evasive action by the enemy aircraft. For 24 minutes, W/O Taylor chased a contact. When a visual was obtained, it was seen to be a Ju 88, and throwing out *Düppel* (*Window*). The Mosquito overshot and contact was lost. A 199 Squadron Stirling crew obtained a visual on a Fw 190 dead astern at 450 yards. Both the rear and mid-upper gunners opened fire before the enemy fighter could attack.

On 23/24 December, 61 aircraft of 100 Group supported operations by Bomber Command when 105 heavies attacked cities in Germany. Low-level *Intruders* had no combats but took advantage of the moonlight to bomb and strafe a variety of aerodromes and any other targets. Again the aerial victories went to the Swannington squadrons. A contact was obtained by F/L G. C. Chapman and F/L J. Stockley of 85 Squadron at 8 miles range and 11,000 ft in the Mannheim area, which turned out to be a Bf 110. After a prolonged dogfight, Chapman finally shot it down just south of Mainz. Crews from 157 Squadron scored two victories this night: F/L R. J. V. Smythe and F/O Waters destroyed a Ju 88 about 10 miles west of Koblenz while 'Ben' Benson and Brandon destroyed a Ju 88.

On Christmas Eve, the Mosquito squadrons in 100 Group celebrated the festive season in style, knocking down five enemy aircraft and damaging three on the ground. Bomber Command dispatched 228 aircraft to Bonn and Köln while 86 aircraft of 100 Group supported the operation. Low-level *Intruders* covered enemy airfields and carried out *Ranger* operations in the Breslau area. Locomotives, rolling stock and motor transport were bombed and strafed by the Mk IV AI Mosquito squadrons operating as low-level *Intruders*. Meanwhile, W/C H. C. Kelsey DFC, the new 515 Squadron CO, and F/O Edward M. 'Smitty' Smith took off from Little Snoring in the afternoon for a night *Intruder* operation. Edward Smith recalls:

We had been interested in night-fighter training areas and felt the Breslau area might be fruitful. We landed at Laon/Juvincourt to refuel as this station was supposed to provide facilities for Bomber Command aircraft. On arrival we found some panic on there as the Battle of the Bulge had just started. However, we managed to make arrangements to refuel and have a quick meal before starting off at 16:50 hours across S Germany, passing near Bayreuth all quite low level; 200–300 ft.

The CO and his navigator reached Rosenborn airfield at 19:52 hours. It was not lit, but several aircraft were seen parked around the perimeter. Kelsey made several low runs over the airfield but, as there was

*Mosquito NS933 crewed by F/O Glenn Graham RCAF and F/L Ayling of 515 Squadron, at Little Snoring. (Tom Cushing Collection)*

some ground haze with poor visibility, he decided to continue his patrol and return to Rosenborn later. They had the same problems at Ohlau airfield so they returned to Rosenborn. Several Ju 52 transports were seen parked at the south end of the airfield while a single He 111 was parked on the north side near a radio station. Kelsey took the Heinkel first, broadside on, from 1,300 ft down to 150 ft, breaking off at 200 ft range. Kelsey's cannon shells ripped into the Heinkel but it did not catch fire. Then the crew turned their attentions to the Ju 52s and a lone Ju 88. Again Kelsey attacked from broadside on, breaking off the attack at 200 ft range at a height of 150 ft. Kelsey claimed one Ju 52 and the Ju 88 as 'damaged'. Smith adds, 'On the way back we damaged two trains severely in the Prague area.'

The Mk X AI Mosquitoes, meanwhile, enjoyed almost total air superiority over the Nachtjagdgeschwader this night. A Bf 110 was chased through several orbits by S/L James Benson DFC and F/L Lewis Brandon DFC of 157 Squadron before the night-fighter ace fired two bursts at the fleeing enemy machine's port exhausts. A second burst set the engine on fire and Benson was forced to veer violently away to avoid the flying debris. The Bf 110 crashed about 10 miles west of Mainz at 18:36 hours. Twenty minutes later, Capt Sven Heglund and F/O Robert Symon of 85 Squadron destroyed a Bf 110 in the Wiesbaden area. The Messerschmitt crashed 20 miles north of Frankfurt. Four minutes later, F/L Jimmy Mathews and W/O Alan Penrose of 157 Squadron blasted a Ju 88 of 5/NJG2 out of the sky, 3 miles south-west of Köln. Three men bailed out before the aircraft crashed near Roermond.

At 19:05 hours, S/L Dolly Doleman and F/L Bunny Bunch of 157 Squadron saw an aircraft 'hit the deck' dead below them near Siegen. Doleman reported:

Things seemed pretty dead, so we went

towards Cologne and just as we arrived, obtained a contact; range 6 miles well below. Overhauled fairly quickly and just managed to slow down into an ideal position, where we identified an Me 110 doing an orbit at 9,000 ft. I think the crew must have been full of the festive spirit as we were directly up moon at 600 ft when we opened fire with a very long burst. The pride of the Luftwaffe caught fire immediately, but we gave them another burst just for fun. He went down and pranged just west of Cologne at 19:05.

The Bf 110 was G9+OT of 9./NJG1, flown by Hptm Heinz Strüning, *Ritterkreuz mit Eichenlaub* (Knight's Cross with Oak leaves) and 56 night victories in NJG 1 and NJG 2. It crashed at Bergisch Gladbach/Rheinland. The Bordfunker and Bordschütze bailed out safely but Strüning hit the tail of his Bf 110 and was killed. His body was found two months later.

Doleman and Bunch immediately had another contact at 10 miles, well above them. They chased at 'full bore'. At debriefing Doleman reported:

Luckily the tyke dived down and we closed in very rapidly, eventually slightly overshooting, about 50 yards to port, having a wizard view of another Me 110. We did a hard port orbit and picked him up at 3 miles. By this time we were at 8,000 ft going NW slap across the Ruhr. We closed in and identified again and opened fire from about 500 ft with a long burst. He caught fire and pieces of debris fell off including one quite large piece. He continued flying evenly, so we gave him three more bursts, when he went down in the Duisburg area at 1921 hours.

The aircraft, G9+GR of 7./NJG1, crashed near Soppenrade at 19:22 hours due to 'engine failure'. The pilot and Bordfunker survived; Gfr Wilhelm Ruffleth was injured. Doleman characteristically concluded. 'Cannot write any more as there is a party on in the mess.' The night's bag was good reason for Yuletide celebration, especially since no operations were flown on 25/26 December or 26/27 December.

Also over Christmas, 462 (RAAF) Squadron, the last unit to join 100 Group, and equipped with Halifax BIIIs, transferred to Foulsham airfield, initially as part of the Window Force. The reaction of crews commanded by W/C D. Shannon DFC to being taken off bombing operations in 4 Group in order to drop strips of silver paper in 100 Group is unknown, but bombs were carried until installation of *Airborne Cigar* was completed in March and the Aussies could begin jamming operations over the Reich.

Staying at The Crown in Fakenham over Christmas were six wives and girlfriends of 23 Squadron crews. At lunch time on 28 December, F/O Lewis Heath, a pilot, who was on leave, volunteered to go to Snoring

to collect the mail. He did not return until the following day. His wife Pauline asked, 'Where have you been?' Lewis smiled and said, Oslo Fiord! Despite protests he and his navigator, F/Sgt Jack Thompson, had been told they were 'On' for an escort to Norway for Halifax mine-layers of 6 Group!

On 31 December/1 January five aircraft were destroyed, two of them the first victories using ASH. The first went to S/L C. V. Bennett DFC and F/L R. A. Smith of 515 Squadron. In the Lovns Bredning area during an *Intruder* patrol to Grove, Bennett and Smith's Mosquito was fired at with tracer from Oblt August Györy's Ju 88 of 4./NJG2. Bennett returned fire at 400 yards with a 2-second burst of cannon and strikes were seen on the port wing. A second burst cut the Ju 88 in two. Györy spun in and dropped into Lim Fiord. 515 Squadron received a congratulatory signal from AVM Addison; "Heartiest congratu-

*With Serrate's effectiveness rendered useless by the introduction of SN-2 equipment in German night-fighters, Nos 141, 169 and 239 Squadrons were taken off Serrate operations and switched to day and night Ranger sorties. As can be seen by 141 Squadron's 'Ranger Effort' they were very successful. (Author)*

| DATE | CREW | | RESULT |
|---|---|---|---|
| 21st Feb '45 | Young | Sanderson | |
| | Riner | Farnfield | |
| 24th Feb '45 | Young | Sanderson | |
| | Brearley | Sheldon | 1 Ju 88 b |
| 26th Feb '45 | Edwards | Lynn | 1½ Bandit D |
| | Brearley | Sheldon | |
| 28th Feb '45 | Burrowman | Griffiths | |
| 14th Apr '45 | Winn | Scott | |
| | Harriott | Barker | |
| | Riner | Farnfield | |
| 14th Apr '45 | Drew | Williams | |
| 16th Apr '45 | Drew | Williams | ½ Bandits |
| 17th Apr '45 | Brearley | Sheldon | |
| 18th Apr '45 | Bates | Field | 1 ½ Bandit |
| | Drew | Williams | 1 ½ Bandit |
| | Winn | Scott | 1 ½ Bandit |
| 23rd Apr '45 | Bates | Field | 1 ½ bandit |
| 24th Apr '45 | White | Allen | 1 ½ Bandit |

## 141 SQUADRON RANGER EFFORT

| DATE | CREW | | RESULT |
|---|---|---|---|
| 20th March '43 | W/c Braham | Blackburn | |
| | F/o Le Boutte | Parrott | |
| 22nd March '43 | W/c Braham | Blackburn | |
| 10th April '43 | W/c Braham | Blackburn | |
| 15th April '43 | F/o Thornton | Hall | |
| | sgt Judge | Blower | |
| 10th April '45 | W/c Braham | Blackburn | |
| | sgt Frost | Towler | |
| | F/L Maltby | Watts | |
| 17th April '43 | F/o Le Boutte | Parrott | |
| 18th April '43 | F/L Davis | Williams | x2 |
| 19th April '43 | F/o Sawyer | Smith, A. | x 2 |
| | F/o MacAndrew | Wilk | |
| 20th April '43 | F/o Kelsey | Smith, E. | |
| 23rd April '43 | F/o Le Boutte | Parrott | |
| 18th May '43 | F/L Maltby | Watts | |
| 17th Sept '44 | F/o Winn | Scott | |
| | F/L Anderson | Osborn | |
| | F/L Bates | Cadman | |
| | F/L Thatcher | Calvert | |
| | F/o Fisher | Watkins | |
| | F/L Rice | Rogerson | |
| 28th Sept '44 | F/o Edwards | Lynn | D |
| 30th Sept '44 | F/L Rice | Rogerson | |
| | F/L Anderson | Osborn | D |

*85 and 157 Squadrons found rich pickings among the Nachtjagdgeschwader in December 1944, particularly the Messerschmitt Bf 110 Gruppen. 85 Squadron shot down 13 Bf 110s and 157 Squadron, eight. The 110s pictured here are Bf 110G-4d/R3s of 7/NJG 3 with Lichtenstein FuG 220 SN-2 and low-drag aerials.*

lations on opening the batting for the Ashes". During the New Year's party which followed they were joined by S/L J. Tweedale and F/L L. Cunningham of 23 Squadron, who scored their Squadron's first victory using ASH, having destroyed a Ju 88 of NJG5 at Alhorn. (On 13 January Bennett and Smith were lost when they went down in the North Sea on the way home.) It brought the number of victories during the month to 37. It is no coincidence that 85 Squadron, which claimed 18 victories, and 157 Squadron, which claimed 13, were the only squadrons in 100 Group which were equipped with the excellent Mk X AI radar. *Intruder* incursions over Luftwaffe bases were being made with haunting regularity and there was much 'joy' as the predators enjoyed rich pickings from among the returning flocks of unsuspecting, weary, Nachtjagdgeschwader crews.

*ASH-equipped Mosquito RS566 of 515 Squadron at Little Snoring. On 31 December/1 January, S/L C. V. Bennett DFC, with F/L R. A. Smith, of 515 Squadron obtained the first ASH victory, when they destroyed a Ju 88 of NJG2 piloted by Oblt August Györy during an Intruder patrol to Grove. 23 Squadron scored its first victory using ASH when a Ju 88 was shot down at Alhorn this same night. (Tom Cushing Collection)*

# CHAPTER 11

# *NO JOY?*

At times when hope was fading,
They would patient vigil keep,
Rejoicing if their crew returned
But often they would weep.
They wept for those who ere the sun
Had warmed the fresh turned clod,
Had fought in their last battle
And were at peace with God.

S. F. RUFFLE

Crews of the Gruppenstab and the VIIIth and IXth Staffeln of III./NJG2 at Marx/Varel were given the usual meteorological and signals briefing on 31 December and the CO told the crews that, in view of the suitable weather conditions, an RAF raid was to be mounted that night. At 18:00 hours, his eight Ju 88s were ordered to take off. The first to take off was 4R+OS and sat at the end of the runway awaiting the signal when an Mosquito *Intruder* dropped a bomb which exploded on the runway about 30 metres from the Junkers. No damage was apparently suffered by 4R+OS and it took off after a short delay. The crew made for Hannover and soon they saw the first cascade flares. On arrival, they saw the incendiary bombs and fires. A four-engined bomber was seen to be held in searchlights and heading south-west. The *Naxos* and SN-2 of 4R+OS had been u/s for some time and the four-engined aircraft was lost. The Ju 88 first turned west-north-west in the hope of finding the bomber stream, but after 15 minutes the starboard engine cut out. It was a coolant leak, caused by the *Intruder*'s bomb.

The *Intruder* was crewed by Lewis Heath and Jack Thompson of 23 Squadron which had taken off from Little Snoring at 17:00 hours on 1 January. The Ju 88 pilot turned due east to return to Marx/Varel but soon afterwards, the crew, believing themselves to be over German territory and anxious to find their exact whereabouts, fired a recognition signal followed by two 'reds' which they repeated. They were then

162

surprised by a night-fighter attack from aft. The pilot lost control and all the crew bailed out. They all landed in Allied territory and were taken prisoner. The foregoing was extracted from one of the crew on interrogation and subsequently Air Commodore Chisholm hoped that F/O Heath would be credited with a destroyed enemy aircraft as it was considered that 4R+0S was hit by splinters from bombs dropped on the airfield by the Mosquito crew before take off.

On 1/2 January, when eight Halifaxes of 462 Squadron flew their first spoofing operation in 100 Group, Mosquitoes on bomber support covered heavy operations over Germany. Eight crews in 85 Squadron participated in a maximum effort in the Kiel and Ruhr areas while the Main Force attacked the Mittelland Canal, rail yards at Vohwinkel and Dortmund. Dickie Goucher and Tiny Bulloch chased a contact for 11

minutes before obtaining a visual. It was a Ju 188. Dickie Goucher gave the Junkers a couple of bursts and it fell in flames, crashing 10 miles north of Münster. Almost immediately, Tiny Bulloch got a second blip on his Mk X scope apparently dropping *Düppel*. Goucher got closer and they could see that their enemy was a Ju 88G. Dickie Goucher gave it a long burst from dead astern as the Junkers turned to port. Flying flaming debris struck the Mosquito causing it to vibrate badly and lose height. Goucher jettisoned his drop tanks and the port tank came over the top of the wing, damaging the tail plane and at the same time shearing off the pitot head. They landed safely at Brussels/Melsbroek and were flown home in a C-47 the next day.

Four Mosquitoes of 239 Squadron carried out low-level *Intruder* patrols. One of these, flown by F/O Walker with F/O J. R. Watkins, crashed on return at Narford

*Halifax BIII MZ913 Z5-N* Jane *of 462 (RAAF) Squadron which began operations in 100 Group on 1/2 January, and by the war's end had lost 23 Australian and 20 RAF aircrew on spoof and jamming operations. Note* ABC *transmission aerial under the nose. (via Jerry Scutts)*

Hall just north of RAF Marham and both were killed. One of the six Mosquitoes dispatched by 141 Squadron on a high-level ASH patrol was forced to land in France with oxygen trouble. Another, flown by F/L Ron Brearley with F/O John Sheldon, took off at 17:10 hours on a low-level *Intruder* patrol to the airfield at Lüneburg. They crossed in at Egmond, Holland at 17:49 hours at 200 ft and flew to Lüneburg arriving at 18:46. The airfield was lit on their approach but the lights were doused as they arrived. Brearley orbited for 10 minutes and as there was no activity flew off to the south. At 19:06 hours he approached the airfield again and again it was lit. The Mosquito orbited about 1 mile away and the crew saw the exhausts of an aircraft taking off but this was then lost. Four searchlights were exposed around the airfield, two pointing in their direction.

Brearley and Sheldon continued to patrol the airfield until 19:40 hours. When crossing Lüneburg airfield at about 100 ft they saw two very small green lights moving along the flarepath. It was an aircraft which had just landed. They executed a tight turn and came in over the flarepath and over the aircraft. Brearley opened fire. Many strikes were seen all over the enemy aircraft but it did not burn. They turned again, giving a longer approach, and once more Brearley opened fire on the German aircraft. Again many strikes were seen resulting in pieces being scattered in all directions. This time the German night-fighter burst into flames and burned furiously. Searchlights were exposed all over the area and flak came up all around them. Brearley took evasive action and then stood off and watched the enemy plane burn before setting course for home at 19:45 hours.

Meanwhile, F/O Frank Bocock and F/Sgt Snogger Rogers of 515 Squadron had found little joy in recent weeks. They had flown their nineteenth operation on 28 December, a flak patrol off Jelöy island in Norway in support of a raid by Lancasters. Strong winds had blown them south to the northern tip of Denmark on the way home. On the 30th, they flew all the way to

*Mosquito FB VIs of 515 Squadron at Little Snoring. Nearest aircraft is PZ347 3P-K. (Tom Cushing Collection)*

*F/L R. T. 'Dickie' Goucher of 85 Squadron, who, with F/L C. H. 'Tiny' Bullock, shot down two enemy aircraft north of Münster on the night of 2/3 January 1945. The second aircraft was Ju 88 G-6 Wrk Nr 621364 2Z+CP of 5./NJG6. It crashed at Dortmund killing Oblt Hans Steffen (pilot), Uffz Josef Knon, Uffz Helmut Uttler and Uffz Friedrich Krebber. (R. T. Goucher)*

Stavanger where they dropped flares over Lista airfield only to discover there were no aircraft, 'not even a light'. Adding to their frustration was the fact that no RAF bombers were headed that way either. (Much later, Frank Bocock was told that agents were being dropped in Norway that night.) Long missions over water were flown at 150 feet above the surface of the sea using the radio altimeter. In complete contrast, their op on 7 January, to Hailfingen in *J-Jig*, was at very high level indeed! Bocock was forced to climb to 23,000 ft to get above cloud. The heating failed and the temperature registered −37 °C outside, or 70° of frost. Rogers was so cold that he wrapped his hands around the bulb on the *Gee* box to try to warm them. They landed back at Snoring after 4 hours. Bocock and Rogers came through but there were periods when the 'chop rate' became very high. Frank Bocock recalls, 'You learned not to be so damned inquisitive some times.'

On 12 January, two Mosquito VIs of 169 Squadron gave high-level and ASR support for a raid by Lancasters on Bergen, Norway. Nearing the target, NS998 encountered five Fw 190s. Undaunted, he attacked two of them and damaged one. In NT176, S/L John Wright was chased by the Fw 190s. Two days later, the first five Mk XIX Mosquitoes arrived at Great Massingham from Swannington and joined A Flight for high-level patrols and intruding. A Flight had been flying *Serrate* patrols since November, while B Flight, which operated Mk VIs, used *Serrate* and *Perfectos*. No. 169 Squadron flew its first Mk XIX Mosquito operation on 21 January. This same night, 239 Squadron operated Mk XXX Mosquitoes for the first time.

Meanwhile, on 14/15 January, the main Bomber Command thrust was aimed at a synthetic oil plant at Leuna near Merseberg, railway yards at Grevenbroich, and an oil store at Dülmen. Ron Brearley with John Sheldon of 141 Squadron again proved successful. Brearley wrote later:

We contacted the bomber stream at the front line and overhauled them at a height of 20,000 ft. On reaching the target area we proceeded eastward through defended area between the banks of searchlights for 7–8 minutes, then struck north in the hope of intercepting enemy fighters from the Berlin area. An airfield was seen lit, subsequently identified as either Jüterbog or Pretsch, but which doused on our approach.

We patrolled, sweeping north and south, for some time, noting three horizontal searchlights pointing south near Wittenberg. At 21:30 hours, 15 minutes after the

*515 Squadron pilots and navigators pose for the camera. (Frank Bocock)*

Merseberg bombing had finished, an ASH contact was achieved at 13,000 ft, 2½ miles, which we followed down to 6,000 ft before losing it in ground returns. Enemy aircraft was losing height rapidly and obviously heading for aforesaid airfield which was plainly visible and which now fired a green Very light. (The flarepath was unusually wide, about 300 yards with aircraft landing close to left hand line of lights. Hangars and buildings plainly seen in light of flares). Smelling blood and knowing that none of our *Intruders* was operating thus far afield, we rapidly knocked off the remaining height and orbited the airfield at 1,500 ft. Navigation lights of an aircraft were seen on the approach, between the 'artificial horizon' and flarepath, at 21:35 hours, so with a twitching thumb we turned hard port and came down in a diving quarter attack, opening fire at 500–600 yards with half ring deflection. Strikes were seen in line with the enemy aircraft, but on the ground as he

neared the runway. This was easily countered by raising the nose and continuing to squirt. Many strikes were seen on him and he hit the deck just off the flarepath, bursting into flames immediately. By the light of flares which had been put up, enemy aircraft was seen to be a twin engined job, but these things happen much too quickly for positive identification.

While doing a hard turn over the airfield after this encounter another set of navigation lights was seen at the other side of the circuit, so we kept on the hard turn and hared after him, determined to get as much joy as we could with our seriously diminishing petrol. Deflection and range estimate being somewhat difficult at night we allowed home one and a half rings for luck and fired at 500 yards as we closed in on him from the port side. After a two or three second burst some strikes were seen on him and flame streamed out behind him. Enemy aircraft dived away as we passed behind him and, as we watched, in a somewhat expectant manner, for him to prang. Instead he made a panic circuit and tried to land in spite of reds which were being popped off from the ground. He failed to make it and opened up again, just as our attention was distracted by some flak which hurtled up at us, necessitating evasive action, with the result that we did not see him again. However, yet another 'bod' was seen almost instantly, with his navigation lights on, and once again we gave chase. After our first burst at him he was evidently stirred by strong emotions, for he commenced weaving violently, and we followed as best we could, squirting as opportunity offered in the pious hope that something would hit him. Much to our regret no strikes were observed and he eventually pulled his finger out and switched off his lights.

As our petrol supply was really getting low we had to set course for home immediately, feeling somewhat peeved that we could no longer take advantage of such promising opportunities. Height was gained at 8,000 ft and while still well in enemy territory another enemy aircraft was seen burning navigation lights crossing to port some distance away. We turned after him but he soon switched them off and we turned back on course as a long ASH chase could not be contemplated even if we could have picked him up, in view of diminishing petrol. What a situation! Several lighted airfields were seen on the way back, and about 06.00E port radiator temperature was seen to be high (110°) Immediately throttled it back to -4 boost and reduced revs in order to nurse it. Temperature remained constant until 04.00E when it shot up right round the clock. Feathered the propeller and proceeded to base to find cloud down to 700 ft and bad visibility. In view of this we had no alternative but to belly-land on the grass. 'G22' of course expired with the port engine and we were 'homed' by Coltishall and base. 215 gallons of petrol in tanks after landing.

Brearley and Sheldon, who were uninjured, submitted claims for one twin-engined aircraft destroyed and one damaged.

Bomber Command attacked Magdeburg and oil plants near Leipzig, and Brux in Czechoslovakia on 16/17 January and 100 Group again flew support. An 85 Squadron Mosquito destroyed a He 219 Owl (the squadron's fourth and final victory during the month), and five Mosquitoes of 239 Squadron made a *Spoof* bombing raid on Stuttgart, while 11 Mosquitoes of 141 Squadron patrolled to Zeitz and Magdeburg. Two of the three crews detailed to patrol the Magdeburg area were F/L D. H. Young and F/O J. J. Sanderson, and F/O R. C. Brady and F/L M. K. Webster. Young wrote up his combat report in a laid back manner, thus:

We patrolled to the north and east of Magdeburg watching it burn somewhat and we continued patrolling the furnace until 22:20 hours when we decided to follow up the bomber stream and set course in that direction. Just as we were leaving Magdeburg at 22:25 hours, our height being 20,000 ft, a contact was got on the starboard side going further starboard, we followed it round the southern side and up the western side of the still furiously burning target, the searchlights very kindly pointing at the aircraft we were chasing. After about half a minute all the searchlights doused simultaneously, (no doubt the Boche told them to put those **** lights out). Shortly after this, having followed him round on to a NE heading (weaving slightly) and closed to about 2,000 ft, I saw a bluish green light being situated inboard of the starboard engine nacelle. I pulled the nose up and pressed the button and precisely two rounds came out. We both nearly burst into tears. Then for some inexplicable reason, I tried the gun master switch and found that it had been flicked off so I put it back on again. By this time I had dropped back to 800 ft but the

Bf 110 continued flying straight and level. I was now afraid I should lose it any second so I closed in again as fast as possible – much too fast – and found myself about to ram the brute so I got him in the sight and opened fire again at what must have been 50 ft. He immediately exploded in a blinding flash, so I pulled back the stick and bounced over the top. A little later I saw the explosion on the ground where he crashed, blew up and burned furiously. We orbited the crash and put its position down. The ASH was now unserviceable so we set course for base and landed at 00:33 hours.

Brady and Webster, meanwhile, were also heading for Magdeburg. As Webster went over to ASH on the 'downward tilt', the Dummer and Sternhuder lakes were picked up, and valuably assisted navigation. They also used the *H2S* side of ASH to reach their patrol point, which was the Brandenburg lake. They obtained an ASH contact at a range of 5 miles, well above them and crossing from port to starboard. Brady recalls:

We chased and after following the aircraft through some mild evasive tactics, obtained a visual, 15 minutes after the initial contact, at 17,000 ft and 1,000 ft range. It was a Halifax. We followed it for a few minutes and it appeared to be orbiting the target of Magdeburg. We carried on with our patrol.

At 22:45 hours whilst patrolling on a westerly vector south of Magdeburg at 14,000 ft, a contact was obtained at 4–5 miles well above and crossing gently to port from starboard. We gave chase and the aircraft appeared to be flying more or less straight and level. Range was closed to 2,000 ft behind, height 17,000 ft. At this point the aircraft appeared to get backward warning of us and began to take violent evasive action, in a way of tight turns with loss of height. We managed to hang on to him but about 1½ miles range. This continued for some time until finally the other aircraft seemed to give

up and flew straight and level. We positioned ourselves dead behind him and at 1 mile range and rapidly closed in and obtained a visual at 1,000 ft range. My 'good man' had the night glasses and identified the aircraft as an Me 110. Upon closing in I noticed a dim yellow light showing from outside the starboard engine nacelle of the enemy aircraft. Range was further closed to about 200 yards and below, so that looking up I was able to confirm the aircraft as being an Me 110. I was still tending to overshoot and was a little to port. I gave the enemy aircraft a one second burst using 20° deflection from 200 ft and strikes were observed on the side of his fuselage. The enemy aircraft immediately fired off colours which lit up the side of the aircraft. I turned away to port to allow the Bf 110 to get ahead of me, which he did, still flying straight and level – quite clueless. We came in behind him and slightly above and at 200 yards opened up with a 5-second burst. Very many strikes were seen on the cockpit and thereabouts. Bits flew off and much black smoke belched out, then the port engine burst into flames. The 110 spiralled down burning furiously and hit the ground with a terrific explosion. It crashed approximately 25 miles SW of Magdeburg at 23:10 hours. We were very short of fuel by this time and headed straight back for base, landing at 01:15 hours.

On 16/17 January F/L Tommy Smith in 23 Squadron, who by now was within two or three operations of completing his second tour, and his navigator, F/O 'Cocky' Cockayne, were on ops. Tommy Smith recalls:

It was a dirty night – thick as a bag up to 16,000 ft – and we went on an ASH patrol to Stendal fighter airfield near Berlin. I used a square search system for nearly an hour, but picked up nothing and when the time was up, we set course for home. At the point when we should have been over the area of the Steinhuder Lake, we came across an airfield where aircraft with nav lights on were taxiing. This was unheard of! I went in to have a bash. There was a chap sitting at the taxi point. He was my target: his nav lights and the hooded runway lights were on. I opened up and saw a good cluster of cannon strikes on the aircraft, and was about to break away when I saw exhaust flames of another aircraft half way up the runway. 'God, someone's taking off! I'll have him,' I thought. (I was trained to recognize an aircraft by the number, type and disposition of its exhaust flames and I reckoned it was a Ju 88.) So instead of breaking off, I closed in and opened up. My muzzle flashes lit up the Hun right under my chin! (I was so close I was practically looking at the back of the pilot's head.) It wasn't a Ju 88; it was an Me 109! (What I had taken for exhausts

of two engines, were the flames from either side of one engine.) Because of the difference in line between my gunsight and the guns beneath my feet, I was shooting low, being so close, and ripped the bottom out of the Me 109. He crashed at the end of the runway.

However, as I was pursuing this chap, I had passed between two flak towers at the downwind end of the runway. Light flak [from 8 guns, the Germans said later] had the cannon flashes to aim at, and my Mosquito was hit coming in over the perimeter track at a height of about 200 ft in a dive. Flak set my right engine on fire and I automatically feathered the prop and pressed the extinguisher button. I zoomed up to 1,000 ft. My mind was running on how to get organized to fly home on one engine, when, all of a sudden the other engine stopped! The first engine was blazing merrily and the prop was feathering and unfeathering. I said to Cocky, 'That's it! Bail Out!' It's not easy to get out of a Mosquito. Cocky was having trouble jettisoning the hatch door. Time and height were running out. I switched on the landing lights. Treetops showed up below. We were too low. I shouted, 'Knock it off. Do your harness up.' Cocky didn't answer. A burst of flame lit up the open hatch. He had bailed out. I found out later that his parachute didn't open fully, and he had broken his neck.

The forest came up and I was skimming over the treetops, and preparing to stuff the nose in while I still had flying speed. I could feel the 'whiffle' which indicated the approach of the stall. Suddenly, there was a field covered in snow. I stuffed it in at about 200 mph. Next thing, I was hurtling along the ground heading for more trees. I thought it was a wood but it was only a line of trees; a windbreak! The trees ripped off the outer wing sections and something, possibly a

*Pat Rooney caricature of Tommy Smith of 23 Squadron, who, with F/O Cocky Cockayne, made a devastating attack on Fassberg airfield on the night of 16/17 January 1945. (Tommy Smith)*

stump, knocked a hole in the cockpit alongside me. I still had my hand on the throttle control and it was ripped away by the tree stump! Then I was out of the trees and into the snow again before the aircraft came to a stop. A feeling of relief came over me. All I could think was 'a forced landing in the dark! What fantastic luck to be alive!'

All I had to do now was lift the roof emergency hatch, climb out, and run away. Except that in the crash, the whole of the seat had come adrift and shot me underneath the instrument panel, and the cockpit cabin was full of earth. The left rudder bar had taken my foot back under the seat and locked it. I had some grim moments trapped in the middle of a bonfire trying to extricate my foot. By the time I got out of the hole the port radiator and its contents were burning fiercely right outside the hole. I crawled out badly burned, and stuffed my face and hands into the snow. When I got up, I found I had a broken leg, caused by the rudder pedal. [He had also lost an eye]. By the light of the fire I could see a farmhouse and crawled over to it. Two soldiers hiding in the hedge, expecting the bombs to explode, carried me into the barn and about an hour later a Luftwaffe ambulance from Fassburg collected me. I was sadly aware that my wartime flying was over.

Tommy Smith was treated at Fassburg

sick quarters. The Germans confirmed his destruction of the two 109s he had shot at and also credited him with another 109 which spun in due to the presence of the intruding Mosquito. It crashed and burnt out, killing the pilot. Tommy stayed at Fassberg for a month before being transferred to Dulag Luft at Frankfurt for another month. He was bombed out by the RAF then transferred to Homemark, a convent hospital being used for RAF PoWs. On 28 March 1945, he and the other inmates were released by the US 3rd Army and flown home from Paris. At the PoW reception centre at RAF Cosford, his assorted burns were treated in hospital. After discharge he was given a posting to Fighter Command HQ at Bentley Priory where the 'Prang Basher' once again took up crash investigation duties. When it came to demob he was invalided out of the RAF and sent to East Grinstead for further plastic surgery. It was there that he met a nursing sister who was to become his wife. Her name was Joy.

After the war, a Feldwebel, who had befriended Tommy when he was blind, sent him photos of Cockayne's grave. It showed Tommy's grave, on the left, waiting for him! Tommy adds, 'The Huns were a tidy-minded lot and would have put the two of us alongside each other. Luckily, I was "late for my own funeral".'

*Mosquito NF XIX TA146 of 157 Squadron, RAF Swannington, which made an emergency belly-landing at the 44th Bomb Group, 8th Air Force base at Shipdham, Norfolk on 17 January 1945 following an in-flight engine failure. A similar outcome in the snow befell Tommy Smith of 23 Squadron at Fassberg this same night. (Jacob Elias via Steve Adams)*

# CHAPTER 12

# *I DANCE WITH GISELA TONIGHT*

*Ganz alleine auf der Reise,*
*Jängt der kleine Kahn am Firmament,*
*Joch das stört in keinster Weise*
*Or ist in seinem Element.*

'DAS LIED VON DER „WILDEN SAU"' BY PETER HOLM

On 21/22 January, 239 Squadron attempted its first ASH patrol when three Mosquitoes from West Raynham supported an attack on Kassel by 76 Mosquitoes, but the Mk XXX returned early with radar problems. The two 141 Squadron Mosquitoes completed their patrols. The following night, 14 Mosquitoes from 141 Squadron and three from 239 Squadron supported Bomber Command operations to Duisburg. One crew reported their first sighting of an enemy jet aircraft. German jets could certainly outpace the Mosquito but their introduction had been too little too late (the first ground units of 100 Group were established on the continent, at Wenduine, Belgium during January), and while on occasions they caused havoc with the US daylight bombing missions, they were less effective against the Mosquitoes at night.

More of a problem was the bad weather, January being the worst month since 100 Group began operations in December 1943. There were 16 days of snow. A big freeze from 19–31 January prevented many operations. However, 100 Group Mosquitoes destroyed 17 enemy aircraft and damaged three in January. By the end of the month, re-equipment with ASH was almost complete. All of 141 Squadron's Mk XV AI radar and the *Monica* Mk IX backward AI ASH had been fitted and the squadron had only experienced four early returns from 80 sorties; a great tribute to the radar mechanics and their abilities in difficult conditions.

In February, Mosquitoes of 100 Group shot down 10 enemy aircraft, probably destroyed one other, and damaged six. On 1/2 February, W/C W. F. Gibb, 239 Squadron CO, with F/O R. C. Kendall, destroyed a Bf 110. Two more enemy aircraft would fall to the squadron's guns during the month. On 3/4 February, W/C Kelsey DFC, CO of 515 Squadron, with

*239 Squadron personnel outside the crew room at West Raynham. Standing, left to right: W/C W. F. Gibb DSO, DFC, the CO (who on 5/6 March with F/O R. C. Kendall DFC destroyed two Ju 88s at Nürnberg to add to their Bf 110 and a Fw 190 during February); u/k, Dicky Da Costa, W/O Tanner (wearing dark glasses); F/Sgt Briggs; F/L Wimbush and W/O Chalky White. Front row, left to right: u/k; S/L A. J. Holderness (who, with F/L Rowley destroyed a Bf 110 on the night of 7/8 February); Peter Poirette; u/k Aussie. (Graham Chalky White)*

F/L Smith DFC, patrolled Gütersloh to no avail before obtaining a visual on a Ju 88 near Vechta. From astern and below, Kelsey dispatched the Junkers with a short burst of 100 rounds of cannon fire. The starboard engine burst into flames, the port wing outboard of the port engine fell off, and pieces of debris flew back and damaged the Mosquito's air intake and undercarriage doors. Kelsey managed to land safely at Little Snoring. The A Flight Commander in 141 Squadron, S/L Peter Anthony Bates DFC, and his navigator, F/O William Guy Cadman, who had destroyed a Bf 110 on 11/12 September, failed to return from an ASH patrol to Ladbergen on 7/8 February. Bates was 23 years old and Cadman, the son of Maj William H. Cadman MBE of nearby Redenhall, Norfolk, was just 22. Both men are buried at Hannover War Cemetery. Apart from the air-to-air victory, they had destroyed one locomotive, damaged three more, and damaged a ship and a train. On a happier note, on 13 February, Harry White and Mike Allen were posted back to 141 Squadron at West Raynham. Harry was promoted Squadron Leader and became A Flight Commander. He remained with 141 until it disbanded at Little Snoring in September 1945.

On 14/15 February, Bomber Command attacked Chemnitz and an oil refinery at Rositz near Leipzig. Leslie Holland of 515 Squadron recalls:

Our designated patrol airfield was Hailfingen, in the area east of Stuttgart where nearly every town ends with 'ingen'. After we had mooched around the vicinity of the airfield for the best part of an hour, Bob announced that he thought there was something on the *Monica*. A port turn caused an increase in range whereupon I immediately opened the taps and made the turn as steep as possible. The blip disappeared so we started a starboard turn to make a sweep. A head-on contact came up on the ASH at about 2 miles closing fast. As he appeared to be on a parallel course slightly right we went straight into a hard right turn. The bogey must have done exactly the same because he failed to appear on our screen after the turn. Reverse course again and have another go. Sure enough, another head-on. Port turn this time and lose him again. Suddenly, Bob yells into the intercom, 'He's coming in from . . .'

WHOOSH, and a Heinkel 219 flashes by under our nose about 20 ft away – the radar operator clearly visible in the after part of the

*The Mosquito NF Mk XXX (RK953 is seen here), was late in arriving on the* Serrate *squadrons in 100 Group and the first Mk XXX victories were not recorded until February 1945. W/C W. F. Gibb DSO, DFC and F/O R. C. Kendall DFC shot down a Bf 110 on the night of 1/2 February 1945 and a Fw 190 on 20/21 February, and four other victories that month went to Mk XXX crews in 85 and 239 Squadrons.*

canopy. No time to depress the nose and have a squirt, not even to get the ginger on the button. And he's in a 60° bank to his right going to my left, so he's probably got a *Lichtenstein* radar with all-round performance superior to our miserable little ASH, so the only course is to try and outguess him, and at the same time bear in mind that we have now been making inroads at full throttle into our get-home fuel. We make a sweep and try to make a bit of westing. But a break in the clouds reveals that the North Star is to port. I've been steering by the directional gyro compass and it has spun in the tight turns. A quick look at the compass which has just about settled

down confirms the 'astro' observation, and we are actually working our way deeper into enemy territory.

Obviously, our adversary had been expecting us to do exactly as we had intended so we must have ended up going in opposite directions at a separating speed of something over 500 mph. We never saw each other again, which may be just as well considering the performance of his mount and the great superiority of his radar.

Another anti-flak covering mine-laying in Oslofiord at Rygge was made. It was very near the scene of our previous sortie. The cloud cover was low and on this occasion we made our approach over the mountains of

*On the night of 1/2 February 1945, F/L A. P. Mellows DFC (below the prop) with F/L S. L. Drew DFC, both of 169 Squadron at Great Massingham, shot down a Bf 110 incurring the same damage to their Mosquito that had befallen F/L Hedgecoe's Mosquito during his victory on 24/25 March 1944, and the Mosquito crewed by Welfare and Bellis on 11/12 June 1944. (Tom Cushing Collection)*

*On 3/4 February 1945, W/C Kelsey DFC, CO of 515 Squadron, with F/L Smith DFC in RS575 V, shot down a Ju 88 near Vechta from astern and below. RS575 was badly damaged in the encounter but Kelsey managed to land safely at Little Snoring. (Tom Cushing Collection)*

southern Norway. There was a good moon but letting down into the Fiord through a gap in the clouds was a trifle nail-biting. Near the south-east coast we intercepted a Halifax while still below cloud and passed fairly close to him without being seen. The mine-layers were supposed to be Lancs so I expect he was from 38 Group on some clandestine activity.

While 141 did not score during February, they destroyed two enemy aircraft on the ground, damaged two more and destroyed a train and damaged nine more. On 13 February, two of 141 Squadron's favourite sons, S/L Harry White DFC** and F/L Mike Allen DFC**, had arrived back at West Raynham after their stint with the BSDU. On 21/22 February, they flew their first operation since rejoining the squadron but drew a blank. On 23/24 February, a 239 Squadron Mosquito flown by F/Sgt Twigg with his navigator, F/Sgt Turner, overshot as it was landing on the FIDO strip at Foulsham and hit a parked Halifax. Twigg was killed and Turner was injured. Worse, four Halifaxes of 462 (RAAF) Squadron failed to return to the airfield after a

windowing operation in the Ruhr. The following night, W/O E. W. 'Bunny' Adams and F/Sgt Frank A. Widdicombe of 515 Squadron damaged a Ju 88 in the circuit at Bonn. Adams throttled hard back and lowered his flaps to avoid overshooting and gave the Junkers a 2-second burst before he was forced to pull away hard to starboard to avoid hitting the ground.

That same night, 10 Halifaxes of 462 (RAAF) Squadron, each carrying three 750 lb incendiary clusters and a 500 lb GP bomb, were despatched on a special duty *Spoof* and bombing raid in the Neuss area of the Ruhr. Four failed to return. One was *MZ 447 A-Able* flown by F/L Allan J. Rate RAAF and his six crew on their twenty-ninth operation. It carried a 'spare bod'; F/O D. N. Kehoe RAAF, the new Squadron Bombing Leader. Flight Sergeant Reg Gould, air bomber and the only crew member to survive, recalls:

We were in the area of Kreffeld in the Ruhr when we were hit in the port wing by flak which set the wing on fire. I was sitting in the nose of the aircraft on my tubular metal folding seat which covered the escape hatch

174

hatch, dislocating my right shoulder as I went. That was the last time I saw the aircraft.'

Reg Gould was soon taken prisoner and placed in a vehicle with three downed aircrew from F/L F. H. Ridgewell's Halifax.

Sergeant R. G. Hodgson, the flight engineer, who was about 19 years old, was injured. F/O J. R. Boyce RAAF, the wireless operator, was badly burned. His parachute had been on fire. It was obvious that he was in very severe pain as the smell of his burnt flesh was terrible. Later I learned that the third person was P/O W. J. Mann who navigated for Ridgewell's crew. Some time after the war I read a letter from the mayor of Kreffeld in which he spoke of the remainder of my crew and the aircraft being scattered over an area of 100 square metres. They had crashed in Boishiem and had been buried in a cemetery at Bieyelle. Later, they were interred by the Allies in the Reichwald Forest War Cemetery.

Dutch Holland's last trip in February was another unusual one in that it was a close escort for a raid on Wilhelmshaven by Liberators of the 492nd BG, USAAF. Leslie Holland recalls:

It was a sort of trial run to see how they made out on a night sortie and involved about three dozen B-24s. We were to rendezvous with them at a DR position half way out at 20,000 ft and run close escort rather like riding herd. We picked them up easily on our little sets then shut them down after getting visual contact. There was no difficulty in running up one side of their stream, turning and coming back for another

and I could see flames through the navigator's window which wasn't quite blacked out. I had been asked by Alan to take a *Gee* fix for F/Sgt J. Maslin, the navigator. Finding the set placed rather high I had taken my parachute from where it was stored to put on the seat. So by a quirk of fate I had my parachute immediately to hand when we were hit. We were in a very steep dive, doing about 340 mph in an attempt to get from 18,000 ft to below 14,000 ft before crossing the Allied front line which was about 40 miles away. The Allies had started a push and their artillery had orders to open fire on any aircraft flying above 14,000 ft. I faced the rear of the aircraft and baled out backwards but the slipstream was so strong it jammed me on to the back of the escape hatch and my parachute caught on a metal strip. I did not have enough strength to push myself off although I was kicking the underside of the aircraft in a desperate attempt to get clear. I heard Malcolm Husband, the rear gunner, yell 'Dive to starboard'. This was the order used by gunners when an enemy aircraft was attacking. Alan responded immediately and as he did so I was rolled out of the side of the run. There was no room to speak of but enough starlight to see them clearly from about 100 yards on the beam. As we neared the target, we widened our sweep to about 1/2–1 mile in order to intercept any interceptors. (Our radar was now switched on again or in the official code of the period, we were 'flashing our weapon'.) Our separation from the stream incidentally kept us nicely clear of the large-calibre flak which was now coming up by the bucketful.

They turned for home without any spectacular disasters and we resumed our role of guard dogs back to our rendezvous, feeling we had done a fairly good job even if we hadn't run into any fighters, but, after our return, a message came through from the American group, 'Where the hell were you guys?' Ah well, I suppose night vision isn't learned in a day (or night). This addendum is of course slightly apocryphal and they were grateful for our support.

Leslie Holland recalls that on 2/3 March:

There was a full moon, which was a deterrent to a Main Force effort but on such occasions experienced intruder crews were allowed to go on a night *Ranger*. Generally, a distant target would be chosen at which

worthwhile aircraft could be found on the ground or even with luck in the air. All such ventures had to be approved by Group HQ and they were usually given the OK if not either too footling or too foolhardy – like an attack on the *Tirpitz*. Several hours would be spent poring over intelligence reports and air photographs. Our little efforts were very tame in comparison. The target selected as our primary was a seaplane base on the Baltic coast at Tarnewitz, near Wismar, calling at Gustrow, Ludwiglust and Schwerin. We found no seaplanes although it was brilliant moonlight, bright enough for us to dodge high tension cables and watch our shadow to be sure one didn't become two without our noticing. Bob was keeping a very sharp look-out behind while I did some very easy map reading. However, it was not entirely a fruitless trip because Hagenow provided so many trains in its yards that we used the last burst of our cannon ammo on the water tower which showed gratifying evidence that next day's traffic would be a trifle interrupted.

On 3/4 March 1945, RAF Bomber Command sent two large forces of bombers to Germany. Some 234 aircraft were to raid the synthetic oil plant at

*On 24/25 February, W/O E. W. 'Bunny' Adams and F/Sgt Frank A. Widdicombe of 515 Squadron damaged a Ju 88 in the circuit at Bonn. Adams demonstrates with his hands how he throttled hard back and lowered his flaps to avoid overshooting and gave the Junkers a 2-second burst before he was forced to pull away hard to starboard to avoid hitting the ground. Among the avid listeners are Alan Hyatt, holding a prop blade, and (far right) Bob Young, Leslie Holland's navigator. (Leslie Holland)*

Kamen and a further 222 aircraft would attack the Dortmund–Ems canal at Ladbergen. Altogether, 100 Group dispatched 61 aircraft on RCM sorties this night to jam the German radar and radio networks and thus hamper the enemy flak and night-fighter defences. One of the aircraft was a 192 Squadron Halifax piloted by W/C Donaldson. His tail gunner was Gunnery Leader Jack Short, who had returned to Foulsham in February after a Gunnery Leader's Course at Catfoss.

We went out in daylight, surrounded by Lancasters PF 5 Group – the 'Death or Glory Boys', who were to punch a hole in the canal. Our lone Halifax caused a great deal of interest. They must have wondered if we had the right raid! It was a comfortable feeling though being with all these aircraft in daylight. At the target there was altostratus at 15,000 ft; bloody annoying because the searchlights silhouetted us against the cloud and we were picked up by the ack-ack. I saw three Lancs go down, one fairly close, in flames. [From these two raids, seven Lancasters were lost.] We were keyed up. Donaldson tipped the Halifax on one wing to look underneath for fighters. If suddenly your right wing crumples . . . but we

encountered no opposition, and we headed back to Foulsham at 10,000 ft.

This night the Luftwaffe mounted. Operation *Gisela*, an attack by 142 Ju 88Gs and almost 60 other twin-engined night-fighters on returning RAF aircraft and their airfields in eastern England. The operation, suggested by Major Heinz-Wolfgang Schnaufer, the top scoring night fighter pilot, who finished the war with 121 victories, was to have taken place at the end of February but details of the plan were obtained and the British made it known by broadcasting the contemporary hit tune 'I Dance With Gisela Tonight' on the Allied propaganda station 'Soldatensender Calais'. *Gisela* had therefore been postponed until the British relaxed their vigilence. German intruders were active on several occasions early in 1945 and more than once had successfully infiltrated the returning bomber stream. They now employed the same tactics and penetrated the airspace over some of the 100 Group stations, Foulsham included. Jack Short continues:

I will always remember the WAAF girl's voice in the Foulsham tower. 'You're clear to circle and orbit at 6,000 ft,' she said.

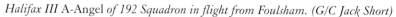

*Halifax III A-Angel of 192 Squadron in flight from Foulsham. (G/C Jack Short)*

*Halifax* Sleepy Gal *of 192 Squadron at RAF Foulsham. (G/C Jack Short)*

Donaldson was the last back and we were the top of the stack. There were 4–5 more Halifaxes underneath at 500 ft intervals. We could see Foulsham airfield illuminated below. Donaldson started a left orbit. I suddenly saw a 2-second set of tracer well beneath the aircraft, then more, in one direction. Then a ball of fire. This poor girl on the R/T screamed, 'Bandits! Bandits!' The airfield lights were doused. She yelled out Weston Zoyland, the diversion airfield, in plain language. Then there was total silence.

The aircraft Jack Short had seen was Halifax Mk III LV955 'G' of 192 Squadron, piloted by F/O E. D. 'Robbie' Roberts. Roberts had taken off from RAF Foulsham at 20:00 hours for a lone ELINT operation over the North Sea to search for possible navigational aids which it was thought might be associated with air-launched V-1s and their guidance to targets in the UK. The Halifax carried out its assigned task and returned to Norfolk. At about 01:00 hours, the two Main Forces were also over-flying the area. *G-George* arrived back over Foulsham. Robbie Roberts recalls:

When we arrived, the airfield lighting was on and after calling the tower for permission to land I began to lose height down into the circuit when given the OK to 'pancake'. My navigation lights were on and wheels lowered. The next thing, a cry over the radio from the control tower said, 'Bandits overhead!' and the lighting went out on the ground. I hit the switch to turn off the navigation lights and turned away from the circuit.

Roberts was instructed to turn to starboard. Whilst flying at an altitude of 1,200 ft, a Ju 88 night-fighter attacked. The pilot continues:

The attack appeared to come from below us. It looked like that from the tracer. The aircraft was hit and both inner engines were put out of action and the aircraft caught fire. Sgt Ken Sutcliffe, the mid-upper gunner, reported streams of flame as the petrol leaking from the wing tanks ignited. I thought that there would be a chance for some to escape by parachute and gave the order for an emergency parachute escape, provided I could keep the aircraft under some sort of control. [Only F/O R. G. Todd, the special wireless operator, was able to bale out successfully, injured.] At 1,000 ft I ordered all the crew back to the normal crash positions and told them to sit tight as it was too low by then to attempt any further parachute escapes. We suffered a further attack and this resulted in the extremely messy death of the wireless operator, W/O William Clementson, who was in his crash position in the cockpit, and also the disintegration of the instrument panel. I grappled with the controls and tried to maintain some sort of stability, looking for a field in which I could make a crash-landing. I can remember passing over some trees in the boundary of the field and pulling everything back in my lap in an endeavour to make a belly-landing, which apparently did come off.

*G-George* crash-landed in flames at Ainlies Farm, Fulmodeston near the Mosquito fighter base at Little Snoring, setting a haystack and two huts on fire. Only two men survived, dragged clear by local people; Roberts suffered a crush-fractured spine and burns, and did not regain consciousness until two weeks later. After treatment at RAF Hospital Ely and East Grinstead, where he underwent plastic surgery under the famous Sir Archibald McIndoe and thus became a member of the famous Guinea-pig Club, was discharged from the RAF in 1947. The

mid-upper gunner, Sgt Ken Sutcliffe, survived with burns to his body and face. Navigator F/O William Darlington, Flt Engineer, Sgt John Anderson, and Air Bomber, F/Sgt Reginald Holmes, were found dead in the burnt-out wreckage. The aircraft was almost completely destroyed. The rear gunner, 34-year-old Sgt Richard Grapes, was found dead with his parachute unopened, either killed due to lack of altitude, or enemy fire as he jumped. Jack Short accompanied his coffin to Liverpool.

All told, the Luftwaffe intruders shot down 20 aircraft over England, including five which crashed in Norfolk. Liberator 'B' of 223 Squadron was in the circuit at Oulton when tracer was fired at it. Although hit, the B-24 was able to land safely. Pilot Officer Bennett in a 214 Squadron Fortress was about to land when he was told to go around again as his A Flight Commander, S/L Bob Davies, was approaching on three engines. Bob Davies recalls:

Our return to Oulton in the early hours of 4 March was normal, the individual aircraft switching on their navigation lights some

*Wreckage of Halifax Mk III LV955 G-George of 192 Squadron, piloted by F/O E. D. 'Robbie' Roberts, which crash-landed in flames at Ainlies Farm, Fulmodeston, near the Mosquito base at Little Snoring, on the night of 3/4 March 1945, after being attacked by a Ju 88 night-fighter. (via Bob Collis, Norfolk & Suffolk Aviation Museum)*

*Crew of the ill-fated Halifax Mk III LV955 G-George of 192 Squadron. Front row, centre: F/O E. D. 'Robbie' Roberts. William Darlington, flight engineer Sgt John Anderson and Air Bomber F/Sgt Reginald Holmes were found dead in the burnt out wreckage. (via Bob Collis, Norfolk & Suffolk Aviation Museum)*

time before we crossed the Norfolk coast. As I approached Oulton I heard control give P/O Bennett clearance to join the circuit. I called saying I was on three engines and was told to come straight in. A few moments later Bennett, who I think was on longish finals, was told to go round again as I was turning long finals and was cleared to land on runway 45. I saw Bennett climbing away, and above me, to my right. Then I saw a fairly long burst of cannon fire and his No. 2 engine and wing caught fire. I lost sight of him still climbing and turning right. At this time I heard the tower say 'Bandits! Bandits! Switch off all lights'. All airfield lights were extinguished. I had landed by now and was stationary. I switched off my navigation lights, or so I thought. However, my rear gunner said, 'There is still a white light shining somewhere above me!' I told him it was impossible as both my flight engineer, F/O Fitzsimmonds and I had checked all switches and they were definitely 'off'. While we started madly to check again all the switches the two of us began to feel very naked and also very panicky as we were expecting to be blown apart at any moment. I finally found the small switch which controlled the white formation light situated at the very top of the vertical stabilizer and switched it off. All ten of us only dared to

breathe again when we finally found our blacked-out dispersal.

However, the night, and the fright, were not yet over. As my Hillman pick-up was parked at dispersal, I drove with my flight engineer to the still fiercely burning wreck which must have roughly impacted in a flying position. [Bennett's Fortress was shot down by Lt Arnold Döring of 10/NJG3 from Jever. It was his twentieth victory.] The fuselage (or what was left of it) had broken off aft of the radio room and also aft of the beam gun position. I could not believe any of the crew had survived but both waist gunners, Sgt Alastair McDirmid and W/O R. W. Church, had 'walked' from the blazing inferno. They had been taken to sick quarters where I spoke briefly to them.

### Don Prutton of 223 Squadron adds:

The intruder, which we learned later, was a Junkers Ju 88, then did a sharp turn and sent a few rounds in the direction of Flying Control [a cannon shell penetrated a safe near a wall which Dick Gunton, 214 Squadron Engineering Officer, was sheltering behind] before all the lights on the airfield were switched off. The CO, who was in the tower, had left his Humber staff car outside with the spotlight on; a zealous airman immediately

*The devastated area of Dresden pictured on 22 March 1945. On 13/14 February 1945, Dresden was bombed by 796 Lancasters and nine Mosquitoes in two separate attacks; 1,478 tons of HE and 1,182 tons of incendiaries were dropped creating a firestorm similar to the one at Hamburg in July 1943. Another 311 bombers of the 8th AF followed with a raid the next day. (Geoff Liles)*

kicked it in but his prompt action was not greatly appreciated by the 'old man'.

The 'zealous airman' was Dick Gunton, who, unable to find the off switch, had resorted to swift action. Gunton related the events next morning at the Cushing household at the Old Hall, Thursford. Eight-year-old Tom listened avidly to the family friend who at Christmas had taken him in his pride and joy, a red MG sports coupé, to see *Holiday Inn* at a Norwich cinema. Gunton, who hurt his foot kicking in the glass because 'it was tougher than expected' confided that he did it because the beam was shining on his beloved MG and he didn't want it shot to bits by the Ju 88! Don Prutton concludes: 'Aircraft still airborne were diverted to another airfield, but were followed by the Junkers 88. He inflicted some more damage before being chased off by our fighters. We heard later that he was shot down somewhere in the north of England.'

Mosquito XIX MM640 of 169 Squadron flown by S/L V. J. Fenwick with F/O Pierce was shot down and both crew killed. Dutch Holland and Bob Young had just landed at Snoring from an air-interception training exercise, left their fully armed Mosquito on its dispersal hard standing, parked their gear in the 515 Squadron hut and were 'sauntering back up the lane towards the

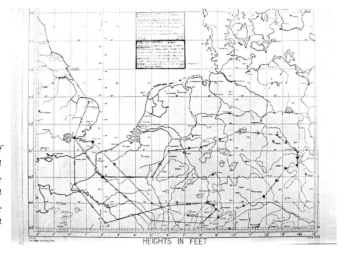

*The Spoof routes flown by Geoff Liles and his crew of 214 Squadron, on the nights of the Dresden operation, 13/14 February 1945, and the Pforzheim operation, 23/24 February 1945. (Geoff Liles)*

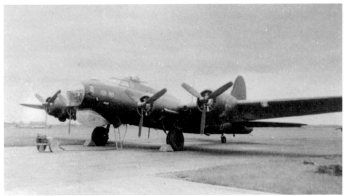

Messes'. Dutch Holland recalls:

There were several returning aircraft in the vicinity all making very familiar noises when we noticed that one was being followed by an aircraft with a distinctly unfamiliar note. I had just time to say to Bob, 'By God it's a Jerry!' when a stream of tracer streaked across and, as they were only at about 1,500 ft, [we] could see the flicker of strikes. The stricken aircraft had its landing lights on ready for joining the circuit and was naturally not expecting any trouble. The lights went into a descending curve out of sight behind the trees. No flak, no fire.

Halifax NA107-T of 171 Squadron, piloted by S/L Procter, the B Flight Commander, was brought down by a Ju 88 while heading for North Creake at 3,000 ft on returning from a *Mandrel* sortie and crashed at Walnut Tree Farm, South Lopham after the crew of eight parachuted out at around 1,000 ft. The mid-upper gunner sustained a broken ankle while the flight engineer, F/Sgt Jaking, 'apparently under the impression that there was no hope of survival, and anxious to save time and money in transportation', glided into a cemetery! Leslie Holland concludes:

As a result of these incursions, a system of stand-by night-fighters dispersed over several adjoining airfields was set up with crews already in the aircraft, engines warmed up ready to respond to any repeat performance. We also did stand-by patrols when the Main Force was returning if not on ops ourselves. However, no further trade came our way when we were ready for them,

*S/L Bob Davies (holding Rhett the 214 Squadron mascot) and Dick Gunton (in white shirt), 214 Squadron Engineering Officer, are pictured all smiles with gunners and RAF personnel at Oulton. On the night of 3/4 March 1945, when the Luftwaffe mounted Operation Gisela, Gunton kicked out the spotlight on W/C McGlinn's Humber staff car during the strafing of the airfield. (Tom Cushing Collection)*

*A wind-swept Leslie Holland in front of his Mosquito D-Dog at Little Snoring. Note the ASH nose radar housing and bat symbol, swastikas and locos indicating strafing victories painted on the side of the forward fuselage. (Leslie Holland)*

but our own vigilance was redoubled when we ourselves came back into the circuit. Minimum exposure of airfield lighting became the rule and navigation lights were, for a time, not used. This in itself involved a certain amount of risk due to the small distance separating airfields in East Anglia. There were 20 airfields north of a line between Norwich and King's Lynn and most were involved in night operations. The circuits alternated left and right so that they meshed like the gears of an enormous watch. Some of the intruders were caught by home-defence night-fighters, mostly to those fitted with Mk X AI (SCR 720).

*In February 1945, 199 Squadron at North Creake converted from the Stirling to the Halifax, making it an all-'Hallybag' station with 171 Squadron. The Halifax BIII pictured here is J-Johnny, captained by F/L Chilcott (below nose aerials, hand on hip). Standing, left to right: 'Scotty', WOP No. 2; Bill Whitworth, flight engineer; Jack McCann RCAF, bomb-aimer; Bob Thompson, navigator; Chilcott; Jim Pearce, gunner; Jock Clark, WOP-AG. The other crew member missing from this photo is Vic Policheck RCAF, gunner. (via Steve Smith)*

# CHAPTER 13

# ASHES TO ASHES

*No, it won't start because it's over-rich. And the burning smell is from one of my beautiful new starter-armatures, due to you keeping your thumb on the starter button far too long – sir*

During early March 1945, Luftwaffe intruders made brief but damaging reappearance over eastern England and many Mosquito crews talked confidently of

getting more victories. At West Raynham, the nights went by with excitement at fever pitch because 239 Squadron were chasing its fiftieth victory. On the night of 5/6 March, W/C W. F. Gibb, the CO, and F/O R. C. 'Killer' Kendall made quite sure of their claim to the fiftieth by destroying two Ju 88s, one at Chemnitz flown by Obstlt Walter Borchers of NJG5, the other at Nürnberg. Their return was particularly memorable for two treasured lines. On climbing unhurriedly out of the aircraft, Killer Kendall seemed quite unmoved by the noisy throng that greeted him, and was heard to remark in acid tones, 'I still say it's a bloody awful set'. The Wing Commander was more verbose and his delight as he described how he had accounted for both his victims was glorious to see. 'But why,' he asked in conclusion, 'why do I always hit them in the port engine?'

March produced rich pickings for the Mosquito *Intruders*. On the 6/7 March, F/O S. J. Bartlam and F/O A. A. Harvey of 515

*Final 239 Squadron Record of Victories, which is on display at the RAF Museum, Hendon. (Author)*

*239 Squadron aircrew and groundcrews pictured at West Raynham.* Top row, left to right: *1–2 u/k groundcrew; Sgt West; W/O Dave Brochie; W/O Chalky White; u/k Belgian; P/O Paul Falconer; F/L R. C. 'Killer' Kendall DFC; P/O Jamie Jameson; u/k; F/O Frazer; u/k; W/O Chick Ellinor; Sgt Peel; u/k; u/k.* 2nd row, left to right: *u/k; F/O 'Spider' Webb; Cliff Rind RCAF; F/L Woolton; F/L Smith; u/k; Da Costa; u/k; F/L Freddy Wimbush; Rowley; F/O Pete Poirette; u/k; Terry Glasheen RAAF; 'Honest John' Bridekirk RAAF.* 3rd row, left to right: *u/k; radar officer RAAF; F/L Al Deere; F/L Hawley Adj; W/C W. F. 'Wally' Gibb DSO, DFC, CO; S/L Dennis Hughes DFC; F/L Dennis Perks DFC; u/k; u/k.* Front row, left to right: *u/k; F/Sgt Dai Rees; F/Sgt Ferguson; F/Sgt Andrews; F/Sgt L. 'Spic' Spicer; F/Sgt Arthur Briggs; F/Sgt Brogan; W/O Tony Tanner; W/O 'Dagwood' Wooding. W/C Gibb and F/O Kendall destroyed two Ju 88s on 5/6 March 1945. S/L Hughes with F/L Perks shot down a Ju 188 at Nürnberg on 16/17 March. (Graham Chalky White)*

Squadron destroyed a Ju 52 and damaged two other enemy aircraft on the ground at Greifswald and Barth airfields during a *Freelance* low-level *Intruder* patrol of the Baltic coast in support of an attack by 336 aircraft of 5 Group on Sassnitz. At Griefswald, Bartlam and Harvey attacked north to south, and many strikes were seen on the Ju 52, an unidentified aircraft and a tractor. Bartlam pulled out of his dive at 400 ft and flew on to Barth where a second aircraft was damaged. The lights at Stalag Luft 1 at Barth were doused during the main attack by the heavies and again when Bartlam and Harvey attacked the airfield. It

must have been a tonic for the PoWs at the infamous Stalag Luft.

On 7/8 March, F/O Lewis Heath and F/Sgt Thompson of 23 Squadron surprised a Fw 190 near Stendal. Heath closed to 150 yards and fired a 2-second burst. Strikes were seen on the port wing, root and fuselage. It exploded on the ground 6 miles south of the airfield. This night a heavy bombing raid on Dessau destroyed the first two prototypes of the Ju 88 G-7 high-performance night-fighter *Moskitojäger* (Mosquito destroyer). On the following night, F/L Ian Dobie and W/O G. R. 'Grimmy' Grimstone DFM of 85 Squadron

*Mosquito Mk VI* B-Bertie *of 23 Squadron at Little Snoring. Note the 23 Squadron eagle emblem on the crew door. (Tom Cushing Collection)*

destroyed a Ju 188 near Hamburg. Shortly afterwards, they were shot down by flak near Koblenz. Dobie bailed out successfully and wandered into the American lines. Grimmy Grimstone was found with his parachute open but burnt, still attached to his body within 50 yards of the wreckage.

On 14/15 March, American pilot F/O (2/Lt) R. D. S. 'Hank' Gregor with his navigator/radar operator, F/Sgt Frank Baker, were on a lone 141 Squadron ASH patrol in the Frankfurt–Mannheim area in support of the bombers attacking Zweibrücken, near Saarbrücken when they picked up a contact coming into land at Lachen airfield. Gregor planned to intersect just short of the runway when a 'flood' lit the runway and the enemy aircraft was seen. Gregor reported:

My angle off was about 60° and range 2,000 ft so I opened fire at the 'silver shape' giving it one ring deflection and then spraying the area. We rapidly closed range to 100 ft and just as we started to pull out, the enemy aircraft exploded under our nose, illuminating the area. Almost immediately, light flak, not too accurate, came up at us, and a searchlight coned us. We dodged the searchlight by turning into it and diving. Frank then yelled 'The ASH altitude line's gone, Hank' so I hooked back on the stick and we left for home. Frank saw all the lights go out after the attack.

It was 141 Squadron's final air-to-air victory of the war.

The following night, 15/16 March, Capt Eric Fossum and F/O S. A. Hider of 85 Squadron closed in below a contact at 200 ft in the Hannover area. Hider used his night glasses and identified the bogey as a Ju 88. Fossum dropped back to 600 ft astern and level, and pumped a 2-second burst into the enemy machine. Strikes could be seen between the fuselage and port engine. The Norwegian fired a second burst. This time the Junkers exploded and the port engine burst into flames. Hider, watching the dying moments through his glasses, saw one crew member bail out of the doomed machine. Fossum, however, closed in for a third burst at 600 ft range. He did not want any of the crew to escape. Fossum blasted the machine again until a bright explosion appeared in the fuselage but Hider, still peering through his night glasses, saw two more crew abandon the doomed Ju 88 before the *coup de grace*. On the same night, F/L Jimmy Mathews and W/O Alan Penrose of 157 Squadron bagged a Ju 88 20 miles south of Würzburg, while on 16/17 March, S/L D. L. Hughes and F/L R. H. Perks of 239 Squadron destroyed a Ju 88 flown by Maj Werner Hoffmann (53 victories) near Nürnberg. On 18/19 March, F/L F. D. Win and F/O T. P. Ryan of 85 Squadron destroyed a Bf 110; W/O Taylor and F/Sgt Radford of 157 Squadron destroyed a Ju 88; and W/C W. F. Gibb and Killer Kendall of 239 Squadron destroyed a

*On 18/19 March 1945, W/C W. F. Gibb DSO, DFC and F/O R. C. 'Killer' Kendall DFC destroyed a He 219 and another Uhu was destroyed on the night of 20/21 March by F/L G. C. Chapman and F/Sgt J. Stockley of 85 Squadron. The Owl pictured has both* Lichtenstein *SN-2 and C-1 radar. Fortunately for the Mosquitoes, up until May 1944, only I./NJG 1 was equipped with the He 219. NJG 10, an experimental anti-Mosquito Gruppe based at Werneuchen near Berlin, became the second Uhu unit to be formed. (via Hans-Peter Dabrowski)*

He 219 Owl. Nachtjadgeschwader crews had little defence against the Mosquitoes. Even their SN-2 AI band could now be jammed since several Fortresses of 214 Squadron had each been fitted with six installations of the latest development of *Piperack*.

Advances by the Allied Armies made most of the month's operations comparatively deep penetrations, and it was not easy to confuse the German plotters once the Main Forces had passed the early stages of their routes over enemy territory. This was overcome in the latter part of the month by splitting the *Window* Force, and by operating the Mandrel aircraft in the double role of Mandrel and *Window*. By these means, and with the co-operation of the American 492nd BG, it was possible to make several feint attacks simultaneously on widely separated areas. The supporting fighters of 100 Group could do little about enemy fighters which occasionally got into the stream and shot down a number of bombers, because they were flying well away from the bomber stream owing to the difficulty of operating AI in the midst of the *Window* and bomber echoes. It became clear that AI Mk X could be used for close escort provided the Mosquitoes flew above the bombers where the H2S and *Window* interference was least. It was decided to try again a close escort of the stream, and it was hoped that with experience the crews would become better able to operate among *Window* and bomber echoes. The first close escort of the bomber stream was carried out in March.

On 20/21 March, no less than three feint attacks took place in support of the Main Force attack on Bohlen. The *Window* Force left the Main Stream soon after crossing the front line, and made for Kassel, which was bombed. Further on, when closer to the true target, another *Window* Force broke off and bombed Halle. The third feint force was provided by the Mandrel screen which, after the passage of the heavies, re-formed into a *Window* Force and attacked Frankfurt with flares. Flight Lieutenant G. C. Chapman and Flight Sergeant Jimmy Stockley of 85 Squadron took off from

Swannington at 01:45 hours in their Mosquito XXX on a high-level escort of bombers to Bohlen. While en route to patrol, a *Perfectos* contact was obtained at 02:55 hours just after passing Hamm at 12 miles range and 12,000 ft. Chapman wrote later:

Range was closed to 1 mile but no AI contact was obtained, and the range started to increase again, so deciding that the contact must be below, we did a hard diving turn to port, down to 9,000 ft and finally, D/F'd on to the target's course at 7 miles range. We closed in to 6 miles range and an AI contact was obtained at 6 o'clock. The target was climbing and we closed in rapidly and obtained a visual at 900 ft, height 13,000 ft. The target was still climbing straight ahead and was identified with the night glasses as a Me 110. It had a pale blue light between the starboard nacelle and fuselage. I closed in to 600 ft and pulled up to dead astern when the Hun started to turn to port. I gave it a ½-ring deflection and a 3-second burst, whereupon the enemy aircraft exploded in the port engine in a very satisfactory manner, with debris flying back. It exploded on the ground at 03:05 hours

25–30 miles NW of Kassel. All this excitement was too much for the Perfectos which went u/s unfortunately, so we set course for the rendezvous with the bomber stream.

Chapman and Stockley reached the bomber stream at 03:22 hours. Their patrol was uneventful until the stream left the target at 04:00 hours. Chapman continues:

I noticed to port and 15 miles south a ball of yellowish flame take off and climb very rapidly (Plauen airfield). I thought it was a flare or a V-2 (a little out of position) until it started emitting a meteor tail several hundred feet long. We turned port towards it, and lost height to 7,000 ft, that being the height of this phenomenon as far as I could judge, and continued watching. It travelled in a NW direction very fast and suddenly to our astonishment fired off some RPs [rocket projectiles], four single and one pair, in the general direction of the departing bomber stream. We were pretty amazed at all this and decided that it must be a Me 163. I continued turning port and got behind it. It was vectoring 275° by this time and doing about 260 IAS and using the AI to check

*On 24/25 March, Dutchman F/O M. Huls and Belgian F/O Joe Kinet (pictured) of 515 Squadron flew a night Ranger to the Stendal area where at Buch dummy landing ground they destroyed a Fw 190 before making for home, dropping 40 4 lb incendiaries on Hustedt airfield north of Celle, en route (Tom Cushing Collection)*

range we closed in to 1,000 ft and visually identified a twin-engined aircraft with rocket apparatus slung under the fuselage – an He 219. [The He 219 V14 Uhu carried a BMW 109-003 turbojet, used in the He 162 Salamander programme, below the fuselage.] Considerable quantities of flames and sparks were flying back preventing me from identifying the tail unit, so I decided to open fire at that range. I gave it several longish bursts as two of the cannon had stoppages and was gratified to see an explosion take place somewhere in the fuselage and debris fly back. The enemy aircraft nosed straight down through the patchy cloud and exploded on the ground with a tremendous glare.

Chapman and Stockley landed back at Swannington at 06:52 hours to claim a Bf 110 and He 219 destroyed.

On 24/25 March, F/O M Huls and F/O Kinet of 515 Squadron flew a night *Ranger* to the Stendal area. Their presence caused consternation. Or did it? The flarepath was lit and doused three times but was identified as Buch landing ground, classified as a dummy in the Intelligence Section's 'List of Airfields, Vol 1 Germany' back at Snoring. Huls and Kinet dropped two flares and went in at 500 ft to spot three Fw 190s dispersed at the runway threshold. Both men were convinced the dummy landing ground was being used as an

airfield and Huls climbed to 1,500 ft and picked out one of the Fw 190s which he gave a long burst of cannon fire before pulling out at 500 ft. The Fw 190 began to burn fiercely and emit a column of smoke. Huls levelled out and the AA defences opened up but they were well clear before any hits could be registered. Not content with their night's work, on their way home they dropped 40 4 lb incendiary bombs on the east-west flarepath at Hustedt airfield north of Celle which was lit up, and caused fires on the south side of the flarepath.

Meanwhile, F/O Bunny Adams and F/Sgt Frank Widdicombe, who had damaged a Ju 88 the previous month, really went to town on their night *Ranger*, to the München area after a refuelling stop at Juvincourt. They made three low runs over Erding airfield and on the third their shells overshot and struck a hanger but a line of at least six aircraft were seen in the south-west corner. Adams and Widdicombe attacked from north to south and sprayed the entire line. The second aircraft exploded and disintegrated and this was claimed 'destroyed', with four claimed as 'damaged'.

On 30/31 March Leslie Holland and Bob Young were assigned to another anti-flak job. 'As it was not at such a great distance,' recalls Dutch Holland, 'there would be time to look for a bit more trouble elsewhere.'

*F/O Bunny Adams (centre), F/Sgt Frank Widdicombe (left) and Bob Young, all of 515 Squadron, eating cabbages collected during an evasion exercise in Yorkshire. On 24/25 March 1945, Adams and Widdicombe flew a night* Ranger *to the München area and made three low runs over Erding airfield and sprayed a line of aircraft, exploding one and damaging four more. (Leslie Holland)*

*The Mosquito was no match for the Me 262 which, fitted with SN2, was used as a night-fighter to attack the bomber streams. Construction No. 130 056, seen here, was experimentally fitted with SN2 in October 1944 for night-fighter tests, being flown by Oberst Hajo Herrmann of Jagddivision 30. It proved very successful but fortunately for RAF heavy bomber and night-fighter crews, Me 262 night-fighters arrived in too few numbers and too late to seriously affect the outcome. (Hans-Peter Dabrowski)*

*Close up of SN-2 Lichtenstein radar antenna fitted to a Me 262A for night-fighter tests in October 1944. Only one prototype Me 262B-2a with extended fuselage and four MK 108 cannons (two in a Schräge Musik installation behind the cockpit for firing obliquely) was flown before the war ended. The Hirschgeweih (antlers) produced so much drag that speed was reduced by as much as 37 mph. A second prototype, fitted with centimetric radar, never entered production. (via Hans-Peter Dabrowski)*

Then mine-laying was to be carried out in the Weser between Bremen and Bremerhaven, so we were expecting to run into some pretty hot opposition. As it turned out, it proved to be a somewhat tame affair with nothing like the reaction we had provoked up the Oslo Fiord.

As a secondary operation we had elected to poke our nose in at Nordholz, a few miles further north near Cuxhaven. Our briefing maps had been pretty specific about aircraft parking stands in among the trees on the north side of the field. It was easy enough to find after having detoured out to sea round Bremerhaven and looked pretty bare of any 'game'. But we had some flares and incendiaries on board. The flares were dropped first over the middle of the field and showed that nothing had been carelessly left out in the open. So, try the coverts next and see what we could draw from them. The incendiaries were duly laid in a string across the shubbery on the north side and 'OHO, what have we here?'

In amongst the parking bays, several twin-engine aircraft without propellers and no reflections from their noses. More than likely Me 262s. This is where the handiness of the Mosquito comes in because a lot has got to be done before the fires go out. Steeply round for a low run with a short burst which hits a trifle short but just time to correct and cover the pens with strikes. Round for another run and by this time the gun crews, probably a trifle out of breath, have got to their posts and are answering back. But this is too good to miss, so back for a couple more runs by which time there is a confused cloud of smoke and fire. We reckon we have done enough to claim one Me 262 destroyed and two damaged, and head for home once more. And on the way out we see an odd thing, a submarine flying a balloon. We don't know whose it is, so refrain from attacking and do not call attention to it until debriefing. My guess is that it was an Allied submarine with an aerial raised by the balloon for signals monitoring.

Somewhere in Holland, flying at about 1,000 ft we were startled to see a V-2 rise off its pad about a mile in front of us. I slipped off the safety catch but it rose at an unbelievable rate into the clouds at about 2,000 ft, lighting up the whole sky in a weird flickering brilliant violet glow. We couldn't trace the pad but made a note of the map references so that someone could come and have a look in daylight; but some of the sites were mobile. I have also been near to being on the receiving end of those beasties and the sudden arrival has a shocking effect much worse than the ones you hear coming.

Although late in the European war, higher authority was viewing with increasing interest the importance of the *Mandrel* and *Window* feint forces. In April, the Mandrel squadrons, 171 and 199, were authorized to increase their strength by four more aircraft each, and on several occasions a small force, usually 20–24 heavy bombers, was allocated from either 4 or 7 Group to support the *Window* Force. Mosquito PR XVIs replaced the Mk IVs in 192 Squadron; their aircraft had been fitted with *Dina* and *Piperack* jamming equipment earlier that year. The Liberators of 223 Squadron were also to be replaced by new Fortresses, the old and worn B-24s having shown themselves too slow to keep up with the British bombers. Later in the month, with the front line beginning to advance further into Germany, the *Mandrel* screen formation was discarded and these aircraft flew with the bombers on three occasions, and the Mosquitoes' targets became more and more distant.

On 1/2 April 1945, four 515 Squadron Mosquitoes took part in a night *Ranger* operation in the München and Augsburg–Ingolstadt areas from their forward base at Juvincourt. Howard Kelsey and Smitty Smith stooged around many airfields in the München area but found no fighters and failed to make any ASH contacts. Kelsey attacked a factory with incendiary bombs and caused terrific explosions and a large fire. Bunny Adams and Frank Widdicombe attacked seven Bf 109s on the ground at Erding with cannon fire and damaged one before attacking Lechfeld airfield, causing fires and explosions. Leipheim airfield was attacked by S/L John Penny and F/O Whitfield, and Lt E. J. Van Heerden SAAF and F/O J. W. Robson. The South African and his navigator were killed when their Mosquito was shot down by an AA battery manned by Hitler Youth. Penny proceeded to Neuburg where he found nothing. Returning to Leipheim, he bombed the dispersals with incendiary bombs and attacked and damaged a truck at Ertingen before turning for home.

Operations were flown even further afield, to the Czech border, as Leslie Holland recalls:

Several Main Force attacks were made on points where there were railway concentrations in order to disorganize the movement of troops from the eastern front. In support of one of these we were assigned to patrol the airfield at Plauen, which is pretty near the Czech border. As it happened, the winds took advantage of the 2½ hours to target to increase and get round to the south. I couldn't claim with confidence that we had located our assigned airfield because a large marshalling yard which appeared beneath us convinced us that we were at Pilsen. There was a great deal of activity and it seemed a good idea to illuminate the scene a little better. There

*The first experimental German jet night-fighter unit was called* Kommando Stamp, *which was created on 28 January 1945 with 10 Me 262B trainers, redesignated -1a/U1 fitted with FuG 218 Neptun and FuG 350 radar, four Mk 108 cannons and drop tanks under the nose. This unit was later redesignated* Kommando Welter *(in April 1945 it became 10/JG 11) after Staffelkapitän Oblt Kurt Welter who was given orders to defend Berlin. Welter scored three of his unit's eight Mosquito kills and finished the war with 61 victories, 35 of them Mosquitoes. (via Hans-Peter Dabrowski)*

W-William *and crew in 223 Squadron at Oulton pose next to a 214 Squadron Fortress. In April 1945, 223 Squadron, which was equipped with Liberators, received a number of Fortress IIs and IIIs including KJ121. Note the waist gun interrupter gear used to prevent the tail being shot off at night; the* Window *chute (underside far left), and the* Jostle IV *transmission mast (for jamming German R/T transmissions) atop the fuselage. Crew* (left to right): *F/Sgt Benn Buff, beam gunner; Sgt Sam Leach, tail gunner; F/O Joe Doolin, wireless operator; F/O Hal Booth, navigator; F/L Gordon Bremness, pilot; Sgt Murdo McIver, beam gunner; Sgt Don Prutton, flight engineer. Sgt Roy Storr, mid-upper gunner. (Don Prutton)*

were, we thought, a flare and incendiaries in the fuselage bay, but dropping these from 500 ft gave us a considerable surprise. The flare turned out to be a 250 lb bomb with contact fuse but fortunately splinters and debris passed us by. The incendiaries proved more true to form. (In fact the load had been changed after the briefing.) At the least we certainly made a hole in the tracks and carried on the good work by damaging some of the locos and rolling stock with cannon fire.

*Richard Moule RCAF of the 515 Squadron Radar Section at Little Snoring early in 1945. ASH radar equipment was carried in the nose of the Mosquito after the Browning machine-guns were removed. ASH could electronically search the skies to a distance of 20–30 miles ahead with a 180° horizontal sweep, 20° above and below flight path. This enabled the navigator to home in on the target so that the pilot could obtain a visual, day or night. Destruction of the target often followed. (Richard Moule via Tom Cushing)*

Having more or less established our position (as we thought), it was then necessary to think about the rather long trek home. Shortly after this, an area of scattered conflagrations to starboard of our track led us to make a tentative identification of Leipzig, which had been the Main Force target. This meant that it was Chemnitz and not Pilsen which we had treated in such cavalier fashion and we were making both much more northing than we wished and slow progress over the ground. After about another hour it was becoming apparent that our fuel state would need careful management. In view of the increased and adverse wind it seemed best to keep at a fairly low altitude and pull back the revs a bit. Much later, the north German islands began to drift past aggravatingly slowly. It now looked as though we might have a problem and some nice calculations began to occupy the fingers of both hands. It would be very much touch and go. Fifty miles out, the gauges were pretty near their marks. A

Mayday from here should get us a clear run through the Norfolk anti-*Diver* belt. This would ensure a straight descending run into the first airfield that could receive us – Coltishall. The fuel pressure warning lights were on during the approach and the touch of the wheels on the asphalt was accompanied by the exaltation we had been delaying for the last 5 minutes. As we turned off the runway the engines stopped.

On 3/4 April, eight Mosquitoes of 157 Squadron made a *Spoof* raid on Berlin in support of 8 Group Mosquitoes. Over the Big City, F/L J. H. Leland was coned by the searchlights and a Me 262, seeing its chance, made four attacks on the Mosquito. Two strikes were recorded on Leland's engines but he escaped his pursuer after spinning his aircraft and heading flat out for friendly territory. On 4/5 April, 141 Squadron dispatched its first Mosquito XXX sortie when three joined 12 from 239 Squadron in a bomber support operation

*This Hitler Youth AA gun crew was responsible for shooting down Mosquito VI PZ249 flown by Lt Van Heerden SAAF and F/O Robson of 515 Squadron on 4 April 1945. They were the first and last these young Germans shot down during the whole war. (Tom Cushing via Peter G. Horner)*

for the heavies attacking synthetic oil plants in southern Germany. This same night, F/L C. W. 'Topsy' Turner and 20-year-old F/Sgt George 'Jock' Honeyman, from Edinburgh, both of A Flight in 85 Squadron, took off from Swannington at 22:38 hours for a high-level escort of the *Window* Force. Escort was only a loose term because in the dark it was not possible to fly any kind of formation over long distances. Turner and Honeyman were new boys who had joined the squadron in November when they were somewhat dazzled by the arrays of 'gongs' worn by aces such as Burbridge and Skelton (DSO* and DFC* each) and A. J. 'Ginger' Owen and McAllister (DFC*, DFM). These crews finished the war with 21 and 15 victories respectively. They flew their freshman op on the night of 29 December 1944 and would fly 17 ops together on the Mosquito. It was Turner's first tour as a pilot. He had been a gunner on Hampdens and had been shot down twice.

Topsy Turner piloted the Mosquito on a course of 090°. On crossing into enemy territory at the Dutch coast, they began their climb to their tasked height of 20,000 ft. After nearly 2 hours, they reached their patrol area north-west of Magdeburg. All the time Jock was scanning the AI and all the other interception aids. Their Mosquito was equipped with Mk X radar, which George Honeyman considered:

probably the best AI of WWII . . . It could be operated down to circuit height of 1,000–1,500 ft. In addition, there were two additional displays. *Perfectos,* a small diameter cathode ray tube fitted in the AI visor, displayed enemy IFF transmissions. Only left or right indications were given but the transmitting aircraft could be detected at a much greater range than was possible

using AI which relied on the echo from the fighter aircraft's own transmission. *Monica,* fitted at the bottom of the instrument panel, showed on its display aircraft coming from behind from a range of 1–2 miles. Every day the Y-Service provided the enemy colours of the day and we carried similar cartridges for the Very pistols, to try to confuse enemy Bofors fire which was usually encountered on *Intruder* sorties at low level over enemy airfields. The only navigational aid was *Gee* which could only be received as far as Holland because of enemy jamming. From there it was DR based on a detailed flight plan.

At approximately 22:38 hours, Jock Honeyman picked an AI contact and immediately began his commentary to Topsy who had a visual range of only 800–1,000 yards, depending on moonlight conditions.

Contact 3½ miles, 20°. Starboard, crossing starboard to port . . . Turn port . . . Go down. Range now 2 miles, 10°. Starboard – harder port. Target now 12 o'clock, 5° above, 1 mile. Level off, ease the turn. Now steady; 800 yards 12 o'clock, 10° above; 600 yards, 12 o'clock 15° above – throttle back; 12 o'clock,

*F/Sgt George 'Jock' Honeyman, navigator with F/L C. W. 'Topsy' Turner in 85 Squadron, who shot down a Junkers Ju 188 on the night of 4/5 April 1945. (George Honeyman)*

20°, minimum range – hold that speed. Can't you see him?

Topsy called 'Visual.' He opened up the throttles and slowly closed in on a gently weaving target, adjusting his gunsight and switching on his camera-gun. At 100 yards, there was no Type F response (an infrared telescope which could pick up a light source fitted under the tail of RAF bombers but invisible to the naked eye because the light was covered by a black shield, known as Type Z). Using night binoculars, the target was identified from underneath as a Ju 188. Topsy dropped back to 200 yards to open fire when a black object, possibly a single-engined fighter, whistled across their bows at about 100 ft. Both men ducked smartly. Turner continues:

After multiple curses and bags of brow-mopping, we saw our quarry still ahead and I opened fire from 200 yards astern with 5° deflection, obtaining strikes on the port engine. Two more short bursts made the Hun burn nicely. It spun and crashed, burning fiercely on the ground, west of Magdeburg.

At 01:30 hours, *C-Charlie* landed back at Swannington after 4 hours 40 minutes in the air. This was their one and only kill of the war.

On 9/10 April, W/C Kelsey, the CO 515 Squadron, and Smitty Smith, flew an *Intruder* to Lübeck, a night-fighter base which was still active. Edward Smith recalls:

After a while we spotted a Ju 88 taking off in dark conditions and had difficulty keeping it in radar contact and slowing down sufficiently to keep behind it. The Ju 88 was climbing very hard (probably with flaps). However, it was shot at and we saw several strikes. (After the war I was with 85 Squadron at Tangmere and visited Lübeck and whilst there I was told there was

somewhere about, the remnants of a Ju 88 from the appropriate time.) After that all was quiet and we headed off towards Hamburg. I spotted an aircraft coming in behind us. We feinted to the right then circled hard to port, coming in behind him in part moonlight. We had no trouble in shooting the Ju 188 down. We continued over Hamburg and dropped the *Intruder* load of two 500 lb HE and 160 incendiaries.

The were definite signs that the end of the war could be in sight but as Leslie Holland in 515 Squadron recalls:

W/C Kelsey and 100 Group between them seemed determined that we should not become bored during its last throes. On 15/16 April Schleissheim, the airfield at Munich, was selected for special attention probably because it was a likely transit point for German staff movements now that Allied armies were closing in from east and west. Be that as it may, it was supposed to have been a co-ordinated attack but I do not recall it as having been a particularly well planned operation. We had the usual feeling that it was Bob and I alone against the Third Reich. In the absence of any general target illumination we used our own incendiaries to light up the area round the airfield buildings. Incidentally, it's a hell of a long way to Munich and we just took it for granted that we would find the place. That we did so without any great difficulty is a credit to Bob. Features on the airfield were recognizable from the photos we had studied at briefing. The object of the exercise being to create mayhem, we used our 20 mm guns on the airfield buildings, concentrating on the control tower which cannot have been too pleasant for its occupants.

After this little gesture, we climbed to about 2,000 ft and flew round Munich trailing our coat, looking for anything that might turn up. Having left behind the light flak at low level which had been hardly enough to mention, it was noticeable that the heavy guns undoubtedly disposed round the city did not seem over-concerned with one or two relatively innocuous Mosquitoes droning around, even though we might have been pathfinders. They probably couldn't set their fuses for that level. We once flew at about 2,000 ft right across the Ruhr (accidentally) without a shot being fired. Bob said it was because they couldn't believe that a hostile aircraft would do anything so stupid. There might have been balloons but the thought didn't occur to us at the time.

While over the northern purlieus of Munich, Bob picked up a contact on our level, range about 1 mile and out to our right. Having turned sharply towards the supposed position of the bogey (it could have of course been one of our own aircraft), a light came into view which was evidently on the aircraft we were tracking. It was not difficult to get into a position behind it but we came near to running into it as it was evidently doing very much less than our 240 mph. A wide S turn brought us back behind it and although our speed was very much reduced, we were still too near and closing too fast. As we passed beneath, the fixed landing gear of a Ju 52 could be seen distinctly but the white light made it almost impossible to pick out any other features against the moonless sky. It seemed to be doing about 120 mph in a slow turn round an airfield beacon, probably in a holding orbit until things had settled down at Schleissheim.

It didn't take too long to decide that although it was a transport aircraft and might be unarmed (some did carry defensive armament) there was no doubt in our minds that the chance that it could be carrying top brass or war material meant that it must be attacked. The next approach brought us into firing position and a burst of 20 mm was aimed at each of the wing engines. As we

passed, it had already begun a descending turn and there appeared to be fire in the wing engines. We did not see it again and the trace disappeared from our radar.

[No.] 515 had more casualties than any other squadron in 100 Group. I suppose there was a tendency to avoid dwelling on the fact if someone 'got the chop'. It just seems that it didn't happen very often and most of our particular mates came through OK.

There remained one more task before hostilities ceased in the wide-ranging activities of 515 Squadron. On 14/15 April, 515 Squadron and 23 Squadron flew the first Mosquito Master Bomber sorties in 100 Group, dropping green TIs and orchestrating attacks by 18 Mosquitoes of 141 and 169 Squadrons which carried a new, even more sinister form of aerial bomb for the first time, going under the code-name *Firebash*.

*23 Squadron and 515 Squadron Victory scoreboard which is displayed on a wall of Little Snoring Church. (Author)*

# CHAPTER 14

# *FIREBASH*

*The fires are grey; no star, no sign*
*Winks from the breathing darkness of the carrier*
*Where the pilot circles for his wingman; where,*
*Gliding above the cities' shells, a stubborn eye*
*Among the embers of the nations, achingly*
*Tracing the circles of that worn, unchanging No –*
*The lives' long war, lost war – the pilot sleeps.*

'THE DEAD WINGMAN' BY RANDALL JARRELL

The quaint English locomotive steamed through the enchanting Norfolk countryside, tugging its carriages behind it. In one of the 1st-class compartments, Winnie Winn DFC, 141 Squadron CO, *en route* to his station at West Raynham, sat opposite a USAAF officer. They were alone in the compartment and were soon in animated conversation, the American exchanging pointers on the daylight air war, and Winn extolling the merits of night bombing. During the course of the conversation the American told Winn that the 8th Air Force intended to drop napalmgel (petrol thickened with a compound made from aluminium, naphthenic and palmitic acids – hence 'napalm' – to which white phosphorous was added for ignition) on enemy installations. Winn was excited at the prospect of using this lethal weapon on enemy airfields. Before the day was out, the dynamic RAF officer had obtained permission to use his squadron to drop the gel in Mosquito 100-gallon drop tanks, providing he could obtain his own supplies.

Winn made a call to the 8th Air Force and 40-gallon and 50-gallon drums of napalmgel soon began arriving at West Raynham, courtesy of the Americans. At first armourers, pumped it into drop tanks using hand pumps but then the Americans obliged with petrol-driven mechanical pumps and the operation became much easier. Armourer LAC Johnny Claxton, at that time one of the longest-serving members of 141 Squadron's groundcrews, recalls that a 1 lb all-way phosphorous fuze was fitted in each tank to ignite the napalmgel on impact. The fuze was called all-way because no matter how the tank fell the fuze would ignite the contents.

In the afternoon of 6 April, W/C Winn carried out the first of three trials of types of napalmgel when he flew low and parallel with the main No. 1 runway and dropped 100 gallon drop tanks on the grass. These trials caused enormous interest and the station and aircrew crowded in the control tower while the groundcrews climbed on to the roofs of the hangars in order to get a better view of the explosions. It was decided that crews who would drop napalmgel required no additional training because they had carried out enough low-level attacks with bombs or cannon over many months; no special tactics were to be employed. Enthusiasm and keenness to get on the night's napalmgel programme reached a fever pitch. When six aircraft were asked for, a dozen were offered – and accepted! Petrol and range was reduced so that each Mosquito could carry two 100-gallon drop tanks of napalmgel but, even so, they would have to land at Juvincourt, Melsbroek or Mannheim. No one was unhappy about this arrangement as it offered the possibility of being stranded on the Continent for days!

Napalmgel came in three different consistencies – thick, medium and thin. Winnie Winn carried out two further trials over West Raynham's grass expanses, on 12 and 13 April, in front of large audiences. As a result of the trials, it was discovered that the thick gel failed to ignite.

The following night, 14/15 April, 18 Mosquito VIs and XXXs were dispatched from West Raynham. Twelve were from 141 Squadron and six from 239 Squadron, some of which were detailed to provide support for the 512 bombers attacking Potsdam just outside Berlin. This was the first time the Big City had been attacked by heavies since March 1944, although Mosquito bombers had continually attacked it. Seven Mosquitoes of 141 Squadron flew high-level Mk X AI patrols in support of the Potsdam raid but also covered the remaining five 141 Mosquitoes which would carry out the first napalmgel *Firebash* raid on night-fighter airfields at Neuruppin near Potsdam and Jüterbog near Berlin.

Winnie Winn with R. A. W. Scott in a Mk VI led the formation of five napalmgel aircraft to Brussels/Melsbroek for refuelling before setting course for the Berlin area where they were to be supported by bomb and incendiary carrying Mosquitoes of 23 Squadron which also supplied the 'Noload' leader, the Master Bomber, for the Neuruppin raid. Master of Ceremonies, S/L H. V. Hopkins, provided 'excellent support' and Winn dropped his canisters from 800 ft. He was followed by F/O R. W. A. Marriott and F/O N. Barber, and F/O W. P. Rimer and F/O H. B. Farnfield. All six napalm bombs exploded near the hangars

*Mosquito Mk XXX flown by Graham Chalky White of 239 Squadron over Hamburg at the end of the war after hostilities had ended.*
*(Graham Chalky White)*

and engulfed the airfield in flame and smoke. A row of six buildings burned merrily and lit up the night sky as all three Mosquitoes, unburdened now, returned to strafe the airfield with cannon fire. Red tracer every fifth shell zeroed in on buildings and bowsers, one of which exploded in a huge flash of flame near a hangar. Rimer and Farnfield strafed the hapless base three times from 2,000 ft to 500 ft in all, helped in no small measure by TIs dropped just south-east of the airfield by the Master Bomber.

At Jüterbog, F/L M. W. Huggins, the Master of Ceremonies, with F/O C. G. Stow, a 515 Squadron 'Sollock' aircraft (Master Bomber), was unable to help much and no TIs were seen to drop which scattered over about a 10-mile area. Ron Brearley with John Sheldon and F/L E. B. Drew with F/O A. H. Williams thundered low over the German countryside and had to toss their napalm bombs on the estimated position of the airfield. One of Brearley's drop tanks hung up so he dropped the port tank containing 50 gallons of napalmgel from 300 ft and headed west. (Returning with a napalmgel tank still attached was, as one could imagine, 'pretty dicey'. On a later *Firebash* op, one tank that would not release over the target, fell off on the West Raynham runway on the aircraft's return. These hang-ups occurred due to deposits of napalm on the release unit, and at the joint between the tank and the mainplanes.) Drew meanwhile, was forced to climb to 5,000 ft and position on *Gee*, following the failure of the TIs and flares, before he dropped down to 1,000 ft and roared over the base with the two 100-gallon drop tanks ready to rain death and destruction. The two fire-bombs exploded among rows of buildings in the north-west corner of the airfield and were still burning 13 minutes later as he twice strafed buildings amid light and inaccurate flak. All five fire-bomber Mosquitoes landed back at

Melsbroek for refuelling before returning to West Raynham, no doubt highly delighted with their night's work.

On 17 April, Johnnie Bridekirk and Terry Glasheen, a universally popular Australian crew crashed when taking off from Brussels/Melsbroek airfield in the early hours of the morning. The Mosquito went up in flames, and those who saw the crash say that they never expected the crew to escape with their lives. However, Terry Glasheen put up a magnificent show by dragging his pilot clear of the flames, and there is no doubt that his level-headedness and courage prevented a terrible tragedy. Terry Glasheen was back on the Squadron within a comparatively few days but Johnny Bridekirk suffered extensive burns and was condemned to many weary weeks in hospital.

The second *Firebash* raid by 141 Squadron was flown on 17/18 April. Bomber Command was also abroad this night, with attacks by 5 Group on railway yards at Cham, Germany. Five 141 Squadron Mosquitoes, each armed with 100-gallon napalmgel drop tanks, and led by W/C Winnie Winn, were to head for Schleissheim airfield just north of München, after a refuelling stop at St Dizier. However, after landing at St Dizier, Winn was delayed with refuelling problems when petrol had to be brought 60 miles by road. He decided that by the time they got off and found the target they would be unable to see the markers, and opted for an attack on München instead. However, a bad storm front scrubbed this option and he and Scott were forced to return to England.

The three remaining napalm-armed Mosquito crews battled through solid cloud and violent thunderstorms to Schleissheim but Rimer and Farnfield were forced to abort after losing *Gee*. After vainly trying to climb above the thick cloud, S/L Thatcher was also forced to abandon the mission. Another crew, F/O J. C. Barton with Sgt L.

Berlin, fought their way through the storm front and hurled their napalm bombs among airfield buildings, then, obtaining permission from the 23 Squadron Master Bomber, strafed the airfield on a return low-level run. Roy Brearley with John Sheldon climbed to 10,000 ft to escape the worst of the weather, and diving down on pinpoints provided by 'Noload' they added fuel to the flames with their two napalm bombs. They fell among two hangars and exploded. They called up the Master Bomber before returning and strafing hangars, buildings and rolling stock, then exiting the area to allow 23 Squadron to add their bombs and incendiaries to the conflagration.

Meanwhile, Mosquitoes of 85 Squadron patrolled Schleissheim and Fürstenfeld-brück airfields. Wing Commander Davison, 85 Squadron CO since W/C K. 'Gon' Gonsalves had been posted in January, destroyed a Ju 88 in the München area using *Perfectos*. On the following night, 18/19 April 1945, seven 141 Squadron Mosquitoes each carrying two 100-gallon drop tanks filled with napalm, eight Mosquitoes of 169 Squadron from Great Massingham, four Mosquito IVs of 23 Squadron and four of 515 Squadron from Little Snoring, and one 141 Squadron aircraft for high-level Mk X AI patrol over the target, flew to the forward base at Juvincourt in France for a *Firebash* raid on München/Neubiberg airfield. The eight Mosquitoes from 23 and 515 Squadrons and the eight Mosquitoes of 169 Squadron were to drop flares and HE on München/Neubiberg with 141 adding to the destruction.

The raid was in full swing when 141 Squadron, led once more by Winn, arrived at München/Neubiberg with their napalm loads. F/L Drew and P/O A. H. Williams were ready to commence their-low level bomb run at 700 ft but had to wait 25 minutes before they could take their turn. To add insult to injury, one of their fire-

bombs refused to release. Drew climbed to 7,000 ft and tried to shake it loose and finally got it safely away just north of München. On the instructions of 'Noload Leader', the Master Bomber, W/O Ronald G. Dawson and F/O Charles P. D. Childs, an all New Zealand crew in *Winball 7*, went in for their fire-bombing run. The 24-year-old pilot and his 32-year-old navigator/radar operator had joined 141 Squadron on 22 January and this was their tenth op. It was the last they would complete. As they hurtled into the attack they heard in their headphones the Master Bomber's warning of accurate light flak but pressed bravely on. Just as they reached their drop point *Winball 7* was hit by flak. The New Zealanders' Mosquito appeared to climb and some 10 seconds later crashed in flames near an autobahn north-west of the airfield. One of the tanks seemed to ricochet into the air and fall back into the burning pyre. They were the last casualties on 141 Squadron in WW2.

On 19/20 April, three squadrons of Mosquitoes flew a napalm raid against Flensburg airfield on the Danish border. Six Mosquito Mk VIs of 515 Squadron marked the target with green TIs and flares, and dropped incendiaries and 500 lb HE bombs. The CO of 515 Squadron, Howard Kelsey, with Smitty Smith, was Master Bomber. Three Mosquito VIs of 169 Squadron took off from Great Massingham and flew to West Raynham to load up with napalm tanks for their first napalm attack. The same aircraft also carried two 500 lb bombs beneath their wings. No. 141 Squadron were unable to carry bombs on its Mk XXX Mosquitoes as well as napalm tanks because they did not have bomb racks or the release mechanisms fitted in the bomb-bay behind the cannons. For the same reason, 169 Squadron were unable to use their Mk XIX Mosquitoes. The attack was very successful with good work by the Master Bomber. Flensburg was plastered and strafed from end to end, and smoke

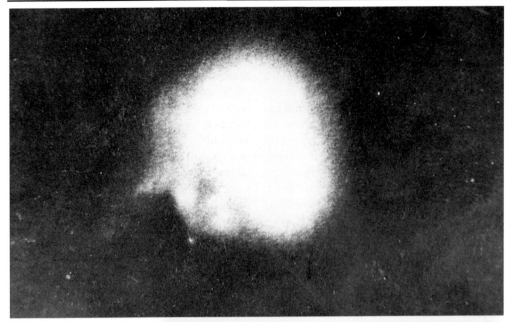

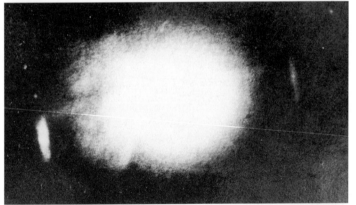

*Camera-gun sequence showing W/C Howard C. Kelsey DFC\* and F/L E. M. Smith DFC, DFM of 515 Squadron showing the last moments of the crew of a Do 217 which they destroyed at Libeznice, 6 miles north of Prague on 24/25 April 1945. Kelsey and Smith thus earned the distinction of getting the first (23/24 December) and last kills in 100 Group. (Tom Cushing Collection)*

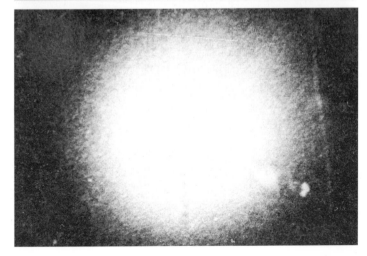

and flame made observation of the final result difficult. Count Bernadotte, the head of the Swedish Red Cross, was at this time using the airfield to fly back and forth between Sweden and Germany for secret negotiations with Heinrich Himmler who hoped to extract a separate surrender. The Count, and his chauffeur, narrowly escaped death during the attack.

Further napalmgel attacks were carried out on 22/23 April. Jagel was attacked by Mosquito XXXs of 141 Squadron, three Mosquitoes of 169 Squadron and four Mosquitoes of 515 Squadron, led by Master Bomber S/L J. H. Penny, with F/O J. H. Whitfield, who dropped green TIs and incendiaries. Flak greeted them and a 141 Squadron Mosquito flown by F/L G. M. Barrowman with W/O H. S. Griffiths, suffered severe damage in the starboard

wing and inner fuel tank. They returned to England hugging the German and Dutch coasts, keeping the Frisians in sight to port, and landed safely at Woodbridge. Five Mosquitoes of 141 Squadron with napalm tanks, and five Mosquitoes of 23 Squadron with S/L H. V. Hopkins as Master Bomber, bombed Westerland airfield on Sylt. Hopkins, aware that his TIs would not be seen because of the thick cloud over the target, instructed the Deputy Master Bomber to drop incendiaries. By 23 April, the British Second Army had arrived opposite Hamburg and on the next day its advanced units were on the west bank of the Elbe ready for the last thrust to Lübeck and Kiel. On 23 April, as part of the support operation for the ground troops, five Mosquitoes of 23 Squadron flew to Melsbroek with six napalm Mosquitoes of

*S/L H. V. 'Hoppy' Hopkins of 23 Squadron (right), pictured here with his CO, W/C Philip Russell (far left) and local farmer's daughter, Sheila Whitehead on the occasion of her wedding to Duncan Sherriff RNZAF of 23 Squadron. On 22/23 April 1945, Hopkins was Master Bomber for a* Firebash *attack on Westerland airfield on Sylt when five Mosquitoes of 141 Squadron carried napalm and five Mosquitoes of 23 Squadron carried incendiaries. Hopkins, aware that his TIs would not be seen because of the thick cloud over the target, instructed the Deputy Master Bomber to drop incendiaries. (Tom Cushing Collection)*

*To the victor the spoils. A Me 262 trainer converted to night-fighter and equipped with FuG 218 Neptun and FuG 350 radar in RAF hands at the end of the war. (Tom Cushing Collection)*

141 Squadron led by W/C Winnie Winn, refuelled and crossed to Lübeck. That night, they plastered the airfield with HE, incendiaries and fire-bombs under the direction of Master Bomber S/L D. J. Griffiths of 23 Squadron. The whole attack took just 10 minutes; the airfield was left burning and devastated. All aircraft returned safely despite light, accurate flak put up by the defenders. That same night, 30 Mosquitoes and seven Lancasters dropped leaflets over eight PoW camps. The war was drawing to a close and the morale of the men behind the wire soared, while, at home, some worried that there would be no more opportunities to fly their Mosquitoes in anger.

On 24/25 April, six Mosquitoes of 141 Squadron carried out a napalm attack on München/Neubiberg airfield again. The 515 Squadron Master Bomber, S/L J. H. Penny, with F/O J. H. Whitfield, again marked for them; other 515 squadron aircraft flew support. During the patrol, F/L J. Davis and F/O B. R. Cronin claimed eight enemy aircraft damaged on the ground during their six strafing and bombing runs with two 500 lb and 80 5 lb incendiaries over Kaufbeuren airfield. The aircraft were in the moon shadow of the hangar and positive identification was therefore impossible. A fire broke out in the hangar and could be seen through the open doors. Meanwhile, at Neubiberg, S/L Harry White DFC** with F/L Mike Allen DFC** also claimed the destruction of a single-engined enemy aircraft on the ground; it was also the last recorded victory for 141 Squadron in WW2. White and Allen dropped their napalm bombs with the safety pins still in but they exploded on impact and caused 'a good fire'. The raid was doubly gratifying for White and Allen who had patrolled the very same area in Beaufighters from August 1943.

On 25 April, special permission was granted for a single Halifax of 192 Squadron, with a full bomb load, to join 359 Lancasters on a raid on the SS barracks and Hitler's bunker at the Eagle's Nest. On 26 April, Bremen was taken by the British Army. On 25/26 April, the *Firebash* Mosquitoes attacked München/Reim airfield while four Mosquitoes of 515 Squadron with Lt W. Barton SAAF as Master Bomber, attacked Landsberg. Mosquitoes of 169 Squadron also took part in the raid on Landsberg. F/O J. K. 'Sport' Rogers, navigator to F/L Phil Kelshall, recalls:

For this operation we flew to RAF Oulton where our drop tanks were filled napalm. We returned to Massingham where the aircraft, a Mosquito VI (224) was armed with two 500 lb bombs and cannons loaded with

*F/L John 'Gracie' Fields (left), and Lt W. Barton SAAF (right) who was the 515 Squadron Master Bomber on 25/26 April for the Firebash raid on Landsberg.*

ammo. In the afternoon we flew to Juvincourt where we refuelled and waited for nightfall – the operation took place in moonlight, so navigation was easy. We flew at low level and made initial rendezvous with all the other aircraft at the north end of the Steinhuder Lake and checked in with Master Bomber.

At the agreed time made by the Master Bomber we made rendezvous over the airfield. We had all been assigned a call-sign in numerical order. At the appropriate time, the Master Bomber called in the first aircraft to drop napalm tanks – calling '01 clear' as it dropped its tanks and then at 10 second intervals the remainder of the aircraft followed to drop their napalm tanks. This routine was adopted to avoid collision over the target area which in this raid were the hangars and adjacent aircraft parking areas which had been previously illuminated with flares and target markers. Also in attendance were anti-flak aircraft to suppress the flak. Having dropped the napalm, we returned to orbit the airfield and when the last aircraft had completed its drop of napalm, the Master Bomber called for the 500 lb bombs to be dropped in the same sequence as before. Having completed the bomb-drop and again returned to orbit, the Master Bomber called for cannon fire, again in the

same sequence – the target area was a mass of flame by this time and the cannons were used to spray the area in the pass over the target. This completed the operation and we returned to Juvincourt – elapsed time 3 hr 40 min – where we stayed the night and returned to Massingham the next day.

Next day another consignment of 100-gallon drop tanks arrived at West Raynham. Word spread quickly that a final *Firebash* fling was in the offing. On 2 May, the British Second Army having crossed the Elbe now moved on to Lübeck and units of the British 6th Airborne Division reached Wismar on the Baltic and made contact with the Russian Army. The war was all over bar the shouting but Leslie Holland in 515 Squadron wrote:

May 2nd, and still, as far as we were concerned, there was no let up in the determination to break the regime that had been our mortal enemy for so long. Crusaderish? It was a pretty general feeling among aircrews at that time now that the end was in sight. With only five days to go before VE Day, 515 undertook just one more very hairy job.

Large convoys of ships were now

*The final 100 Group operation of the war took place on 2/3 May 1945 when a record 106 aircraft took part in napalm attacks on Flensburg and Hohn airfields in Schleswig-Holstein, Westerland and Jagel. 515 Squadron crews also dropped 50-gallon 'thermite' cylindrical bombs on Sylt; Leslie Holland, who flew this operation, has captured the scene in his very impressive painting of the raid.*

assembling at Kiel on the Baltic, and it was feared that they were to transport German troops to Norway to continue the fight from there. It was decided therefore that Mosquitoes of Bomber Command should attack Kiel on 2/3 May and this would be the very last operation of the war for Bomber Command. Some 126 Mosquitoes from 8 Group of the Pathfinder Force would follow in the wake of 16 Mosquitoes of 8 Group and 37 Mosquitoes of 100 Group in attacks on the Kiel area. Support for the night's operations would be provided by 21 *Mandrel/Window* sorties by 199 Squadron Halifaxes while 11 Fortresses of 214 Squadron and nine B-17s/B-24s of 223 Squadron would fly *Window*/jamming sorties over the Kiel area. At Foulsham, 10 Halifaxes of 462 Squadron would carry out a *Spoof* operation with *Window* and bombs against Flensburg while some of the 19 Halifaxes of 192 Squadron carried out a radio search in the area. Others dropped *Window* and TIs, and some also carried eight 500 lb bombs. Five Mosquitoes of 192 Squadron were also engaged in radio frequency work.

At North Creake, AVM Addy Addison was present during the take off of 39 aircraft, 18 of them Halifaxes from 171 Squadron, also heading for Kiel on *Mandrel/Window* operations. He expressed his satisfaction at the size of the final effort.

All told, a record 106 aircraft of 100 Group took part. Eight Mosquito XXXs of 239 Squadron took off from West Raynham for high-level and low-level raids on airfields in Denmark and Germany, while six Mosquitoes of 141 Squadron were to make napalm attacks on Flensburg airfield with 14 napalm-armed Mosquitoes attacking Hohn airfield. Master of Ceremonies at Flensburg would be F/O E. L. Heath of 23 Squadron while Master Bomber at Hohn was S/L D. J. Griffiths. Four Mosquitoes of 23 Squadron would drop incendiaries on Flensburg prior to the arrival by 141 Squadron, and seven more from 23 Squadron would bomb Hohn with incendiaries before the arrival of 141 Squadron's Mosquitoes. Meanwhile, 169 Squadron's Mosquitoes, plus four from 515 Squadron with F/L McEwan as Master Bomber with F/O Barnes, would raid Jagel. Four other Mosquitoes of 515 Squadron, with W/C Howard Kelsey as Master Bomber, would drop incendiaries on Westerland airfield on Sylt. Dutch Holland in 515 Squadron has written:

Just what was brewing at the Westerland I have never been able to find out precisely. It couldn't have been that it was a particularly active night-fighter base because I don't remember any patrols being assigned there, but it was believed that suicide missions

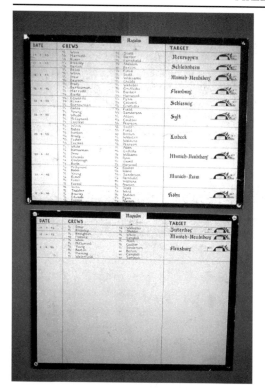

*141 and 239 Squadrons dropped napalm on German airfields during the closing weeks of April and May 1945, and their success is reflected here in their final Victory Score boards which once hung in the headquarters building at West Raynham. (Author)*

his own pinpoint and ETA, and there was still enough light to make out the odd island as we approached Sylt. A marker was to be dropped on one of them to ensure complete synchronization at the target. All aircraft duly arrived at their stations and the minutes began to drag by. For some reason Kelsey wasn't ready to open the attack and we were acutely aware that immediately the airfield became encircled by orbiting aircraft the Jerries must have been fully alerted and dashed out to man every gun on the place. The covers were off and there was one up the spout of every weapon they possessed when the cue to start was finally given. I don't know what form the signal took as I was too uptight to record an impression. The runs were to follow in very quick succession, a matter of seconds only and after that each aircraft was to engage the defences.

The first one in was greeted by a cone of tracer that looked like a tent of sparks flying upwards, meeting and then spreading like the poles of a tepee. Thinking to take advantage of their diverted attention I cut in at full belt to cross the airfield, heading for some large hangars clearly visible in the south-east side but by the time we were half way, the whole shower swung in our direction. Things happened pretty fast from then on. I pressed the release when I judged the aim about right and almost immediately as we turned sharply away the whole hangar erupted in an enormous ball of fire out of the roof, doors and windows. I couldn't help hoping even at that moment that there was nobody in it but all else was driven from our minds by a sharp BONK in the tail at which the aircraft began to vibrate violently and the stick to try and shake itself out of my hand. (The cause of the vibration was that the

were being planned by the Luftwaffe, presumably against heads of state or centres of government. Whatever it was it must have been something out of the ordinary to make it necessary to try and burn up everything on it. At the briefing it was announced that a new type of bomb would be used, referred to as 'thermite'. It was a 50-gallon cylinder carried on the wing racks. A warning was given that it would ignite on contact and great care must be exercised not to cause premature ignition. In other words – 'For God's sake don't have a prang with these on board!' Each aircraft was detailed to take up an assigned position round the island at a designated time; great emphasis on the time. At a given signal the attack would commence with a bomb run by the CO, followed by the rest at very short intervals, criss-crossing the field from different directions at height intervals of 50 ft. Bob and I were to come in No. 3 at 150 ft.

It was still full daylight when we left Little Snoring in a loose gaggle, each making for starboard elevator had been shot through at the spar and the resulting overbalance was causing a flutter. It was gradually coming apart and just lasted out the return to Snoring.)

Clearly this was no time to think about 'giving supporting fire' which turned out to be about as dangerous from risk of collision as from flak. So we excused ourselves and informed the assembled host that we had been hit and were pulling out. Still at about 100 ft we turned seawards and immediately found ourselves flying horizontally down the beams of a battery of searchlights. If they did shoot anything further in our direction we were heartily glad not to see any tracer probably on account of the brightness of the lights. There was a bank of mist offshore a mile or two and the shadows of our aircraft in several discs of light were plain to see on its surface. Anything in the way of violent

evasive action was out of the question and the minute it took to reach cover seemed like an hour. Losing all visual references on entering the mist then rendered us dependent on instruments which were all snaking about so much that only the artificial horizon could be seen at all clearly. However, taking stock and realizing that apart from whatever was causing the alarming vibration, all else seemed to be more or less in order. We found that by reducing speed down to about 150 mph it was possible to gain a little height and think about a course for home. Bob, I may say, appeared to remain unperturbed throughout apart from impolite observations about the parentage of some anti-aircraft personnel.

During the napalmgel attack on Jagel, F/O R. Catterall DFC and F/Sgt D. J. Beadle of 169 Squadron were killed when

*Messerschmitt Bf 110G-4d/R3 discovered by American troops near an autobahn leading to München at the end of the war. These final production aircraft were fitted with low drag aerials for the FuG 220B Lichtenstein SN-2d radar and were equipped with nose-mounted Mk 108 and MG151/20 cannons. (via Hans-Peter Grabowski)*

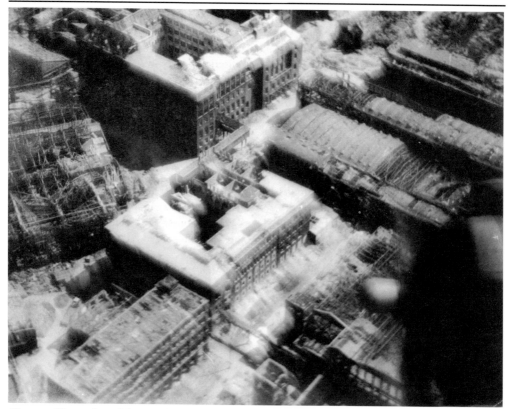

*Krupps of Essen viewed from a 100 Group Halifax during a Cook's Tour of the continent after the ending of hostilities. (John Crotch)*

their Mosquito was shot down by flak. Flight Sergeant John Beeching, a pilot in the Squadron, who was on leave at the time but learned the details later, wrote:

The commander of the German flak battery who shot the aircraft down later wrote to Catterall's mother saying that had he known that the end of the war was only two days' away he would not have opened fire, which is all right to say, but as our blokes were dropping Napalm I cannot imagine anyone standing by to watch that!

Two Halifaxes from 199 Squadron collided over Kiel with the loss of all 16 crew. During a run on Westerland, a Mosquito in 515 Squadron flown by F/L Johnson with F/O Thomason was hit but the pilot landed safely at Woodbridge

on one engine. Two Mosquitos in 169 Squadron, one flown by S/L Wright, the other by F/O Keith Miller, the Australian cricketer, returned to Great Massingham each with a tank hung up but both landed safely. (On 28 June, Miller lost an engine near Bircham Newton. He extinguished the fire and put down at Great Massingham where he overshot and crashed. He and his navigator were unhurt. Immediately afterwards, Miller jumped into his car, and headed for London where he proceeded to score 50 not out at Lords!)

Earlier, on the afternoon of 6 May, Flight Sergeants Williams and Rhoden crashed on a cross-country training flight at Devil's Dyke (Spitalgate) near Brighton. Both men were killed. They were 169 Squadron's final casualties of the war. With Hitler dead and the European war over, celebrations got into full swing before crews began training for the Japanese war, got demobbed, or transferred to other duties in the service. Leslie Holland of 515 Squadron recalls:

There followed three weeks of flights to observe bomb damage in Germany and a few practice flights before 515 broke up and we took our aircraft up to Silloth and left them forlornly standing in a row. That flight doesn't appear in my logbook. While the House of Commons was being told on the afternoon of the 7th that cessation of hostilities was imminent, they may have heard a Mossie go over at 500 ft and if they or the milkman whose horse gave him a bit of trouble at Sudbury Hill wondered who was the lunatic up there – well, now they know.

Geoff Liles, a Fortress pilot in 214 Squadron, recalls:

On VE-Day minus one, I approached W/C Bowes for his permission to take my groundcrew on a round trip of 'Happy Valley' to show them the results of their labours in keeping the kites flying. This was approved and actually resulted in the two of us flying at low level and in very loose formation, crammed full with sightseers. It was something that I don't think any of us will ever forget.

'Dutch' Holland concludes:

May 9th dawned bright and clear with only one drawback: I was orderly officer. I was awakened by a sergeant of RAF Police standing beside my bed staring straight ahead through the peak of his cap announcing that it was believed that an officer from Little Snoring had made off with the Union Jack which had been flying at the King's Lynn Steam Laundry and if it was returned, no more would be said. If the sergeant would give me a few minutes I

*Mosquito NS594 of 515 Squadron flown by Chris Harrison pictured at the end of the war.*

*Celebration photo taken at Oulton at the end of the war with an effigy of the Axis Powers specially constructed for VE-Day. (Bill Bridgeman)*

would join him in the search for said item. He dutifully departed and as I was hoisting myself out of the pit, noticed that my bed had for a quilt a very large Union Jack. It was quite a night.

Squadron Leader John Crotch was specially chosen to fly Air Commodore Rory Chisholm on 21 May, and Air Vice-Marshall Addison on 28 May, to Schleswig and return in Halifax IIIs. During 25 June

– 7 July 1945 Exercise *Post-Mortem* was carried out to evaluate the effectiveness of RAF jamming and *Spoof* operations on the German early warning radar system. Simulated attacks were made by aircraft from four RAF groups including 100 Group, the early warning radar being manned by American and British personnel on this occasion. *Post-Mortem* proved conclusively that the counter-measures had been a great success.

*Halifax BIII PN375 FE-X of 199 Squadron (note the Mandrel masts below the fuselage) after take off from North Creake for partici-pation in* Post-Mortem, *an exercise which proved the overwhelming success achieved by 100 Group in the final 18 months of the war. (via Jerry Scutts)*

AVM Addison (third from right) on the viewing stand at Little Snoring at the end of the war when a silver trophy was presented by the 'Queen Bee' WAAF to the contingent at the station. (Tom Cushing Collection)

On 5 July, John Crotch flew Brig Gen W. R. Peck, the commander of the US 2nd Air Division at Ketteringham Hall, Norfolk, to Denmark to inspect the underground fighter headquarters at Grove and see the tests at Schleswig, returning on 7 July.

Meanwhile, on 25 June Tim Woodman flew to Germany and Denmark with F/L Neville and F/L Bridges.

At Grove I was walking back across the airfield after inspecting some of their aircraft when I passed four Luftwaffe airwomen in white shorts and grey skirts. Typical Fräuleins. They stood smartly to attention but looked pretty boot-faced at having lost the war. 'OK sweethearts,' I said, 'Your time will come again.' How right I was.

But what disasters they must have gone home to.

This stained-glass window in Ely Cathedral is a memorial to the crews of RAF Groups who flew from East Anglia in WW2, including 100 Group. The roll of honour lists 525 men killed while serving in 100 Group. (Author)

# 100 (SD) GROUP ORDER OF BATTLE

| Squadron | Aircraft | 1st Op in 100 Group | Station |
|---|---|---|---|
| 192 | Mosquito BIV/BXVI<br>Wellington BIII<br>Halifax BIII/V<br>Mosquito II | December 1943 | Foulsham |
| 141 | Beaufighter VI<br>Mosquito II/VI/30 | December 1943 | West Raynham |
| 239 | Mosquito II/VI/30 | December 1943 | West Raynham |
| 515 | Mosquito II/VI | December 1943 | Little Snoring<br>Great Massingham |
| 169 | Mosquito II/VI/XIX | 20 January 1944 | Little Snoring |
| 214 | Fortress BII/III | 20/21 April 1944 | Sculthorpe<br>Oulton |
| 199 | Stirling III<br>Halifax BIII | 1 May 1944<br>February 1945 | North Creake |
| 157 | Mosquito XIX/30 | May 1944 | Swannington |
| 85 | Mosquito XII/XVII | 5/6 June 1944 | Swannington |
| 23 | Mosquito VI | 5/6 July 1944 | Little Snoring |
| 223 | Liberator VI<br>Fortress BII/III | 19 September 1944 | Oulton |
| 171 | Stirling BII<br>Halifax BIII | 15 September 1944 | North Creake |
| 462 (RAAF) | Halifax BIII | 13/14 March 1945 | Foulsham |
| 1473 Flight | | | |
| 692 Flight | | | |
| 1694 Flight | | | |
| 1699 Flight | | | |
| Bomber Support Development Unit | | | |
| The *Window* Research Section | | | |

# 100 GROUP FIGHTER CLAIMS DECEMBER 1943 – APRIL 1945

| | AI Mk IV HLP | | | Non-Radar LLP | | | | AI Mk X HLP | | | AI Mk X LLP | | | AI Mk XV HLP | | | AI Mk XV LLP | | | |
|---|---|---|---|---|---|---|---|---|---|---|---|---|---|---|---|---|---|---|---|---|
| | Dis | M | Claims | Dis | M | Claims Air | Claims Ground | Dis | M | Claims | Dis | M | Claims Air | Dis | M | Claims | Dis | M | Claims Air | Claims Ground |
| Dec 1943 | 11 | 1 | 1:0:1 | | | | | | | | | | | | | | | | | |
| Jan 1944 | 41 | 1 | 4:0:0 | | | | | | | | | | | | | | | | | |
| Feb 1944 | 89 | 3 | 4:0:2 | | | | | | | | | | | | | | | | | |
| Mar 1944 | 135 | 4 | 6:0:2 | | | | | | | | | | | | | | | | | |
| Apr 1944 | 175 | 4 | 12:0:0 | 66 | 3 | 3:1:0 | | | | | 3 | 0 | | | | | | | | |
| May 1944 | 212 | 2 | 18:0:1 | 117 | 6 | | | 3 | 0 | | 179 | 0 | 10:0:3 | | | | | | | |
| Jne 1944 | 330 | 2 | 17:1:1 | 138 | 2 | 1:0: | 1 | 23 | 0 | | 37 | 0 | 2:0:0 | | | | | | | |
| Jul 1944 | 338 | 2 | 19:0:5 | 252 | 2 | 4:0:0 | | | | | | | | | | | | | | |
| Aug 1944 | 331 | 1 | 7:0:2 | 222 | 1 | 0:0:4 | | | | | | | | | | | | | | |
| Sept 1944 | 240 | 3 | 1:0:0 | 232 | 4 | 20:1:10 | 6:0:12 | 167 | 2 | 7:1:4 | 69 | 0 | 2:0:1 | | | | | | | |
| Oct 1944 | 308 | 0 | 4:0:4 | 173 | 2 | 1:1:0 | 1:0:2 | 163 | 3 | 5:1:1 | 75 | 0 | 1:0:0 | | | | | | | |
| Nov 1944 | 296 | 1 | 2:0:1 | 182 | 2 | 0:0:2 | 0:0:3 | 211 | 1 | 12:3:3 | | | | | | | | | | |
| Dec 1944 | 116 | 0 | | 172 | 1 | 1:0:0 | 1:0:3 | 278 | 1 | 35:1:4 | 4 | 0 | | 84 | 0 | 3:0:1 | 54 | 0 | 1:0:0 | |
| Jan 1945 | 40 | 1 | | 47 | 0 | | 1:0:0 | 177 | 0 | 0:11:2 | | | | 169 | 1 | | 78 | 2 | 2:0:0 | 1:0:0 |
| Feb 1945 | | | | | | | | 287 | 1 | 9:0:2 | 26 | 0 | 0:1:0 | 48 | 0 | 1:0:0 | 192 | 1 | 1:0:1 | 0:0:2 |
| Mar 1945 | | | | | | | | 347 | 2 | 11:0:2 | 36 | 1 | | 15 | 0 | | 213 | 3 | 1:1:1 | 3:0:9 |
| Apr 1945 | | | | | | | | 360 | 2 | 4:1:2 | 97 | 0 | 2:0:1 | | | | 226 | 1 | 4:0:1 | 5:0:0 |

**Dis: Dispatched**   **M: Missing**   Destroyed : Probably Destroyed : Damaged

# 100 GROUP FIGHTER AIR-TO-AIR VICTORIES DECEMBER 1943–APRIL 1945

| Date | Type | Serial No. | | Squadron | Enemy aircraft | Location & other details | Pilot Nav/radar op |
|---|---|---|---|---|---|---|---|
| 23/24 Dec 43 | Beaufighter VIF | V8744 | V | 141 | Ju 88 | near Düren | F/L H. C. Kelsey<br>P/O E. M. Smith |
| 28/29 Jan 44 | Mosquito II | HJ941 | X | 141 | Bf 109 | near Berlin | F/O H. E. White DFC<br>F/O M. S. Allen DFC |
| 28/29 Jan 44 | Mosquito II | HJ644 | | 239 | Bf 110 | near Berlin | F/O N. Munro<br>F/O A. R. Hurley |
| 30/31 Jan 44 | Mosquito II | HJ712 | | 141 | Bf 110 | near Berlin | F/L G. J. Rice<br>F/O J. G. Rogerson |
| 30/31 Jan 44 | Mosquito II | HJ711 | P | 169 | Bf 110 | Brandenburg area | S/L J. A. H. Cooper<br>F/L R. D. Connolly |
| 5/6 Feb 44 | Mosquito II | HJ707 | B | 169 | Bf 110 | North Sea off UK | P/O W. H. Miller<br>P/O F. C. Bone |
| 15/16 Feb 44 | Mosquito II | DZ726 | Z | 141 | He 177 | Berlin | F/O Harry E. White<br>F/O Mike Allen |
| 20/21 Feb 44 | Mosquito II | DZ270 | | 239 | Bf 110 | near Stuttgart | F/O E. A. Knight<br>F/O D. P. Doyle |
| 25/26 Feb 44 | Mosquito II | DZ254 | | 169 | Bf 110 | SW of Manheim | F/L R. G. Woodman<br>F/O P. Kemmis |
| 5 Mar 44 | Mosquito VI | | | 515 | He 177 | Brétigny? Melun | W/C E. F. F. Lambert<br>F/L E. W. M. Morgan |
| 18/19 Mar 44 | Mosquito II | HJ710 | T | 141 | 2 x Ju 88 | near Frankfurt | F/O H. E. White DFC<br>F/O M. S. Allen DFC |
| 18/19 Mar 44 | Mosquito II | DZ761 | C | 141 | Ju 88 | near Frankfurt | F/O J. C. N. Forshaw<br>P/O F. S. Folley |

| Date | Aircraft | Serial | Code | Sqn | E/A | Location | Crew |
|---|---|---|---|---|---|---|---|
| 22/23 Mar 44 | Mosquito II | | | 239 | Bf 110 | Frankfurt | S/L E. W. Kinchin / F/L D. Sellars |
| 24/25 Mar 44 | Mosquito II | DD717 | M | 141 | Fw 190 | Berlin | F/L H. C. Kelsey DFC* / F/O E. M. Smith DFC, DFM |
| 30/31 Mar 44 | Mosquito II | DZ661 | | 239 | Ju 88 | Nürnberg | F/Sgt J. Campbell DFM / F/Sgt R. Phillips |
| 11/12 Apr 44 | Mosquito II | DZ263 | | 239 | Do 217 | Aachen | S/L N. E. Reeves DSO, DFC*, / W/O A. A. O'Leary DFC**, DFM |
| 18/19 Apr 44 | Mosquito II | DD799 | | 169 | Bf 110 | Compèigne | F/L R. G. Woodman / F/O P. Kemmis |
| 20/21 Apr 44 | Mosquito II | DD732 | S | 141 | Do 217 | N of Paris | F/L H. E. White DFC* / F/L M. S. Allen DFC* |
| 20/21 Apr 44 | Mosquito II | | | 169 | Bf 110 | Ruhr | F/L G. D. Cremer / F/O R. C. Farrell |
| 22/23 Apr 44 | Mosquito II | W4085 | | 169 | Bf 110 | Bonn area | P/O R. G. Woodman / F/O P. Kemmis |
| 22/23 Apr 44 | Mosquito II | W4076 | | 169 | Bf 110 | Köln | P/O W. H. Miller / P/O F. C. Bone |
| 23/24 Apr 44 | Mosquito II | HJ712 | R | 141 | Fw 190 | Flensburg | F/L G. J. Rice / P/O R. S. Mallett |
| 26 Apr 44 | Mosquito VI | | | 515 | UEA | Gilze airfield | S/L H. B. Martin / F/O J. W. Smith |
| 26 Apr 44 | Mosquito VI | | | 515 | 2 x UEA | (1) Le Culot airfield (2) Brussels Evere | W/O T. S. Ecclestone / F/Sgt J. H. Shimmon |
| 26/27 Apr 44 | Mosquito II | W4078 | | 239 | Bf 110 | Essen | F/O W. R. Breithaupt / F/O J. A. Kennedy |
| 27/28 Apr 44 | Mosquito II | W4076 | | 169 | Bf 110 | SE of Strasbourg | P/O P. L. Johnson / P/O M. Hopkins |
| 27/28 Apr 44 | Mosquito II | | | 239 | Bf 110 + Ju 88 | Montzon–Aulnoye | F/O R. Depper / F/O R. G. C. Follis |
| 27/28 Apr 44 | Mosquito II | DD622 | | 239 | Bf 110 | Montzon–Aulnoye | S/L N. E. Reeves DSO, DFC* / W/O A. A. O'Leary DFC**, DFM |
| 8/9 May 44 | Mosquito II | DD799 | | 169 | Bf 110 | Braine le Comte | S/L R. G. Woodman / F/O P. Kemmis |
| 10/11 May 44 | Mosquito II | W4078 | | 239 | Bf 110 | near Courtrai | F/O V. Bridges DFC / F/Sgt D. G. Webb DFM |

| Date | Aircraft | Serial | Letter | Sqn | E/A | Location | Crew |
|---|---|---|---|---|---|---|---|
| 11/12 May 44 | Mosquito II | HJ726 | Z | 141 | Ju 88 | N of Amiens | F/L H. E. White DFC* / F/L M. S. Allen DFC* |
| 11/12 May | Mosquito II | DZ240 | H | 141 | Ju 88 | SW of Brussels | F/L L. J. G. LeBoutte / F/O R. S. Mallett |
| 12/13 May 44 | Mosquito II | W4078 | | 239 | Bf 110 | Hassel–Louvain | F/O W. R. Breithaupt / F/O J. A. Kennedy |
| 12/13 May 44 | Mosquito II | W4092 | | 239 | Ju 88 | Belgium | F/O V. Bridges DFC / F/Sgt D. G. Webb DFM |
| 15/16 May 44 | Mosquito II | DZ478 | | 169 | Bf 110 + 2 x Ju 88 | Cuxhaven area | P/O W. H. Miller / P/O F. C. Bone |
| 22/23 May 44 | Mosquito II | DZ309 | | 239 | Bf 110 | Dortmund | F/L D. E. Hughes / F/O R. H. Perks |
| 22/23 May 44 | Mosquito II | | | 169 | Bf 110 | Groningen area | W/C N. B. R. Bromley OBE / F/L P. Truscott |
| 24/25 May 44 | Mosquito II | DZ265 | | 239 | Bf 110 | Aachen | F/L D. J. Raby DFC / F/Sgt S. J. Flint DFM |
| 24/25 May 44 | Mosquito II | DZ297 | | 239 | Ju 88 | 15 miles ESE of Bonn | F/O W. R. Breithaupt DFC / F/O J. A. Kennedy DFC |
| 24/25 May 44 | Mosquito II | DZ309 | | 239 | Bf 110 | Aachen | F/L D. E. Hughes / F/O R. H. Perks |
| 27/28 May 44 | Mosquito II | DD622 | | 239 | Bf 110 | Aachen | S/L N. A. Reeves DSO, DFC / P/O A. A. O'Leary DFC**, DFM |
| 27/28 May 44 | Mosquito II | HJ941 | X | 141 | Bf 109 | W of Aachen | F/L H. E. White DFC* / F/L M. S. Allen DFC* |
| 31/1 Jun 44 | Mosquito II | DZ297 | | 239 | Bf 110 | near Trappes | F/O V. Bridges DFC / F/Sgt D. G. Webb DFM |
| 31/1 Jun 44 | Mosquito II | DZ256 | U | 239 | Bf 110 | W of Paris | F/L D. Welfare DFC* / F/O D. B. Bellis DFC* |
| 1/2 Jun 44 | Mosquito II | DZ265 | | 239 | Bf 110 | N France | F/L T. L. Wright / P/O L. Ambery |
| 5/6 Jun 44 | Mosquito II | DD789 | | 239 | Ju 88 | Frisians | F/O W. R. Breithaupt DFC / F/O J. A. Kennedy DFC |
| 5/6 Jun 44 | Mosquito II | DZ256 | U | 239 | Bf 110 | N of Aachen | F/L D. Welfare DFC* / F/O D. B. Bellis DFC* |
| 8/9 Jun 44 | Mosquito II | DD741 | | 169 | Do 217 | Paris area | W/C N. B. R. Bromley OBE / F/L P. V. Truscott |

| Date | Aircraft | Serial | Letter | Sqn | EA | Location | Crew |
|---|---|---|---|---|---|---|---|
| 8/9 Jun 44 | Mosquito II | DD303 | E | 141 | UEA | Rennes | F/O A. C. Gallacher DFC / W/O G. McLean DFC |
| 11/12 Jun 44 | Mosquito II | DZ256 | U | 239 | Bf 110 | N of Paris | F/L D. Welfare / F/O D. B. Bellis |
| 11/12 Jun 44 | Mosquito XIX | MM642 | R | 85 | Bf 110 | Melun airfield | W/C C. M. Miller DFC** / F/O R. O. Symon |
| 12/13 Jun 44 | Mosquito XIX | MM630 | E | 157 | Ju 188 | Fôret de Compiègne | F/L J. G. Benson DFC / F/L L. Brandon DFC |
| 12/13 Jun 44 | Mosquito XIX | | | 85 | Bf 110 | near Paris | F/L M. Phillips / F/L D. Smith |
| 13/14 Jun 44 | Mosquito II | DZ254 | P | 169 | Ju 88 | near Paris | W/O L. W. Turner / F/Sgt F. Francis |
| 14/15 Jun 44 | Mosquito II | DZ240 | H | 141 | Me 410 | N of Lille | W/O H. W. Welham / W/O E. J. Hollis |
| 14/15 Jun 44 | Mosquito XIX | MM671 | C | 157 | Ju 88 | near Juvincourt | F/L J. Tweedale / F/O L. I. Cunningham |
| 14/15 Jun 44 | Mosquito XIX | | Y | 85 | Ju 188 | SW of Nivelles | F/L B. Burbridge / F/L F. S. Skelton |
| 14/15 Jun 44 | Mosquito XIX | | J | 85 | Ju 88 | near Creil | F/L H. B. Thomas / P/O C. B. Hamilton |
| 15/16 Jun 44 | Mosquito XIX | | C | 85 | Bf 110 | St Trond airfield | S/L F. S. Gonsalves / F/L B. Duckett |
| 15/16 Jun 44 | Mosquito XIX | MM671 | C | 157 | Ju 88 | Creil–Beauvais–Cormeilles | F/L J. O. Mathews / W/O A. Penrose |
| 16/17 Jun 44 | Mosquito II | W4076 | | 169 | Ju 88 | Pas de Calais | F/O W. H. Miller DFC / F/O F. Bone |
| 17/18 Jun 44 | Mosquito XIX | | | 85 | Bf 110 | Eindhoven–Soesterberg | F/O P. S. Kendall DFC* / F/L C. R. Hill |
| 17/18 Jun 44 | Mosquito II | W4092 | | 239 | Ju 88 | near Eindhoven | F/L G. E. Poulton / F/O A. J. Neville |
| 21/22 Jun 44 | Mosquito II | DZ290 | | 239 | He 177 | Ruhr | F/O R. Depper / F/O R. G. C. Follis |
| 21 Jun 44 | Mosquito VI | PZ203 | X | 515 | Bf 110 | Eelde airfield | S/L P. W. Rabone DFC / F/O F. C. H. Johns |
| 23/24 Jun 44 | Mosquito XIX | | Y | 85 | Ju 88 | | F/L B. A. Burbridge / F/L F. S. Skelton |

| Date | Aircraft | Serial | Code | Squadron | Enemy | Location | Crew |
|---|---|---|---|---|---|---|---|
| 24/25 Jun 44 | Mosquito II | DD759 | R | 239 | Ju 88 | Paris–Amiens | F/L D. Welfare DFC* / F/O D B Bellis DFC* |
| 27/28 Jun 44 | Mosquito II | HJ911 | A | 141 | Ju 88 | Cambrai | S/L G. J. Rice / F/O J. G. Rogerson |
| 27/28 Jun 44 | Mosquito II | DZ240 | H | 141 | Ju 88 | S of Tilburg | W/O H. Welham / W/O E. Hollis |
| 27/28 Jun 44 | Mosquito II | DD759 | R | 239 | Me 410 | E of Paris | F/L D. Welfare DFC* / F/O D. B. Bellis DFC* |
| 27/28 Jun 44 | Mosquito II | | | 239 | Fw 190 | near Brussels | W/C P. M. J. Evans / F/O R. H. Perks DFC |
| 27/28 Jun 44 | Mosquito II | DD749 | W | 239 | Ju 88 | near Brussels | F/L D. R. Howard / F/O F. A. W. Clay |
| 27/28 Jun 44 | Mosquito VI | PZ188 | J | 515 | Ju 88 | Eindhoven | P/O C. W. Chown / F/Sgt D. G. N. Veitch |
| 28/29 Jun 44 | Mosquito VI | NT150 | | 169 | Bf 110 | near Mücke | P/O H. Reed / F/O S. Watts |
| 30 Jun 44 | Mosquito VI | PZ203 | X | 515 | He 111 | Jagel/Schleswig | S/L L. P. Rabone / F/O F. C. H. Johns |
| 30 Jun 44 | Mosquito VI | PZ188 | J | 515 | Ju 34 | | P/O C. W. Chown RCAF / F/Sgt D. G. N. Veitch |
| 30/1 Jul 44 | Mosquito VI | DZ265 | | 239 | Ju 88 | Le Havre | F/L D. J. Raby DFC / F/Sgt S. J. Flint DFM |
| 4/5 Jul 44 | Mosquito II | DZ298 | C | 239 | Bf 110 | NW of Paris | S/L N. A. Reeves DSO, DFC / P/O A. A. O'Leary |
| 4/5 Jul 44 | Mosquito VI | PZ163 | | 515 | Ju 88 | near Coulommiers | W/O R. E. Preston / F/Sgt F. Verity |
| 4/5 Jul 44 | Mosquito II | DD725 | G | 141 | Me 410 | near Orleans | F/L J. D. Peterkin / F/O R. Murphy |
| 4/5 Jul 44 | Mosquito II | | | 169 | Bf 110 | Villeneuve | F/L J. S. Fifield / F/O F. Staziker |
| 5/6 Jul 44 | Mosquito II | DZ298 | | 239 | Bf 110 | near Paris | S/L N. E. Reeves / W/O A. A. O'Leary |
| 5/6 Jul 44 | Mosquito VI | NT121 | | 169 | Ju 88 | S of Paris | F/O P. G. Bailey / F/O J. O. Murphy |
| 7/8 Jul 44 | Mosquito II | HJ911 | A | 141 | Bf 110 | NW of Amiens | S/L G. J. Rice / F/O J. G. Rogerson |

| Date | Type | Serial | Code | Sqn | E/A | Location | Crew |
|---|---|---|---|---|---|---|---|
| 7/8 Jul 44 | Mosquito II | DD789 | | 239 | Fw 190 | Pas de Calais | W/C P. M. J. Evans / F/L T. R. Carpenter |
| 7/8 Jul 44 | Mosquito II | W4097 | | 239 | 2 x Bf 110 | Paris | S/L J. S. Booth DFC* / F/O K. Dear DFC |
| 7/8 Jul 44 | Mosquito II | DZ298 | | 239 | Bf 110 | near Charleroi | F/L V. Bridges DFC / F/Sgt D. G. Webb DFM |
| 10 Jul 44 | Mosquito VI | PZ188 | J | 515 | Ju 88 (shared) | Zwichilnahner airfield | F/L R. A. Adams / P/O F. H. Ruffle |
| 10 Jul 44 | Mosquito VI | PZ420 | O | 515 | Ju 88 (shared) | Zwishilnahner airfield | F/O D. W. O. Wood / F/O Bruton |
| 12/13 Jul 44 | Mosquito XIX | TA401 | D | 157 | Ju 88 | SE of Etampes | F/L J. O. Mathews / W/O A. Penrose |
| 14 Jul 44 | Mosquito VI | RS993 | T | 515 | Ju 34 | Stralsund, NE Germany | F/L A. E. Callard / F/Sgt E. D. Townsley |
| 14/15 Jul 44 | Mosquito XIX | | | 157 | Bf 110 | 20 miles NE of Juvincourt (anti-Diver) | Lt Sandiford RNVR / Lt Thompson RNVR |
| 14/15 Jul 44 | Mosquito VI | NT112 | M | 169 | Bf 109 | Auderbelck | W/O L. W. Turner / F/Sgt F. Francis |
| 20/21 Jul 44 | Mosquito VI | NT113 | | 169 | Bf 110 | near Courtrai | W/C N. B. R. Bromley OBE / F/L P. V. Truscott DFC |
| 20/21 Jul 44 | Mosquito VI | NT146 | | 169 | Ju 88 | Hamburg area | P/O H. Reed / F/O S. Watts |
| 20/21 Jul 44 | Mosquito VI | NT121 | | | Bf 110 | Courtrai | F/L J. S. Fifield / F/O F. Staziker |
| 23/24 Jul 44 | Mosquito II | HJ710 | T | 141 | Ju 88 | SW of Beauvais | P/O I. D. Gregory / P/O D. H. Stephens |
| 23/24 Jul 44 | Mosquito VI | NS997 | | 169 | Bf 110 | near Kiel | F/L R. J. Dix / F/O A. J. Salmon |
| 23/24 Jul 44 | Mosquito II | DZ661 | | 239 | Bf 110 | Kiel | F/O N. Veale / F/O R. D. Comyn |
| 25/26 Jul 44 | Mosquito VI | RS961 | H | 515 | Me 410 | Knocke, Belgium | S/L H. B. Martin DSO, DFC / F/O J. W. Smith |
| 25/26 Jul 44 | Mosquito VI | PZ178 | | 23 | UEA | Laon Pouvron | F/L D. J. Griffiths / F/Sgt S. F. Smith |
| 28/29 Jul 44 | Mosquito II | HJ712 | R | 141 | 2 x Ju 88 | Metz/Neufchâteau | F/L H. E. White DFC* / F/L M. S. Allen DFC* |

| Date | Aircraft | Serial | Letter | Squadron | Enemy aircraft | Location | Crew |
|---|---|---|---|---|---|---|---|
| 28/29 Jul 44 | Mosquito II | HJ741 | Y | 141 | Ju 88 | Metz area | P/O I. D. Gregory / P/O D. H. Stephens |
| 8/9 Aug 44 | Mosquito II | DZ256 | U | 239 | Fw 190 | St Quentin | F/L D. Welfare DFC* / F/O D. B. Bellis DFC* |
| 8/9 Aug 44 | Mosquito II | ? | | 239 | Bf 109 | N France | F/L D. J. Raby DFC / F/Sgt S. J. Flint DFM |
| 8/9 Aug 44 | Mosquito VI | NT156 | Y | 169 | Fw 190 | E of Abbeville | F/L R. G. Woodman / F/L P. Kemmis |
| 10/11 Aug 44 | Mosquito VI | NT176 | H | 169 | Bf 109 | Dijon | F/O W. H. Miller DFC / F/O F. C. Bone |
| 12/13 Aug 44 | Mosquito VI | NT173 | | 169 | He 219 | near Aachen | F/O W. H. Miller DFC / F/O F. C. Bone |
| 16/17 Aug 44 | Mosquito VI | HR213 | G | 141 | Bf 110 | Ringkobing Fiord | W/O E. A. Lampkin / F/Sgt B. J. Wallnutt |
| 26/27 Aug 44 | Mosquito VI | NT146 | T | 169 | Ju 88 | near Bremen | W/O L. W. Turner / F/Sgt F. Francis |
| 29/30 Aug 44 | Mosquito II | W4097 | | 239 | Ju 88 | near Stettin | F/L D. E. Hughes / F/L R. H. Perks |
| 6/7 Sep 44 | Mosquito VI | PZ338 | A | 515 | Bf 109 | Odder, Denmark | W/C F. F. Lambert / F/O R. J. Lake AFC |
| 11/12 Sep 44 | Mosquito XIX | | Y | 85 | Ju 188 | Baltic Sea | S/L B. Burbridge DFC / F/L F. S. Skelton DFC |
| 11/12 Sep 44 | Mosquito VI | HR180 | B | 141 | Bf 110 | SW of Mannheim | F/L P. A. Bates / P/O W. G. Cadman |
| 11/12 Sep 44 | Mosquito XIX | MM630 | E | 157 | 2 x Ju 188 | Zeeland | S/L J. G. Benson DFC* / F/L L. Brandon DFC |
| 11/12 Sep 44 | Mosquito XIX | | A | 85 | Bf 109G | Limburg area | F/L P. S. Kendall DFC* / F/L C. R. Hill DFC |
| 12/13 Sep 44 | Mosquito XIX | MM643 | F | 157 | Bf 110 | | S/L R. D. Doleman / F/L D. C. Bunch DFC |
| 12/13 Sep 44 | Mosquito II | | | 239 | Bf 110 | Ranschhack | F/O W. R. Breithaupt DFC / F/O J. A. Kennedy DFC |
| 13/14 Sep 44 | Mosquito XIX | | D | 85 | Bf 110 | near Koblenz | F/L W. House / F/Sgt R. D. McKinnon |
| 17/18 Sep 44 | Mosquito XIX | | J | 85 | 2 x Bf 110 | crashed east of Arnhem | F/O A. J. Owen / F/O S. V. McAllister DFM |

| Date | Aircraft | Serial | Letter | Sqn | Enemy aircraft | Location | Crew |
|---|---|---|---|---|---|---|---|
| 26/27 Sep 44 | Mosquito VI | PZ301 | N | 515 | He 111 | Zellhausen airfield | S/L H. F. Morley<br>F/Sgt R. A. Fidler |
| 28/29 Sep 44 | Mosquito XIX | | Y | 85 | Ju 188 | | F/L M. Phillips<br>F/L D. Smith |
| 29/30 Sep 44 | Mosquito XIX | | | 157 | Me 410 (prob) | 10 miles ESE of Yarmouth | F/L Vincent<br>F/O Mony |
| 6/7 Oct 44 | Mosquito VI | NT234 | W | 141 | Ju 88 | S of Leeuwarden | F/L A. C. Gallacher DFC<br>P/O G. Mclean DFC |
| 7/8 Oct 44 | Mosquito XIX | MM671 | C | 157 | Bf 110 | W of Neumünster | F/L J. O. Mathews<br>W/O A. Penrose |
| 8 Oct 44 | Mosquito VI | PZ181 | E | 515 | Bf 109 | Eggebek, Denmark | F/L F. T. L'Amie<br>F/O J. W. Smith |
| 11 Oct 44 | Mosquito II | DZ256 | | 239 | seaplane | Tristed | F/L D. Welfare DFC*<br>F/O D. B Bellis DFC* |
| 14/15 Oct 44 | Mosquito XIX | | Y | 85 | 2 x Ju 88G | Gütersloh airfield | S/L B. Burbridge DFC<br>F/L F. S. Skelton DFC |
| 14/15 Oct 44 | Mosquito VI | PZ245 | | 239 | Fw 190 | Meland | F/L D. R. Howard<br>F/O F. A. W. Clay |
| 15/16 Oct 44 | Mosquito XIX | | D | 85 | Bf 110 | | F/L C. K. Nowell<br>W/O Randall |
| 19/20 Oct 44 | Mosquito XXX | NT250 | Y | 141 | Ju 88 | SE of Karlsruhe | F/L G. D. Bates<br>F/O D. W. Field |
| 19/20 Oct 44 | Mosquito VI | PZ175 | H | 141 | Ju 88 | NW of Nürnberg | F/O J. C. Barton<br>F/Sgt R. A. Kinnear |
| 19/20 Oct 44 | Mosquito XIX | TA404 | M | 157 | Ju 88 | 49°20' N 092°02' E | S/L R. D. Doleman<br>F/L D. C. Bunch DFC |
| 19/20 Oct 44 | Mosquito XIX | | Y | 85 | Ju 188 | Metz | S/L B. Burbridge DFC<br>F/L F. S. Skelton DFC |
| 19/20 Oct 44 | Mosquito VI | PZ275 | | 239 | Bf 110 | Strasbourg | W/O P. O. Falconer<br>F/Sgt W. G. Armour |
| 28/29 Oct 44 | Mosquito II | PZ245 | | 239 | He 111 | Dummer Lake | F/L D. R. Howard<br>F/O F. A. W. Clay |
| 29 Oct 44 | Mosquito VI | PZ344 | E | 515 | Fw 190<br>Ju 34 | Hechingen, nr Stuttgart<br>Staubing | F/L F. T. L'Amie<br>F/O J. W. Smith |
| 29 Oct 44 | Mosquito VI | PZ217 | K | 515 | Bf 110 | Ingolstadt | P/O T. A. Groves<br>F/Sgt R. B. Dockeray |

| Date | Aircraft | Serial | Code | Enemy aircraft | Sqn | Location | Crew |
|---|---|---|---|---|---|---|---|
| 1/2 Nov 44 | Mosquito XIX | | R | Ju 88 | 85 | 20 miles E of Mulhouse | F/O A. J. Owen<br>F/O J. S. V. McAllister |
| 4/5 Nov 44 | Mosquito XIX | TA401 | D | Bf 110 | 157 | Osnabrück | W/C K. H. P. Beauchamp<br>F/O Monoy |
| 4/5 Nov 44 | Mosquito II | | | Bf 110 | 239 | Bochum | F/L J. N. W. Young<br>F/L R. H. Siddons |
| 4/5 Nov 44 | Mosquito VI | TA401 | D | Bf 110 | 169 | Bochum | S/L R. G. Woodman<br>F/O A. F. Witt |
| 4/5 Nov 44 | Mosquito XIX | | Y | Ju 88G<br>Ju 88<br>Bf 110<br>+ Ju 88 | 85 | 30 miles E of Bonn<br>5 miles SE of Bonn airfield<br>N of Hangelar airfield | S/L B. Burbridge DSO*, DFC*<br>F/L F. S. Skelton DSO*, DFC* |
| 4/5 Nov 44 | Mosquito XIX | | B | Ju 88 | 85 | SE of Bielefeld | F/O A. J. Owen<br>F/O McAllister DFM |
| 6/7 Nov 44 | Mosquito XIX | | N | Ju 188 | 85 | | S/L F. S. Gonsalves<br>F/L B. Duckett |
| 6/7 Nov 44 | Mosquito XIX | | Y | Bf 110 | 85 | | F/L Keele |
| 6/7 Nov 44 | Mosquito XIX | | A | Ju 88 (prob) | 85 | | Capt T. Weisteen |
| 6/7 Nov 44 | Mosquito XIX | TA391 | N | Ju 188 (prob) | 157 | Osnabrück–Minden | F/L H. P. Kelway<br>Sgt Bell |
| 6/7 Nov 44 | Mosquito XIX | TA404 | M | Bf 110 | 157 | E of Koblenz | S/L R. D. Doleman<br>F/L D. C. Bunch DFC |
| 6/7 Nov 44 | Mosquito II | DD789 | | Ju 188 | 239 | Osnabrück | F/O G. E. Jameson<br>F/O L. Ambery |
| 10/11 Nov 44 | Mosquito XIX | TA402 | F | Ju 88 | 157 | Frankfurt–Koblenz | S/L J. G. Benson<br>F/L L. Brandon |
| 10/11 Nov 44 | Mosquito XXX | PZ247 | | Ju 188 | 169 | NE Germany | S/L R. G. Woodman<br>F/O A. F. Witt |
| 11/12 Nov 44 | Mosquito XIX | | | Ju 88 (prob) | 157 | Bonn | F/L J. O. Mathews DFC<br>W/O A. Penrose |
| 11/12 Nov 44 | Mosquito XIX | | B | Fw 190 | 85 | 30 miles SE of Hamburg | F/O A. J. Owen<br>F/O McAllister DFM |
| 21/22 Nov 44 | Mosquito XIX | | N | Bf 110<br>Ju 88 | 85 | near Würzburg<br>Bonn | S/L B. Burbridge DSO*, DFC*<br>F/L F. S. Skelton DSO*, DFC* |
| 30 Nov 44 | Mosquito VI | 242 | | He 177 | 515 | Liegnitz | W/C H. C. Kelsey DFC*<br>F/L E. M. Smith DFC, DFM |

| Date | Aircraft | Serial | Code | Squadron | Enemy aircraft | Location | Crew |
|---|---|---|---|---|---|---|---|
| 30/1 Dec 44 | Mosquito XIX | | | 85 | Ju 88 | | S/L F. S. Gonsalves / F/L B. Duckett |
| 30/1 Dec 44 | Mosquito XIX | | | 157 | Ju 188 | 50° 30' N 09° 20' E | F/L R. J. V. Smythe / F/O Waters |
| 2/3 Dec 44 | Mosquito XIX | | A | 85 | Bf 110 | | Capt T. Weisteen |
| 2/3 Dec 44 | Mosquito XIX | | | 157 | Ju 88 | Osnabrück | F/L W. Taylor / F/O J. N. Edwards |
| 4/5 Dec 44 | Mosquito XIX | MM671 | C | 157 | Ju 88 | Dortmund airfield | F/L J. O. Mathews DFC / W/O A. Penrose DFC |
| 4/5 Dec 44 | Mosquito XIX | | | 157 | Bf 110 | Limburg | F/L W. Taylor / F/O J. N. Edwards |
| 4/5 Dec 44 | Mosquito XXX | | C | 85 | 2 x Bf 110 | Kalsruhe–Germesheim | F/L R. T. Goucher / F/L C. H. Bulloch |
| 4/5 Dec 44 | Mosquito XXX | | B | 85 | Bf 110 | 50 miles ENE of Heilbronn | Capt S. Heglund DFC / F/O R. O. Symon |
| 4/5 Dec 44 | Mosquito XXX | | H | 85 | Ju 88 (85 Sqn's 100th) | near Krefeld | F/O A. J. Owen / F/O J. S. V. McAllister |
| 6/7 Dec 44 | Mosquito XXX | | O | 85 | Bf 110 | W of Münster | F/L E. R. Hedgecoe DFC / F/Sgt J. R. Whitham * (with FIU) |
| 6/7 Dec 44 | Mosquito XIX | MM671 | C | 157 | Bf 110 / Ju 88 | near Limburg / 15 miles SW of Giessen | F/L J. O. Mathews DFC / W/O A. Penrose DFC |
| 6/7 Dec 44 | Mosquito XIX | TA404 | M | 157 | Bf 110 | Kitzingen | S/L R. D. Doleman / F/L D. C. Bunch DFC |
| 6/7 Dec 44 | Mosquito XXX | MM638 | G | BSDU | Bf 110 | W of Giessen | S/L N. A. Reeves DSO, DFC / F/O M. Phillips |
| 12/13 Dec 44 | Mosquito XIX | | A? | 85 | Ju 88 | | Capt E. P. Fossum / F/O S. A. Hider |
| 12/13 Dec 44 | Mosquito XXX | | O | 85 | 2 x Bf 110 | S of Hagen–Essen | F/L E. R. Hedgecoe DFC / F/Sgt J. R. Whitham * (with FIU) |
| 12/13 Dec 44 | Mosquito XXX | | Z | 85 | Ju 88 / Bf 110 | Gütersloh airfield / 2 miles W of Essen | S/L B. Burbridge DSO*, DFC* / F/L F. S. Skelton DSO*, DFC* |
| 17/18 Dec 44 | Mosquito XIX | MM627 | H | 157 | Bf 110 | 51° 12' N 06° 35' E | W/O D. A. Taylor / F/Sgt Radford |
| 17/18 Dec 44 | Mosquito XIX | MM653 | L | 157 | Bf 110 | | F/Sgt J. Leigh |
| 17/18 Dec 44 | Mosquito XXX | | J | 85 | Bf 110 | 40 miles from Ulm | F/L R. T. Goucher / F/L C. H. Bullock |

| Date | Aircraft | Serial | Code | Squadron | Enemy aircraft | Location | Crew |
|---|---|---|---|---|---|---|---|
| 18/19 Dec 44 | Mosquito XIX | MM640 | I | 157 | He 219 | Osnabrück area | F/L W. Taylor / F/O J. N. Edwards |
| 21/22 Dec 44 | Mosquito XIX | TA401 | D | 157 | Ju 88 | N of Frankfurt | W/C K. H. P. Beauchamp DSO, DFC / F/L Scholefield |
| 22/23 Dec 44 | Mosquito XXX | | B | 85 | 2 x Ju 88 + Bf 110 | Saarbrücken area | F/O A. J. Owen / F/O J. S. V. McAllister |
| 22/23 Dec 44 | Mosquito XXX | | P | 85 | Bf 110 | Koblenz–Gütersloh | S/L B. Burbridge DSO*, DFC* / F/L F. S. Skelton DSO*, DFC* |
| 22/23 Dec44 | Mosquito XIX | TA404 | M | 157 | Ju 88 | 5 miles W Limburg | S/L R. D. Doleman / F/L Bunch DFC |
| 23/24 Dec44 | Mosquito XXX | | | 157 | Ju 88 | near Koblenz | F/L R. J. V. Smythe / F/O Waters |
| 23/24 Dec44 | Mosquito XIX | | N | 85 | Bf 110 | Mannheim–Mainz area | F/L G. C. Chapman / F/L J. Stockley |
| 24/25 Dec44 | Mosquito XIX | MM671 | C | 157 | Ju 88G | 3 miles SW of Köln | F/L J. O. Mathews / W/O A. Penrose |
| 24/25 Dec44 | Mosquito XIX | TA404 | | 157 | 2x Bf 110 | Köln/Duisburg | S/L R. D. Doleman / F/L D. C. Bunch DFC |
| 24/25 Dec44 | Mosquito XIX | MM676 | W | 157 | Bf 110 | 50° 38' N 07° 52' E | S/L J. G. Benson DFC / F/L L. Brandon DSO, DFC |
| 24/25 Dec 44 | Mosquito XXX | | A | 85 | Bf 110 | 20 miles N of Frankfurt | Capt S. Heglund DFC / F/O R. O. Symon |
| 31/1 Jan 45 | Mosquito VI | RS518 | L | 515 | Ju 88 | Lovns Bredning | S/L C. V. Bennett DFC / F/L R. A. Smith |
| 31/1 Jan 45 | Mosquito XXX | MT491 | E | 169 (attached to 85) | He 219 | Köln area | F/L A. P. Mellows DFC / F/L S. L. Drew DFC |
| 31/1 Jan 45 | Mosquito VI | RS507 | | 23 | Ju 88 | Alhorn area | S/L J. Tweedale / F/L L. I. Cunningham |
| 1/2 Jan 45 | Mosquito XXX | | R | 85 | Ju 188 / Ju 88G | 10 miles N of Münster / 10 miles E of Dortmund | F/L R. T. Goucher / F/L C. H. Bullock |
| 1/2 Jan 45 | Mosquito XXX | | | 85 | Ju 88 | | F/O L. J. York |
| 2/3 Jan 45 | Mosquito XXX | | N | 169 (attached to 85) | Ju 188 | near Frankfurt | F/L R. G. Woodman / F/L Simpkins |
| 2/3 Jan 45 | Mosquito XIX | TA393 | C | 157 | Ju 88 | 3 miles W of Stuttgart | F/L J. O. Mathews DFC / W/O A. Penrose DFC |

| Date | Aircraft | Serial | Code | Enemy a/c | Sqn | Location | Crew |
|---|---|---|---|---|---|---|---|
| 2/3 Jan 45 | Mosquito XXX | | X | Ju 88 | 85 | 15 miles SW of Ludwigshaven | S/L B. Burbridge DSO*, DFC* / F/L F. S. Skelton DSO*, DFC* |
| 5/6 Jan 45 | Mosquito XXX | | B | Bf 110 | 85 | 25 miles N of Münster | Capt S. Heglund DFC / F/O R. O. Symon |
| 5/6 Jan 45 | Mosquito XIX | TA394 | A | He 219 | 157 | E of Hanover | F/L J. G. Benson DSO, DFC* / F/L L. Brandon DSO, DFC* |
| 5/6 Jan 45 | Mosquito VI | RS881 | C | Ju 88 | 515 | Jagel airfield | F/L A. S. Briggs / F/O Rodwell |
| 14/15 Jan 45 | Mosquito XXX | | Y | Ju 188 | 85 | Frankfurt | F/L K. D. Vaughan / F/Sgt R. D. MacKinnon |
| 14/15 Jan 45 | Mosquito VI | HR294 | T | UEA | 141 | Jüterbog | F/L R. Brearley / F/O J. Sheldon |
| 16/17 Jan 45 | Mosquito VI | RS507 | | Bf 109 | 23 | Fassberg | F/L T. Smith / F/O Cockayne |
| 16/17 Jan 45 | Mosquito XXX | | R | He 219 | 85 | Ruhr | F/L K. D. Vaughan / F/Sgt R. D MacKinnon |
| 16/17 Jan 45 | Mosquito VI | HR200 | E | Bf 110 | 141 | Magdeburg | F/L D. H. Young / F/O J. J. Sanderson |
| 16/17 Jan 45 | Mosquito VI | HR213 | G | Bf 110 | 141 | SW of Magdeburg | F/O R. C. Brady / F/L M. K. Webster |
| 16/17 Jan 45 | Mosquito XIX | TA446 | Q | Ju 188 | 157 | Fritzler | F/L A. Mackinnon / F/O Waddell |
| 1/2 Feb 45 | Mosquito XIX | | | Bf 110 (prob) | 157 | Oberolm | S/L Ryall / P/O Mulroy |
| 1/2 Feb 45 | Mosquito XXX | NT309 | C | Bf 110 | 239 | Mannheim | W/C W.F. Gibb DSO, DFC / F/O R. C. Kendall DFC |
| 1/2 Feb 45 | Mosquito XXX | NT252 | | Bf 110 | 169 | Stuttgart | F/L A. P Mellows DFC / F/L S. L. Drew DFC |
| 2/3 Feb 45 | Mosquito XXX | MV548 | Z | Ju 88 | 85 | | W/C W. K. Davison |
| 2/3 Feb 45 | Mosquito VI | RS575 | V | Ju 88 | 515 | Vechta | W/C H. C. Kelsey DFC* / F/L E. M. Smith |
| 7/8 Feb 45 | Mosquito XXX | NT330 | | Ju 188 | 239 | Ruhr | F/L A. J. Holderness / F/L W. Rowley DFC |
| 7/8 Feb 45 | Mosquito XXX | NT361 | | Bf 110 | 239 | Ruhr | F/L D. A. D. Cather DFM / F/Sgt L. J. S. Spicer BEM |
| 13/14 Feb 45 | Mosquito XIX | MM684 | H | 2 x Bf 110 | BSDU | Frankfurt area | F/L D. R. Howard DFC / F/L F. A. W. Clay DFC |

| Date | Aircraft | Serial | Code | Sqn | Enemy | Location | Crew |
|---|---|---|---|---|---|---|---|
| 14/15 Feb 45 | Mosquito XXX | MV532 | S | 85 | Ju 88 | Schwabish Hall airfield | F/L F. D. Win RNZAF / F/O T. P. Ryan RNZAF |
| 20/21 Feb 45 | Mosquito XXX | NT361 | N | 239 | Fw 190 | Worms | W/C W. F. Gibb DSO, DFC / F/O R. C. Kendall DFC |
| 5/6 Mar 45 | Mosquito XXX | NT361 | B | 239 | 2 x Ju 88 | Chemnitz/Nürnberg | W/C W. F. Gibb DSO, DFC / F/O R. C. Kendall DFC |
| 7/8 Mar 45 | Mosquito VI | | S | 23 | Fw 190 | Stendal | F/O E. L. Heath / F/Sgt Thompson |
| 8/9 Mar 45 | Mosquito XXX | MV555 | | 85 | Ju 188 | | F/L J. A. Dobie / W/O A. R. Grimstone |
| 14/15 Mar 45 | Mosquito VI | HR213 | G | 141 | UEA | Lachen, Germany | F/O (2/Lt) R. D. S. Gregor / F/Sgt F. S. Baker |
| 15/16 Mar 45 | Mosquito XXX | NT309 | | 85 | Ju 88 | Hannover area | Capt E. P. Fossum / F/O S. A. Hider |
| 15/16 Mar 45 | Mosquito XIX | TA393 | C | 157 | Ju 88 | 20 miles S of Würzburg | F/L J. O. Mathews DFC / W/O A. Penrose DFC |
| 16/17 Mar 45 | Mosquito XXX | NT330 | | 239 | Ju 188 | Nürnberg | S/L D. L. Hughes DFC / F/L R. H. Perks DFC |
| 18/19 Mar 45 | Mosquito XXX | NT364 | K | 157 | Ju 88 | Hanau | W/O D. Taylor / F/Sgt Radford |
| 18/19 Mar 45 | Mosquito XXX | NT271 | M | 239 | He 219 | Witten | W/C W. F. Gibb DSO, DFC / F/O R. C. Kendall DFC |
| 18/19 Mar 45 | Mosquito XXX | MV548 | Z | 85 | Bf 110 | | F/L F. D. Win RNZAF / F/O T. P. Ryan RNZAF |
| 20/21 Mar 45 | Mosquito XXX | NT324 | T | 85 | Bf 110 + He 219 V14 | | F/L G. C. Chapman / F/Sgt J. Stockley |
| 3 Apr 45 | Mosquito XXX | | | 239 | Ju 188 | | F/L D. L. Hughes / F/L R. H. Perks |
| 4/5 Apr 45 | Mosquito XXX | MU540 | C | BSDU | Bf 109 | W of Magdeburg | S/L R. G. Woodman / F/L Neville |
| 4/5 Apr 45 | Mosquito XXX | | C | 85 | Ju 188 | near Magdeburg | F/L C. W. Turner / F/Sgt G. Honeyman |

| Date | Aircraft | Serial | Code | Sqn | E/A | Location | Crew |
|---|---|---|---|---|---|---|---|
| 7/8 Apr 45 | Mosquito XXX | | Q | 85 | Fw 190 | NW Moblis | W/C K. Davison DFC, F/L Bunch DFC (157 Sqn) |
| 9/10 Apr 45 | Mosquito XXX | NT494 | N | 85 | Ju 88 | 20 miles W of Lutzendorf | F/L H. B. Thomas DFC, F/O C. B. Hamilton |
| 9/10 Apr 45 | Mosquito VI | RS575 | V | 515 | Ju 188 | SE of Hamburg | W/C H. C. Kelsey DFC*, F/L E. M. Smith DFC, DFM |
| 10/11 Apr 45 | Mosquito XXX | | | 239 | He 111 | | W/O P. O. Falconer, F/Sgt W. G. Armour |
| 13/14 Apr 45 | Mosquito XXX | NT334 | S | 85 | He 219 | Kiel | F/L K. D. Vaughan, F/Sgt R. D. MacKinnon |
| 14/15 Apr 45 | Mosquito XXX | | | 239 | Ju 88 | Potsdam | S/L D. J. Raby DFC, F/O S. J. Flint DFM |
| 15/16 Apr 45 | Mosquito VI | PZ398 | | 515 | Ju 52/3M | near Schleissheim | P/O L. G. Holland, F/Sgt R. Young |
| 17/18 Apr 45 | Mosquito XXX | MV557 | | 85 | Ju 88 | München area | W/C K. Davison |
| 19/20 Apr 45 | Mosquito XXX | 276 | B | BSDU | Ju 88 | S Denmark | F/L D. R. Howard DFC, F/L F. A. W. Clay DFC |
| 21 Apr 45 | Mosquito VI | | | 23 | Ju 188 | | W/O East, F/Sgt Eames |
| 24/25 Apr 45 | Mosquito VI | RS575 | V | 515 | Do 217 | Libeznice, 6 miles N of Prague | W/C H. C. Kelsey DFC*, F/L E. M. Smith DFC DFM |

# INDEX

229